VENTURE CAPITAL FINANCING

Text and Case Studies in Unorganized Environment

DR. CHIMUN KUMAR NATH
Ph.D., M.Com., PGDM
Department of Commerce
Dibrugarh University
Dibrugarh (Assam)

DEEP & DEEP PUBLICATIONS PVT. LTD.
F-159, Rajouri Garden, New Delhi - 110 027

VENTURE CAPITAL FINANCING
Text and Case Studies in Unorganized Environment

ISBN 978-81-8450-384-5

Printed in India at MAYUR ENTERPRISES
WZ Plot No. 3, Gujjar Market, Tihar Village, New Delhi - 110 018

Published by DEEP & DEEP PUBLICATIONS PVT. LTD.,
F-159, Rajouri Garden, New Delhi - 110 027 • Phone : 25435369, 25440916
E-mail : ddpubs@gmail.com • ddpbooks@yahoo.co.in
Showroom :
2/13, Ansari Road, Daryaganj, New Delhi - 110 002 • Telefax : 23245122

Dedicated to

PAPA

Dedicated to

PAPA

Contents

Preface

Entrepreneurs turn to venture capitalist when conventional means of funding are not available and it is not possible in the routine course to procure funds to meet the requirement of equity capital for a contemplated project. Venture capital plays an increasingly important role in the financial system and the economy. Providers of venture capital attempt to identify firms, typically in early or developmental stages, those possess strong potential for profitable growth. Like any providers of finance, venture capitalists monitor the performance of the firms they fund, including prospective involvement in the management and/or governance of said firms. Once the underlying business has sufficiently developed, the venture capitalist typically exit from its investment and diverts funds to new opportunities.

The VCF may be an old concept in some advanced continents like USA and Europe, but it is comparatively a new phenomenon in Asia. Although the first initiative to promote VCF in India was taken in 1973, yet it can be observed that there is a considerable presence of regional imbalances exists among the different states of India in terms of VCF penetration. The picture of venture capital financing is not very encouraging especially in Assam. It has been a recognized fact that to start up business ventures in Assam is difficult and risky due to its geographical location, various socio-economic environmental factors, the infrastructural bottlenecks, etc. Although risk aversiveness is not the motto of VCF but it is astonishing that the author has found a very poor response from the FIs in this part of the country. Moreover, the Government initiative in this direction to develop an environment to harness VC Financing possibilities is totally absent.

Although it is difficult to define an unorganized as well as organized environment, but for the simplicity of the work here I have taken the state of Assam as a representative of such unorganized environment for VCF. It is well known that Assam enjoys a very vital, strategic and sensitive location in the country. The uniqueness stems from its peculiar geo-political and geo-economic dimensions, which complete the already complex mosaic of a multi-ethnic, multi-lingual land with diverse culture. Though having rich resources, Assam has witnessed awfully poor development of venture capital growth. Therefore, a research observation would be to look into the problem of Venture Capital growth in Assam. At the same time it is noteworthy to grasp some more information about the growth of Venture Capital in some of the advance states of India where VCF has taken place in large numbers. Maharashtra is the leading state in terms of Venture Capital movement followed by Gujarat, Tamil Nadu and Karnataka. From the review of literatures it emerges that Karnataka has over the years developed in venturing into this type of capital, and for that reason the present study has made an attempt to monitor the growth of VCF in Karnataka to suggest some methodology of VCF for the state of Assam. Moreover, Karnataka happens to be the state where it has been observed that, before the information technology (IT) revolution since 1995 onwards; there were negligible diffusion of venture capital funding. Predominantly having an agro-based economy, Karnataka has shifted their focus from Agriculture to IT and IT enabled services during the first generation of reforms and has started enjoying the benefits during the second-generation reforms starting from 1995 onwards. Thus, the study has attempted to gather the experiences of Karnataka in the direction of VCF development to suggest a comprehensive methodology of VCF development in Assam as because Assam is still an agrarian economy like pre-1995 Karnataka.

While carrying out this endeavour, I have explored the scholarly works of many eminent authors and researchers. I wish to acknowledge my indebtedness to all of them for their direct or indirect contribution to this work. I would like to put on record my sincerest thanks and gratitude to Dr. Ashit Saha, Reader, Department of Commerce, Dibrugarh University for his invaluable expert guidance, inspiration, help and support without which this work would not have seen its accomplishment.

CHIMUN KUMAR NATH

[illegible] constant encouragement to this work. I am indebted to [illegible] and [illegible] to [illegible] Department of Commerce [illegible] direct and indirect [illegible] and support without which this work would not have been completed [illegible]

[illegible] NATH

Abbreviations

AAR	Authority of Advance Rulings
ADB	Asian Development Bank
AIDC	Assam Industrial Development Corporation
AIFI	All India Financial Institutions
ARDC	American Research and Development Corporation
ASIC	Assam State Industrial Corporation
BPO	Business Process Outsourcing
CBDT	Central Board of Direct Taxes
CEPA	Closer Economic Partnership Agreement
COO	Chief Operating Officer
DNA	Deoxyribonucleic Acid
DtA	Deutsche Ausgleichsbank, Germany
EED	European Enterprises Development
EVCA	European Venture Capital Association
FDI	Foreign Direct Investment
FIs	Financial Institutions
GAIL	Gas Authority of India Limited
GDP	Gross Domestic Product
H.O.	Head Office
IDBI	Industrial Development Bank of India
IFS	International Financial Statistics
IIE	Indian Institute of Entrepreneurship
IIIT-B	Indian Institute of Information Technology, Bangalore
IIM	Indian Institute of Management

IIT	Indian Institute of Technology
IPO	Initial Public Offer
IRR	Internal Rate of Return
ISRO	Indian Space Research Organisation
IT	Information Technology
IVCA	Indian Venture Capital Association
KfW	Kreditanstalt fur Wiederaufbau, Germany
KIDC	Karnataka Industrial Development Corporation
NEC	North Eastern Council
NECON	North Eastern Industrial Consultants Ltd.
NEDFi	North Eastern Development Finance Corporation Limited
NEITCO	North Eastern Industrial and Technical Consultancy Organization
NFSIT	National Venture Capital Fund for the Software and IT Industry
NGO	Non-Governmental Organization
NISIET	National Institute of Small Industry Extension Training
NME	New Molecular Entity
NRI	Non-Resident Indian
NSE	National Stock Exchange
NVCA	National Venture Capital Association
OECD	Organization for Economic Cooperation and Development
PAT	Profit After Tax
PEPI	Private Equity Performance Index
QIB	Qualified Institutional Buyer
R&D	Research and Development
RBI	Reserve Bank of India
RRL-J	Regional Research Laboratory, Jorhat
RRTCITT-G	Regional Research and Training Center on Indian Traditional Treatment, Golaghat
ROI	Return On Investment
ROM	Read Only Memory
RVCF	Regional Venture Capital Fund
SARS	Severe Acute Respiratory Syndrome
SBIC	Small Business Investment Companies
SDR	Société de Développement Régional (France)
SEBI	Security and Exchange Board of India

SIDBI	Small Industrial Development Bank of India
SME	Small and Medium-sized Enterprise
SPV	Special Purpose Vehicle
SWOT	Strength, Weakness, Opportunities and Threats
TDICI	Technology Development and Investment Corporation of India
UK	United Kingdom
USA	United States of America
USP	Unique Selling Proposition
UTI	Unit Trust of India
VAT	Value Added Tax
VC	Venture Capital
VCF	Venture Capital Financing
VC fund	Venture Capital Fund

CHAPTER 1

Introduction to Venture Capital Financing

1.1 PROLOGUE

The concept of venture capital is not new. Venture capitalists often relate the story of Christopher Columbus. In the fifteenth century, he sought to travel westwards instead of eastwards from Europe and so planned to reach India. His far-fetched idea did not find favour with the King of Portugal, who refused to finance him. Finally, Queen Isabella of Spain decided to fund him and the voyages of Christopher Columbus are now empanelled in history.

According to the Encyclopedia Britannica, "venture capital is a capital (as retained corporate earnings or individual savings) invested or available for investment in the ownership element of new or fresh enterprise. It is also called as risk capital and the term Venture Capital was coined for the first time in the year 1943". Thus, venture capital is the risky capital* collected

* It is a capital, bearing a high risk arising out of financing a new technology enterprise or converting an innovative idea into a commercially viable project and in this process the venture capitalist also participate in the equity of such enterprises.

through different sources to invest alongside management participation in rapidly growing industries. Venture capital is an important source of equity for start-up enterprises. Venture capitalists are high risk taking investors and, in accepting high risks, they desire a higher return on their investment. The venture capitalist manages the risk/reward ratio by investing only in those businesses that fits their investment criteria and after having completed extensive due diligence. Venture capitalists have different operating approaches. These differences may relate to the location of the business, the size of the investment, the stage of the enterprise, industry specialization, and structure of the investment and involvement of the venture capitalists in the investees' activities.[1] They generally:

- Finance enterprises with enormous growth or growth potential;
- Purchase equity securities;
- Assist in the development of new products or services;
- Take higher risks with the expectation of getting higher return;
- Have a long-term orientation/gestation to evaluate business sustainability; and
- Besides providing capital gives experienced management support.

In VCF, the management participation by the venture capitalist differs significantly from the management participation by the creditors in case of conventional loans. The venture capitalist participate with ownership stake in the management of the enterprise not only to monitor the growth of the firm (by keeping an eye on the proper utilization of the resources, technological usage, creating and satisfying the needs of the customers, etc.) but also to create a viable exit route preferably through the capital market or strategic sales. Such participation gives the venture capitalist an ease to manage the enterprise according to their wishes so as to safeguard their investment. At the same time the entrepreneurs also receives a support in the management to run the enterprise, which is very much essential because these entrepreneurs though may have bright ideas but may lack in implementing the same. It is normally easy for a venture capitalist to get a viable exit route if the enterprise attains sustainability.

Entrepreneurs turn to venture capitalist when conventional means of funding are not available and it is not possible in the routine course to procure funds to meet the requirement of equity capital for a contemplated project. Venture capital plays an increasingly important role in the financial system and the economy. Providers of venture capital attempt to identify firms, typically in early or developmental stages, those possess strong potential for profitable growth. Like any providers of finance, venture capitalists monitor the performance of the firms they fund, including prospective involvement in the management and/or governance of said firms. Once the underlying business has sufficiently developed, the venture capitalist typically exit from its investment and diverts funds to new opportunities.

1.2 REVIEW ON VCF

Venture capital investments generally are relatively high-risk investments, but may offer the potential for above average returns. Venture capital is a form of intermediation particularly well suited to support the creation and growth of innovative, entrepreneurial companies. Hellmann *et. al.* (2000)[2] (2002)[3], Kortum *et. al.* (2000).[4] It specializes in financing and nurturing enterprises at an early stage of development (start-ups) that usually operated in high-tech industries. For these companies the expertise of the venture capitalist, its knowledge of markets and of the entrepreneurial process, and its network of contacts are most useful to help unfold their growth potential, observed by Bottazzi *et. al.* (2004[5]), Gompers (1995[6]), Hellmann *et. al.* (2002[7]), Lerner (1994[8]), and Lindsey (2003[9]). In contrast, when venture capital is applied to companies at a later stage of their growth, or in companies which operate in technologically mature industries, it has less opportunity to 'make a difference', commented by Michelacci *et. al* (2004[10]).

A report under the auspices of OECD (2000[11]), has identified venture capital as a critical component for the success of entrepreneurial high-technology firms and recommended that all countries should consider strategies for encouraging the availability of venture capital. With such admiration and encouragement from a prestigious international organization* have stimulated for various attempts to create indigenous venture capital industry. The possibility and ease of cross-national transference of institutions has been a subject of debate among scholars, policy-makers, and industrialists during the entire 20th century, if not earlier, Kogut *et. al.*, (1998[12]). National economies have particular path-dependent trajectories, as do their national systems of innovation (NIS). The forces arrayed against transfer are numerous and include cultural factors, legal systems, entrenched institutions, and even lack of adequately trained personnel. Failure to transfer is probably the most frequent outcome, as institutional inertia is usually the default option. In the transfer process, there is a matrix of possible interactions between the transferred institution and the environment. There are four possible interactions: (a) the institution can be successfully transferred with no significant changes to either the institution or the environment just like the VCF experience in Israel. (b) The institutional transfer can fail just like the case of China. (c) The institution can be modified or hybridized so that it is able to integrate into the environment as in the case of UK, Korea, etc. (d) An interaction between the existing institutions and venture capital to modify the environment occurs like the experience of VCF in India. Though (a) and (b) are exclusionary, it is possible for transfer to yield a combination of (c) and (d), Kogut (2000).[13]

Venture capital research has focused primarily on the venture capitalists' investment process, strategy and the relationship of the equity provider to the venture-backed firm. Fewer articles emphasized the entrepreneur or the entrepreneurial firm this research approach can be defined as focusing on the supply side of the equation where the respective of the venture capitalist, or the venture capital industry, is the central concern, Mason *et. al.* (1999).[14] Studies examined the strategies of venture capital firms, the "value added" to entrepreneurial firms by venture capitalists, Sapienza (1992),[15] the effects of team processes in the partnership, Watson (1995),[16]

* On path dependency, refer Arthur (1994) and David (1986). For NIS, refer Lundvall (1992) and Nelson (1993).

and venture capitalist's perceptions of serial entrepreneurs Write *et. al.* (1997).[17] More recent studies employed experimental design techniques and cognitive theory to assess venture capitalist decision-making processes, Zacharakis *et. al.* (2001).[18]

Less research has examined the demand side, or the approaches taken by firms seeking venture capital. A noteworthy exception is a study by Sapienza *et. al.* (1996[19]) that investigated the ways entrepreneurs managed information flows that influenced investors. Till recently, populations of entrepreneurs including women and minorities, remain understudied as observed by Zacharakis *et. al.* (2001).[20] Research about gender of the business owner and financing has focused exclusively on access to debt capital has been observed by Buttner *et. al.* (1988[21]), Riding *et. al.* (1990[22]), and Coleman (2000[23]). A literature review Gatewood *et al.* (2002[24]) found very few academic study that examined the factors that effect entrepreneurs' access to, or utilization of, outside equity funding mostly in the area of Angel Funding. This suggests that the seeking, utilization and strategies of obtaining angel funding is based on the experiences of entrepreneurs.

Becker (1964[25]) in his study has identified another dimension for financing enterprises, i.e. human capital, which consists of achieved attributes that lead to increased levels of productivity. Human capital according to Carter *et al.* (1997[26]) and Dollinger (1994[27]), is not only derived from investments in formal education, occupational experiences and training, but also extends to judgments, insight, creativity, vision and intelligence.

The VCF investors normally preferred technically qualified entrepreneurs instead of generally qualified entrepreneurs for parking venture capital funds. But it has been observed by Hisrich *et. al.* (1983[28]), Honig-Haftel *et. al.* (1986[29]), Brush (1992[30]), Carter *et. al.* (1997[31]) that in past, people in general were more likely to have a liberal arts education instead of training in business, sciences or engineering, thus limiting the scope of the application of venture capital funds. However, it was also observed by them that a general education, regardless of the content, might inspire confidence in investors, especially if augmented by specific business training or work experience.

To the extent that investors rate 'management' in capital seeking companies more favourably if they have experience in funding a venture, and a strong track record in marketing, management, and leadership decision-making, which leads to higher probability of funding success, as revealed by Fried *et. al.* (1988[32]), and Wright *et. al.* (1998[33]).

Kelly (1994[34]) identified that for financing through venture capital, the formation of social capital is necessary. Social capital is a form of non-economic knowledge separate from the foundation of human capital. Distinct from formal learning or instruction, it nevertheless directly impacts the economic behaviours of individuals. Coleman (1988[35]) reveals that social capital emerges from the norms, networks, and relationship of the social structure in which an individual lives. The social capital has the potentiality to produce useful resources for business through the development of sets of obligations and execrations, information channels, and social norms that reinforce certain types of behaviours. Social networks* allow entrepreneurs to go gaining access to opportunities and resources, save time, and tape into advice and normal support that may otherwise be unavailable. Social networks also are important for venture capital firms. Bygrave (1992[36]) described the venture capital industry as closed network, geographically concentrated, and tightly interconnected. It is widely recognized that the core of a venture capital firm's livelihood is deal flow, which the principals learn about through their network of informal contacts as commented by Bygrave (1992[37]), and Alimansky (2000[38]). Thus, the success of VC firms depends on who, as well as what, the principals perceive.

The commonness of the entrepreneur's network structure with that of the venture capitalist may be an important factor in determining the likelihood that the entrepreneur will be able to find private equity funding, has been found by Tybee *et. al.* (1988[39]), and Freear *et. al.* (1992[40]) in their respective studies. Most venture capitalists invest in deals brought to them or

* Social networks include friendship, referral groups and other family members, institutions, etc. It allow entrepreneurs to gain access to opportunities and resources, save time, and tap into advice and moral support that may otherwise be unavailable.

referred by people they know. Few deals originate from plans received 'over the transom'. Therefore, entrepreneurs seeking venture capital increases their chances of receiving it when they know the venture capitalists or those who shepherd deals to them. Aldrich (1989[41]), argued that, 'venture capitalists are probably as important for their broker role as for the funds they provide to struggling entrepreneurs. He also argued that the venture capitalist bring together technical experts, management consultants, and financial planners, who supplement an entrepreneur, but limits the knowledge and experience of it.

Researches suggest that entrepreneurs might be underrepresented in the venture capital social networks. Social network theory posits that people tend to interact with people like themselves. This performance, or 'homophilous' propensity, leads to segregated networks as identified by Brass (1985[42]). Studies showed that the networks of entrepreneurs conformed to homophilous propensity are predominately found in females, Aldrich (1989[43]), Aldrich *et al.* (1989[44]), Brush (1992[45]). Conversely, networks in the investment industry are predominately male. A review of Pratt's Guide to venture Capital Sources (1990) indicated that only 529 of the more than 6086 venture capitalists were women as referred by Hart (1995[46]). With these informations, the likelihood that the network of a female entrepreneur will contain only female equity investors is remote if not absurd. Never the less to make the critical connections in the investing community, entrepreneurs may need to rely on alternative networking strategies.

Obtaining the necessary financing to start and grow a business is generally considered one of the entrepreneur's major problems. While the emphasis in this study is on securing equity capital, it is rarely the only source of capital used by the entrepreneurs. Capital comes from many sources, including personal saving, banks, government programs, venture capital funds, and business angels. Drawing on each of these sources has different ramifications for the business and the business owner. The choice of an appropriate capitalization structure and decisions about the sequencing of capital sources are widely acknowledged as important to venture success.

According to the 'Pecking Order Hypothesis*', debt will be include among the first sources of funding entrepreneur's seek in financing their business. This may be from 'quasi' external sources like credit cards, or from more formal sources like banks or other larger institutional providers. There is conflicting evidence on entrepreneur's experiences in accessing debt financing from institutions, suffer from weaker collateral positions, and believe that they have been discriminated against or received unequal treatment by financing institutions as observed by Goffe *et. al.* (1983[47]), Hisrich *et. al.* (1984[48]), and Olm *et. al.* (1988[49]) in their respective studies.

It seems plausible that the discrepancies in the studies may relate to difference in the level of the entrepreneur's human and social capital. Indeed, Wsaton *et. al.* (1995[50]) found human capital factors such as intention, greater scanning of the environment and more disciplined approach to management distinguished high growth from low growth women led ventures. As entrepreneurs acquired critical experience, their difficulties in accessing debt financing for their business appeared to abate. Furthermore, ventures are seldom funded by a single source, hence experience in obtaining debt or other type of financing would provide a stronger foundation for securing equity capital. Similarly, it is expected that the more extensive and diverse the business owners' social networks, the higher their chances of being introduced to the favourable banking relationship necessary for loan approval.

In addition to financing, bootstrapping appears to be a critical component to venture financing success. As commented by Van Osnabrugge *et. al.* (2000[51]) bootstrapping as an effective strategy for financing a new enterprise's growth build on personal equity and debt. If successful in using bootstrapping, the enterprises purportedly are better positioned to receive private equity investments in later stages of development.

---

* The traditional pecking order theory suggests that the financing source of choice is earnings retention, followed by external debt. External equity is the last resort. This traditional approach can, however, be confronted by the excessive demand for external equity, especially for start-ups. This demand can be explained by the absence of interest costs on the one hand, and fixed payback obligations on the other.

Bootstrapping can free the venture from excessive debt loads that may constrain the company in its early years and hampers its growth. Bootstrapping may be an effective means of preparing a venture for getting outside investment at a latter time. These arguments indicate that some funding sources provide the basis for acquiring other sources. Personal investment may precede bootstrapping, which in turn creates the opportunity to acquire outside equity investment at a later date.

The extent to which Indian entrepreneurs effectively use bootstrapping to position their business for outside funding is nuclear. No studies were found that examined Indian business owners' experience is using bootstrapping to effectively grow their companies. Intuitively though, it would appear that Indian business owners who have industry, management and start-up work experience, together with diverse social networks, are better equipped to effectively use bootstrapping to positions their business attractive investment opportunities for outside investors then business owners without having these experiences and networks. Such human and social capital can provide entrepreneurs, knowledge of bootstrapping strategies, capabilities, access to credit from vendors, or business alliances needed to generate revenue and costs—all bootstrapping techniques that can minimize business risk and demonstrate the hustle that outside equity investors reward. From the various literatures reviewed it emerges *inter alia* that diffusion of human and social capital has been the prime reason for success of venture capital financing.

The above studies emphasizing on human and social capital have been carried out in a different socio-eco-political environments, i.e. carried out in countries like UK, USA, Israel, Germany, etc. Albeit it seems that a similar circumstances relating to growth and diffusion of human and social capital might prevail under the socio-eco-political environment in India, but evidence followed by a systematic study has been found to be non-existent.

Never the less while studying the demand and supply of venture capital funds in its various forms, it has been observed that the success of VCF has been dependent on right diffusion of human and social capital. Here an attempt has been made to understand the VCF not only from the organized environment like Karnataka but also from the unorganized environment like Assam in India. In order to gain experience of VCF in the state where venture capital financing has experienced success up to the global standard, the state of Karnataka has been selected for gaining experience on VCF *vis-à-vis* the kind of growth and diffusion of human and social capital there. Karnataka has been selected because of its agrarian economy prior to the IT boom like that of the prevailing economy of Assam which is predominantly agriculture-based and rural in nature.

1.3 UNORGANIZED ENVIRONMENT

To be very honest the concept of Organized and Unorganized environment to VCF is a relative term to define. By far the strongest and best-substantiated conclusion from economic research on the unorganized environment to VCF is the urgent need to stimulate job-creating growth with the fastest growing population in the world.

Various definitions of entrepreneurship exist. This book adopts a simple one: the creation of new businesses that prosper and create jobs (Kirchho, 1994). Among the first economists to talk about the role of the entrepreneur in economic development was Schumpeter (1934, 1976), with his discussion of entrepreneurial innovation and creative destruction, which serves as a catalyst for economic growth. Schumpeter's work was intellectually motivated by the absence of entrepreneurship from the neoclassical model. The neoclassical approach essentially viewed firms as 'black box' production functions, and therefore de-emphasized the role of individuals within them. It also left little room for distinguishing between firms that were innovative and others that were not.

Contributions to the field of economics by the likes of Whyte (1956) and Galbraith (1952, 1958, 1967) led to the fairly widespread view (influenced by the post depression, post WWII United States) that large firms were a preferred source of employment creation, and presented a model of wealth creation and distribution dominated by large corporations, big government and large labour unions. Meanwhile, development economists were justifying the state-led approach to development they prescribed for the 'third world' based, partly, on their perception of low entrepreneurial capacity there (Hirschman, 1958). In neither approach were there innovative entrepreneurs creating market chaos (Schumpeter, 1939). Instead, the neoclassical approach conceived of systematic, frictionless markets, with buyers and sellers responding to price fluctuations that result in new points of equilibrium. This neater, more easily modeled approach won the day as discussions of the role of entrepreneurship in capitalism were relegated to the handful of academics who studied 'small business'.

Over the past two decades, micro-based research in information economics has seen a departure from the neoclassical understanding of the firm, as models about incentives, innovation, influence, negotiation and renegotiation, power and authority have taken center stage (Jensen and Mecklin, 1976; Hart and Holmströ m, 1987; La.ont and Tirole, 1993; Aghion, 1995; Gibbons, 1997), including key results about how large firms can quell innovation (Holmströ m and Milgrom, 1994; Hart and Moore, 1996). Related research on the problem of agency cost reduction suggested that financial intermediaries, namely banks, play a central role (Diamond, 1984; Fama, 1985; Stiglitz, 1985). Further research has slowly began to show how venture capitalists solve a more extreme form of the agency problem, one that is beyond the monitoring and certification role. This literature highlights two key roles played by venture capitalists: value-added support and governance control (Sahlman, 1990; Admati and P.eiderer, 1994; Berglöf, 1994; Gompers, 1995; Lerner, 1995; Hellmann, 1998; Kaplan and Strömberg, 1999; Hellmann and Puri, 2000). While these contributions mostly focused on the relationship between investors and companies (invested in), a further set of papers sought to explore the role of financial institutions as they .t into the broader economic system (Gilson and Roe, 1993; Gilson, 1996; Roe, 1998; Bebchuk and Roe, 1999).

Of particular relevance to this book is the theory of asset complementarities, first developed by Milgromand Roberts (1990, 1994, 1995), which explains how equilibrium congruence between agents is achieved when agent actions are mutually enhancing.[52] This framework offers an extremely useful endogenous understanding of institutions with multiple equilibria. The key insight here is that an institution, such as a private equity fund in country X, can have impact and is viable depending on what institutional equilibrium exists in country X. A necessary property of any equilibrium with complementarities is that any single deviation is unprofitable. Any initial institutional change has to be accompanied by further changes in the system so that the system can move toward a new equilibrium. If not, some agents either have to be willing to incur losses or their losses have to be covered by the government. Applications of these ideas lead to conclusions about the importance of coupling innovations in financial intermediation (e.g. the creation of private equity funds) with appropriate institutions including ones that facilitate transactions and provide incentives (such as technically 'smart' legislation) and others that create 'deal flow' and bring forward entrepreneurial talent (both linked to educational and business policy interventions).[53] A private equity fund created in an environment with no deal flow and/or inappropriate legislation, for example, does not benefit from the complementarities necessary to move the economic system to new points of equilibrium. In such a setting, the fund itself is of limited effectiveness and viability. These contributions are key to a better understanding of how to promote entrepreneurship for economic development.

In addition to theoretical developments in economics, empirical research on industrialized countries managed to underscore, apparently not without creating controversy with the 'old' school (Kirchoff, 1994), the importance of entrepreneurial firms in job creation (Birch, 1987) and the role of innovative, flexible small firms in economic development from countries throughout the world (Späth, 1993; Schmitz, 1993; Schmitz and Musyck, 1993; Nadvi and Schmitz, 1994). It has also been seen that a simultaneous mushrooming over the past 20 years of literature on the role of micro-finance and micro-enterprises in economic development, especially poverty alleviation.

Much of this literature tells tales of small businesses that attract attention either because they are run by shoe-string entrepreneurs in adverse settings, or because they are managed/owned by especially entrepreneurial women in settings where women do not run businesses, or because they are entrepreneurial in how they manage to operate in the 'informal economy'. In virtually each of these accounts, one finds a discussion of entrepreneurial talent that explains daring innovation, overcoming negative externalities and success in adverse markets. Behind each account lies entrepreneurial talent that the neoclassical 'black box' did not account for.

In addition, the previous decade of bounty on global financial markets played a central role in giving the subject of entrepreneurship a shot in the arm and a polished cachet. As more finance chased fewer ideas, we saw the development of a whole industry of business plan producers and consumers, including the innovator and the professor, the venture capitalist, the consultant and the bankruptcy lawyer. Now that the dust has settled, we know that the popularization of the private equity industry (including its venture capital component), the proliferation of its product range, and the lessons from its failures, have all yielded valuable experience, much of which is carried back to the developing world through young professionals. When they choose to return to their countries, they are keen to apply what they have learned elsewhere.

So three questions emerged here.

What Does it Mean to Focus on Dynamic New Business Creation?

New 'job creation' strategies for an unorganized environment should target first-time job seekers to tackle the most pressing end of the labour market, but should also include policies that target unemployment for those who have already entered the labour market. Among other things (which are not the subject of this book), a focus on dynamic new business creation can help address both needs at the same time, as new businesses tend to absorb all levels of experience.

What is a 'Job'?

All types and levels of employment are our target here,

ranging from the selling of used books among college students, to starting a regional transport sector leader, to conducting advanced scientific or policy work. Furthermore, low-level jobs, especially for first-time job seekers, are a partial education and certainly an investment in experience for higher-level jobs, attainable through concomitant levels of education at every stage. The notion of a job in industrialized economies begins with the high school level summer responsibilities at camps and beaches and extends through the highest ends of the job market, for the same people at different stages in their lives. Nuclear physicists also start out as lifeguards and newspaper delivery boys and girls. This notion is not as present in the Arab world, partly, as it can be learned through some work on poverty assessments with the World Bank, because own school textbooks cast excessive glamour on white-collar jobs, and disdain blue-collar jobs. As a result, many young people are not encouraged to take on early in life, the responsibilities that can prepare them for more sophisticated responsibilities later on in life. The phenomenon of 'queuing unemployment' in many parts of the world is partly a result of this expectation mismatch created partly through inappropriate education from early on.[54]

What is the Difference between 'New' Firms and 'SMEs'?

'New firms' is a concept slightly different, but not excluding the now-established SME concept. Because it is based on firm size, the term SME can include enterprises that .t this category by virtue of their size, but are neither dynamic, nor growing, and therefore are not necessarily competitive, but continue to exist for various reasons, including state subsidies and private sector connections. As such, new firms can become and remain SMEs, but might not be dynamic. But also, new firms that are truly successful can quickly outgrow the SME category if their products and market strategies achieve rapid capture of large market shares. Dynamic and growing firms are what is needed, for example, to begin to address the problem of low levels of incoming FDI flows to the third world.

Thus we can infer that in an unorganized environment there is a need for:

(1) Plan and execute priority areas of 'new generation'

reforms, with individual environmenty priorities and capacities in mind.

(2) Launch new initiatives as part of reforms, to help drive and capitalize on reform momentum. These could be along the lines of the following:

   (a) national/regional entrepreneurship information campaigns;

   (b) international business innovation and knowledge-transfer links. These would have, among other things, the objective of financing the transfer and outsourcing of commercializable business ideas and exchanging best practice on innovation;

   (c) develop national entrepreneurship training programmes for all levels of the job ladder, from micro-finance to high finance. These would be part of action plans that would also include (d) below;

   (d) identify and train trainers for all those interested in working to promote entrepreneurship;

   (e) foster entrepreneurship networks within and across countries in the region, leveraging media tools such as television programmes for entrepreneurship competitions, star entrepreneurs who can serve as role models, and rewards for business innovation in all sectors, across the environment, again at all levels of the job ladder; and

   (f) . . . more, depending on country specificities.

Each economy has its specification and these permeate the economy ranging from the level of sophistication of the financial sector and the relative availability of liquidity, to the types of jobs that need to be created. In countries, such as Morocco, Algeria, Bangladesh and Egypt, with their large low-skilled rural populations, VCF complementarities are the number one priority. In economies such as that of India and North East Region in particular, VCF complementarities are as important as those related to the high value-added end of the labour market, where the brain-drain problem is most pressing. In addition, efforts must be made to encourage innovative education, such as broad-based programmes to encourage entrepreneurship, i.e. how to create economic value, especially jobs, from innovative ideas in all sectors. A whole range of topics can be taught related to innovation, entrepreneurial finance and economics, and small business at all educational levels, including executive education. From the current academic experience in the region, they do not do nearly enough of this. Complementary educational programmes can range from teaching how to write a rudimentary business plan for 'small' finance projects, to encouraging participation in high-tech business plan competitions networked with venture capital, locally, regionally and globally. In this book, we have taken Karnataka as a representative of orgânized environment for VCF due to its advancement of such financing at par with the global standards and Assam as a representative of unorganized environment for VCF due to its discernible growth of VCF.

Notes and References

1. Gill, D. (2003); 'Venture Capital in Selected Countries'. Washington D.C., IFC, pp. 12-22.
2. Hellmann, Thomas, and Manju Puri (2000) 'The Interaction between Product Market and Financing Strategy: The Role of Venture Capital,' *Review of Financial Studies*, New Haven, Vol. 13, No. 4, pp. 959-84.
3. Hellmann, Thomas, and Manju Puri (2002) 'Venture Capital and the Professionalization of Start-up Firms: Empirical Evidence,' *Journal of Finance*, Blackwell Publishing, American Finance Association, Vol. 57, No. 1, *pp*. 169-97.
4. Kortum, Samuel, and Josh Lerner (2000) 'Assessing the Contribution of Venture Capital to Innovation, *Rand Journal*, Santa Monica, CA, Vol. 31, No. 4, pp. 674-92.
5. Bottazzi, Laura, and Marco Da Rin (2004) 'Financing European Entrepreneurial Firms: Facts, Issues and Research Agenda', forthcoming in Christian Keuschnigg and Vesa Kanniainen (eds.) Venture Capital, Entrepreneurship and Public Policy, Cambridge, MA, MIT Press, p. 102.
6. Gompers, Paul (1995) 'Optimal Investment, Monitoring, and the Staging of Venture Capital,' *Journal of Finance*, Blackwell Publishing, American Finance Association, Vol. 50, No. 4, pp. 1461-90.
7. Hellmann, Thomas, and Manju Puri (2002) 'Venture Capital and the Professionalization of Start-up Firms: Empirical Evidence,' *Journal of Finance*, Blackwell Publishing, American Finance Association, Vol. 57, No. 1, pp. 169-97.
8. Lerner, Josh (1994) 'Venture Capitalists and the Decision to go Public,' *Journal of Financial Economics*, Vol. 35, No. 1, pp. 293-16, Available at www.jfe.rochester.edu.jfenh.htm

9. Lindsey, Laura (2003) 'The Venture Capital Keiretsu Effect: An Empirical Analysis of Strategic Alliances among Portfolio Firms,' mimeo, Stanford University, p. 134.
10. Michelacci, Claudio, and Javier Suarez (2004) 'Business Creation and the Stock Market,' *Review of Economic Studies*, Institute of Economics and Statistics, UK, Vol. 71, No. 2, pp. 459-81.
11. OECD (2000). A new economy? The Changing Role of Innovation and Information Technology in Growth. Paris: OECD Publication, Available at *www.oecd.org*.
12. Kogut, B. and Parkinson, D. (1998). Adoption of the Multidivisional Structure: Analyzing History for the Start. Industrial and Corporate Change, Oxford University Press, UK, Vol. 7, pp. 249-73.
13. For a more general conceptualization, refer Kogut (2000).
14. Mason, C. and Harison, R. (1999), Venture Capital: Rationale, Aims & Scope. *Venture Capital*, Routledge Publication, UK, Vol. 1, pp. 1-46
15. Sapienza, H. (1992), When do Venture Capitalist add Value?, *Journal of Business Venturing*, Elsevier, Netherland, Vol. 7, pp. 9-28.
16. Watson, W. (1995), Team International Effectiveness in Venture Partnerships and its Connection to Perceived Success, *Journal of Business Venturing*, Elsevier, Netherland, Vol. 10, pp. 393-411.
17. Wright, M., Rooobbie, K. and Ennew, C. (1997), Venture Capitalists and Serial Entrepreneurs, *Journal of Business Venturing*, Elsevier, Netherland, Vol. 16, pp. 311-32.
18. Zacharakis and Shepherd (2001), The Nature of Information and Overconfidence on Venture Capitalist's Decision-making, *Journal of Business Venturing*, Elsevier, Netherland, Vol. 16, pp. 311-32.
19. Sapienza, H. and Korsgaard, M.A., (1996), Procedural justice in entrepreneur-investor relations. *Academy of Management Journal*, Academy of Management, NY, Vol. 39, pp. 544-74.
20. Zacharakis and Shepherd (2001), The Nature of Information and Overconfidence on Venture Capitalist's Decision-making, *Journal of Business Venturing*, Elsevier, Netherland, Vol. 16, pp. 311-32.
21. Buttner, E.H. and Rosen, B.H., (1988), "Bank loan Officer's Perceptions of Characteristics of Men, Women and Successful Entrepreneurs", *Journal of Business Venturing*, Elsevier, Netherland, Vol. 3, No. 3. pp. 233-39.
22. Riding, A. and Swift, C. (1990), Women Business Owners and Terms of Credit : Some Empirical Findings of the Canadian Experiences. *Journal of Business Venturing*, Elsevier, Netherland, Vol. 5, pp. 327-440.
23. Coleman, S., (2000), Access to Capital and Terms of Credit: A Comparison of Men and Women-owned Small Business. *Journal of Small Business Management*, UK, Vol. 38, pp. 48-52.
24. Women's Entrepreneurship and High Growth Ventures; (1994), An Annotated Bibliography Stockholm; Entrepreneurship and Small Business Research Institute, p. 82.
25. Becker, G.S. (1964), Human Capital, NY: Columbia University Press, pp. 87-104.
26. Carter, N.M. and Allen, K.R., (1997), Size Determinants of Women-owned Business: Choice or Barriers to Resources? *Entrepreneurship and Regional Development*, Vol. 9, pp. 211-20, Available at www.erd.com/journal.

27. Doorlinger, M. (1994), Entrepreneurship: Strategies and Resources, Boston, Mass: Irwin, p. 126.
28. Hisrich, R.G. and Brush, C.G., (1983), The Women Entrepreneur: Implications of Family, Educational and Occupational Experience. In N.C. Churchill, S. Birley, W.D. Bygrave, D.F. Muzyka, C. Wahlbin and W.E. Wetzel, Jr [eds.] Frontiers of Entrepreneurship Research Wellesley, MA: Babson College, pp. 237-39.
29. Honig-Haftel, S. and Martin, L., (1986), is the Female Entrepreneur at a Disadvantage? Thrust: *The Journal for Employment and Training Professionals*, UK, Vol. 7, pp. 49-64.
30. Brush, C.G., (1992), Research on Women Business Owners: Past Trends, a New Perspective and Future Directions. Entrepreneurship Theory and Practice, Baylor University, Waco, Vol. 16, pp. 5-30.
31. Carter, N.M. and Allen, K.R., (1997), Size Determinants of Women—Owned Business: Choice or Barriers to Resources? Entrepreneurship and Regional Development, Vol. 9, pp. 211-20. Available at www.erd. com/ jounral.
32. Fried, V. Hisrich, R.D. (1988), Venture Capital Research; Past Present and Future. Entrepreneurship. Theory and Practice, Baylor University, Waco, Vol. 13, pp. 15-29.
33. Wright, M. and Robbie, K., (1998), Venture Capital and Private Equity: A Review and Synthesis. *Journal of Business Finance and Accounting*, Vol. 25, pp. 521-70, Available at www.blackwell publishing.com/ jounral.asp?ref=0306-686X.
34. Kelly, M. (1993), Towanda's Triumph: Social and Culture Capital in the Transition to Adulthood in the Urban Ghetto. *International Journal of Urban and Regional Research*, Vol. 18, march, pp. 88-111. Available at www.blackwellpublishing.com/jounral.asp?ref=0309-1317.
35. Coleman, J., (1988), Social Capital in the Creation of Human Capital. *American Journal of Sociology*, NY, Vol. 94, pp. S95-S120.
36. Bygrave, W.D., (1992), Venture capital returns in the 1980's. In D.L. Sexton and J. Kasarda [eds.] The State of the Art of Entrepreneurship, USA, p. 187.
37. Bygrave, W.D., (1992), Venture Capital Returns in the 1980's. In D.L. Sexton and J. Kasarda [eds.] The State of the Art of Entrepreneurship, USA, p. 201.
38. Altimansky, B., (2000), Eight ways to ruin your chances of Raising Equity Capital. *Journal of Private Equity*, USA, Summer, Vol. 3, No. 3, pp. 78-83.
39. Tyebjee, T.T. and Bruno, A.V., (1984), A Model of Venture Capitalist Investment Activity. *Management Science*, Michigan University, USA, Vol. 30, pp. 1051-1076.
40. Frrear, J., Sohl, J. and Wetzel, W.E. Jr, (1997), The Informal Venture Capital Market: Milestones Passed and the Road Ahead. In D.L. Sexton and R.W. Smilor [eds.] Entrepreneurship 2000 Chicago: Upstart Publishing, pp. 47-49.
41. Aldrich, H., (1989), Networking among Women Entrepreneurs. In O. Rivchun and D. Sexton [eds.] *Women-Owned Business*, NY: Praeger, pp. 103-32.

42. Brass, D.J., (1985), Men's Women's Networks: A Study of Interaction Patterns and Influence in an Organization. *Academy of Management Journal*, Academy of Management, NY, Vol. 28, pp. 327-43.
43. Aldrich, H., (1989), Networking among Women Entrepreneurs. In O. Rivchun and D. Sexton [eds.] *Women-Owned Business*, NY:Praeger, pp. 103-132.
44. Aldrich, H., Reese, P.R. and Dubini, P., (1989), Women on the Verge of a Breakthrought: Networking among Entrepreneurs in the United States and Italy. Entrepreneurship and Regional Development, Routledge Publication, UK, Vol. 1, pp. 339-56.
45. Brush, C.G., (1992), Research on Women Business Owners: Past Trends, a New Perspective and Future Directions. Entrepreneurship Theory and Practice, UK, Vol. 16, pp. 5-30.
46. Hart, M., (1995), Founding Resource Choices: Influences and Effects. Doctoral Dissertation. Harvard Graduate School of Business, p. 52. Available at http://en.wikipedia.org/wiki/Harvard_Business_School
47. Goffe, R. and Scase, R., (1983), Business Ownership and Women's Subordination; a Preliminary Study of Female Proprietors. *Sociological Review*, Keele University, Vol. 31, pp. 625-48.
48. Hisrich, R.G. and Brush, C.G., (1983), The Women Entrepreneur: Implications of Family, Educational and Occupational Experience. In N.C. Churchill, S. Birley, W.D. Bygrave, D.F. Muzyka, C. Wahlbin and W.E. Wetzel, Jr. [eds.] Frontiers of Entrepreneurship Research, Wellesley, MA: Babson College, pp. 202-12
49. Olm, K., Carsurd, A. and Alvey, L., (1988), The Role of Networks in New Venture Founding for the Female Entrepreneur : A Continuing Analysis. W.A. Long, E. McMullan, K.H. Vesper and W.E. Wetzel Jr. [eds.] *Frontiers of Entrepreneurship Research*, Wellesy, MA: Babson college, pp. 302-18.
50. Watson, W., Ponthieu and Critelli, J., (1995), Team Interpersonal Effectiveness in Venture Partnerships and its Connection to Perceived Success. *Journal of Business Venturing*, Elsevier, Netherland, Vol. 10, pp. 221-31.
51. Van Osnabrugge, M. and Robinson, R.J., 2000, Angel Investing: Matching Start-up Funds with Start Up Companies, San Francisco, Jossey-Bass.
52. To illustrate the notion of complementarity, take two types of assets, a_1 and a_2 (located in firm 1 and firm 2 respectively). These assets are strictly complementary either if access to a_1 alone has no effect on the manager of firm 1's marginal return from investment (i.e. if he needs a_2 as well), or if access to a_2 alone has no effect on the manager of firm 2's marginal return from investment (i.e. he needs a1 as well). Assets a_1 and a_2 are independent if access to a_2 will not increase the manager of firm 1's marginal return from investment if he already has access to a_1, and if access to a_1 will not increase the manager of firm 2's marginal return from investment if he already has access to a_2.
53. 'Deal flow' is a phrase used to denote the availability of a stream of business ideas, typically in the form of business plans that constitute potential investments for providers of finance.
54. A related tragic extreme are the young 'hittis' of North Africa.

Venture Capital Financing : Global Scenario

The modern venture capital industry began to take shape in the post-World War II years. It is often said that people decide to become entrepreneurs because they see role models in *other* people who have become successful entrepreneurs. Much the same thing can be said about venture capitalists. The earliest members of the organized venture capital industry had several role models, including the following three organizations:

I. *American Research and Development (ARD) Corporation*, formed in 1946, whose biggest success was Digital Equipment. The founder of ARD was General Georges Doroit, a French-born military man who is considered "the father of venture capital." In the 1950s, he taught at the Harvard Business School. His lectures on the importance of risk capital were considered quirky by the rest of the faculty, who concentrated on conventional corporate management.

II. *J.H. Whitney & Co*, also formed in 1946, one of whose

early hits was Minute Maid Juice. Jock Whitney is considered one of the industry's founders.

III. *The Rockefeller Family*, and in particular, L.S. Rockefeller, one of whose earliest investments was in Eastern Airlines, which is now de-functioned but was one of the earliest commercial airlines company.

The Second World War had produced an abundance of technological innovation, primarily with millionitary applications. They include, for example, some of the earliest work on micro circuitry. Indeed, J.H. Whitney's investment in Minute Maid was intended to commercialize an orange juice concentrate that had been developed to provide nourishment for troops in the field.

The objective of the present chapter is to highlight the growth and development of venture capital financing (VCF) in: Europe; the United States; and Asia in order to gather experience the trajectory of it. Following these parts, a summary of findings of above studies has been added. The last part of this chapter has been devoted in reviewing the overall global growth and development of VCF with pictorial exhibits.

2.1 THE EUROPEAN EXPERIENCE

According to a European venture capitalist, an experienced intermediary often refers to venture capital as a prerequisite for productivity and employment growth to young enterprises in combination with management support for these enterprises. The role of venture capital in facilitating employment and productivity growth has made venture capital a major target of financial market policies by European governments.

The first attempt of General Doriot in UK, a technical development corporation, launched in 1962, was sold at a loss to the ancestor of 3I. A second attempt in 1965, European Enterprises Development (EED), set-up in Paris, was more successful despite an unsupportive environment. The financial uncertainties of mid-70 have led it to stop its activities in 1976. Its example however had led a number of institutions to get interested in the activity. From 1977, the EED started to study action plans to finance enterprises, *inter alias* high technological start-ups.

Besides a culture unsupportive of entrepreneurial spirit, two of the main practical stumbling blocks came from the poor exit alternatives offered by the stock markets at that time, and from the absence of pension funds in the continent to provide the capital required for the activity (the UK being an exception in that respect). As a consequence, funds developed mainly from banks and financial institutions, funded on their own limited resources and with a very long lifetime that would allow waiting for an exit. In the second part of the 80's, a fad similar to the more recent one led many to think venture capital was easy and their experience, intelligence, and knowledge had lead them to surefire success.

Then came the Gulf war and the recession. The prime focuses for corporations were concentrated on re-structuring and focusing on core activities. Most recent investors suffered from their foray in an activity, which they could not locate the reasons. In France, two of the most illuminating experiences were that of the investment arm of Crédit Lyonnais, and that of the SDRs (Société de Développement Régional). In both cases, the state had to intervene to save what ever was possible. It was a period to ensure their sustainability instead of drawing discussions on the principle of venture capital investing. As a result, the few surviving funds were able to choose among the best projects and set the way for what would become their record performance in years to follow.

Then, came the period of Internet business and Europe started thinking in that line. Very few local investors in Europe were fortunate to adapt the new concept and could sustain. But US VCF companies got the opportunity to start up their business in Europe either in the form of joint ventures or floating European subsidiaries.

The growth curve began to sour in 2000. VCF companies could not manage to innovate a viable model to cope with that situation. Many funds were raised, invested at the peak time, quite a few could manage to fund through self-assured people, which was novel to VCF. Due to intensive competition, the complains came from the start-ups about the behaviour of the VCF companies. As a result, funds were stopped compelling new investments to concentrate on their existing portfolios, with reduced headcount, and started reevaluating their investments. In the ensuing paragraph some research findings gives a detailed views about the state of VCF in Europe in recent times.

Economic theory and recent empirical work provide evidence that financial market failures arise when markets perceive an adverse imbalance in the risk-reward ratio. Mason *et. al.* (1995[1], 2003[2]) identify gaps in the supply of external financing particularly for companies requiring seed, start-up and early stage finance. These difficulties increased for young firms, which are highly innovative and deal with speculative new technologies. A shortage of investors' experience in these technical sectors exacerbates information asymmetries and the potential for substantial agency costs. Both factors reduce the supply of finance. Moreover, technological knowledge is more difficult to finance than other types of firm assets. Due to its intangible character, it does not offer any collateral in credit negotiations. (As yet unproven intellectual property rights are frequently a poor substitute for more easily priced, tangible assets.) Thus, the inherent uncertainty and increased possibility of failure associated with each investment is such that potential investors were reluctant to finance certain categories of young firms regardless of their commercial merits. Such a situation has been termed 'the equity gap' since its first used by MacMillan (1931[3]) investigating the availability of finance to small and medium sized enterprises (SMEs) in the UK over seventy-six years ago. This market failure appears a persistent and endemic problem for both high potential young firms and those governments attempting to encourage the formation of such firms. Some 70 percent of Martin *et. al.* (2003[4]) respondents suggest that venture capital is undersupplied in Germany and in the UK. Governments may decide to address finance gaps by the application of different incentivising policy instruments (e.g. tax-credits, loan guarantees, soft loans or equity) with the goal of establishing a new 'culture' of professional equity financing in Europe via an efficient early-stage VCF. Since 1995, several early-stage VCF companies have been founded in both Germany and the UK. In Germany, national as well as regional banks have been encouraged to create special funds to foster high-growth and innovative firms. While there were some responses from private sector banks in the UK, e.g. The Midland Bank scheme, it has never been on a comparable scale to that of German experience. Not withstanding their scale, Harding (2000[5]) argues that such UK responses to the problem have been ineffective given the poorly functioning early-stage VCF. One consequence of failure has been downswing in venture capital deals. This has encouraged the VC industry in its tendency of allocated a majority of funds towards the higher returns of 'private equity', particularly Management by Objectives or Management by Industries investments. As early as 1995, Murray and Lott noted that 'UK, as the largest and most experienced VC industry in Europe, can in part be characterized by a near universal retreat from investment in new technology-based firms'. Till today the comments has remained valid.

Martin *et. al.* (2003[6]) analyzed different policy instruments designed to strengthen VC financing in Germany and the UK. They ascertained that the scale of public support is more significant in Germany than in the UK. The need for greater support was necessary because the VC market in Germany was immature and risk-averse as well. German federal financial interventions are founded on the central policy role of two public owned banks, called the Kreditanstalt fur Wiederaufbau (KfW) and the Deutsche Ausgleichsbank (DtA). These institutions merged in July 2003, was an important outcome.

While these public banks dominated federal support programmes in Germany, the UK has adopted an alternative strategy to address a similar concern with 'equity gap' issues and their effect on new firm formation and growth. The DTI and Small Business Service established the Regional Venture Capital Funds (RVCFs) in 2000. The goal of this programme is to create one early-stage 'classic' venture capital fund in each of the nine English Regional Development Agency areas. (The other three countries of the United Kingdom have their own economic development programmes for SMEs not administered from London.) These funds explicitly aim to provide start-up and early growth funding in a defined geographical area. Accordingly, they are specifically proscribed from making investments above £ 250,000 per firm at the first round. The RVCFs are not limited to technology investments. This scheme addresses the concerns of Mason *et. al.* (1995[7]), who have observed that the UK (as well as the US and Canada) experiences an equity gap for firms seeking small amounts of formal risk capital. This situation was even worse in regions where there was no local or regional VC industry. Both countries use public finance predominantly at the start-up phases although Germany has more expansion finance under such schemes. One direct consequence of the combining of public policies with private investors' interests was that German VC policy instruments continued to reproduce an uneven regional distribution of VC investment. The policy was highly demand-driven and depended largely on the 'pull' activity of the region. According to its federalist policy perspective, VC policies were to assist the promotion of regional clusters, which were seen as the most promising structure to promote young industries and technologies.

The ability of German policy-makers to influence the establishment of a venture capital market was partly the result of the timing of their interventions in the mid-1990s when high technology investments were booming in a bullish market. German VC funds have been primarily directed at start-up and early-stage investment, whereas private and earlier established VC firms in the UK had increasingly metamorphosed into development capital or private equity investments. Although the espoused aim of UK Government's intervention was to create a high growth knowledge-based economy aided by the establishment of venture capital funds. Harding (2000[8]) has argued that UK VC industry has tended to avoid innovative and high-tech activities, preferring less risky sectors such as consumer goods and services.

However, this analysis has been somewhat superceded by contemporary UK policy events, notably the UK Government's underwriting of the UK High Technology Fund and further investments into the University Challenge Fund. Both financing initiatives were specifically directed at start-up and follow-on finance for young technology-based firms. Similar investment schemes have also been created in the life science industries.

Both countries have seen an increase in equity investments in new technology-based enterprises throughout the 1990s. This trend has been much more pronounced in Germany and has reflected the deliberate and generous treatment that the federal government has given to co-financing both new technology-based enterprises and the VC funds that engage in such activities.

By 2001, Germany had the most active early stage VC market in new technologies in Europe. Yet, this rapid 'progress' also made Germany's immature VC industry uniquely vulnerable to the subsequent international market collapse of the value of technology companies. The report demonstrates that VC policies in Germany and the UK continue to differ substantially. Germany with its traditional reliance on bank-based loan capital has provided a complex variety of public policy measures in an attempt to construct rapidly a VC industry. Such initiatives to provide professionally mediated equity finance, introduced into a SME market strongly characterized by the use of bank guarantees, refinancing loans and mezzanine capital, have not been without their problems. UK policy, in contrast, has traditionally exhibited a stronger market orientation illustrated in its common use of fiscal incentives. The case for policy intervention based on evidence of market failure in UK has been controversial. Since the late 1990s the UK Government decided to increase directly the supply of early-stage venture capital by its own involvement as an investor. Importantly, the UK Government's predilection to use private agents (i.e. rent maximizing VCs) as the conduit has been predominant.

2.1.1 European Experience for Private Equity

Before the mid-1990s, it seemed that venture capital, as a source for financing young enterprises, would never play a significant role in quantitative terms in the 10 private equity markets of Europe. However, in the mid-1990s, a substantial upswing took place in private equity as well as in more narrowly defined venture capital activity. The growth rates of investments in enterprises' early stage of development containing the seed and the start-up stage were particularly high. In the seed stage, the initial business concept is formed and prototypes of new products are developed and compared with competing products in the market. In the start-up stage, production is set-up and an initial marketing campaign is launched, to which the market reaction is carefully analyzed.

Compared to other stages of development, the seed and start-up stage are the most risky stages. Between 1990 and 1999, these investments grew annually by 20 per cent, between 1995 and 1999 even by 46 per cent. In 1995, 0.27 billion Euros went into enterprises' early stage, while in 1999 the respective amount was 2.7 billion Euros. Private equity investments in enterprises that are in their expansion stage also increased, but growth rates were lower than those of the early stage investments. Enterprises in the growth or expansion stage often require very large amounts of external funding, because their cash flow may not generate enough liquidity for firm's growth to be financed internally. Investments in enterprises' expansion stage grew annually by 11.6 per cent per year between 1990 and 1999. The growth rate of investments was comparatively small because the upswing took place in the second half of the 1990s: between 1995 and 1999 the average annual growth rate was 22.4 per cent. Investments in the expansion stage increased from 2.0 billion Euros in 1995 to 6.2 billion Euros in 1999. Thus, expansion stage investments increased more strongly than early stage investments in absolute terms.[9] All the countries considered here differ considerably with respect to investments in enterprises' early stages as per million of GDP (Figure 2.1) even if all the countries experienced a positive development in investment volumes over the observation period.

Relative to GDP, early stage investments are highest in Sweden, the Netherlands and Belgium, while in Austria, early stage investments hardly play a role. The importance of Swedish and Belgian early stage investments relative to GDP in comparison to the other European countries has emerged in till the year 1999, whereas the Dutch market was already the leading country in terms of early stage investments relative to GDP in 1995. European countries also differ with respect to the level of expansion stage investments relative to GDP. The United Kingdom, the Netherlands, and Belgium had the highest levels of investments relative to their GDPs, with more than Euro 1.5 per million of GDP in 1999. In 1995, these three countries were also the leading countries in terms of expansion stage investments relative to GDP. Austria's expansion stage investments, however, accounted for only Euro 0.2 per million

FIG. 2.1

Early and Expansion Stage Investments through Private Equity in Europe

(Per million of GDP)

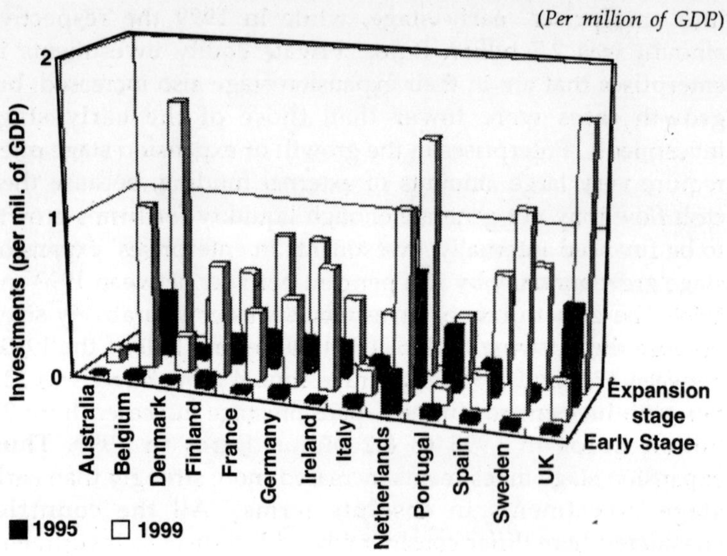

Source : Investment volumes are from EVCA 1991–2000; GDPs are from International Financial Statistics CD ROM IFS (2000).

of GDP followed by Italy and Denmark, with about Euro 0.3 per million of GDP.

The Belgian and the Dutch venture capital markets seem to be the markets, which are comparable to the US market in terms of investments in enterprises' early and expansion stages relative to GDP in 1999. Belgian investments in enterprises' early and expansion stages relative to GDP were not significant in 1995, while Dutch investments had already become somewhat significant in 1995. Dutch early stage investments accounted for Euro 0.25 per million of GDP in 1995, the expansion stage investments for more than Euro 0.7 per million of GDP.

In the data offered by the EVCA, two sets of variables are available which can be used to analyze which types of passive investors are offering capital to European private equity investors. The first set of variables describes the types of passive investors, the so-called sources of funds, such as banks, insurances and pension funds, without considering the possibility of a legal connection between private equity investors and passive investors. The second set of variables combines the investments of private equity investors with the legal connection between them and their passive investors, albeit without identifying the sources of funds. The two most important sources of funds for the European private equity market are banks and pension funds (Figure 2.2). In Europe, the significance of banks decreased over the period of observation, while the significance of pension funds increased. In 1990, banks provided more than 40 per cent of the new funds raised for private equity investments, pension funds, in contrast, made up only about 16 per cent of the new funds. Since the mid-1990s, the situation has changed significantly; since 1995 both types of passive investors have invested on average about a quarter of the new funds rose for private equity investments. These are for

Fig. 2.2
Sources of New Funds

(billion Euros)

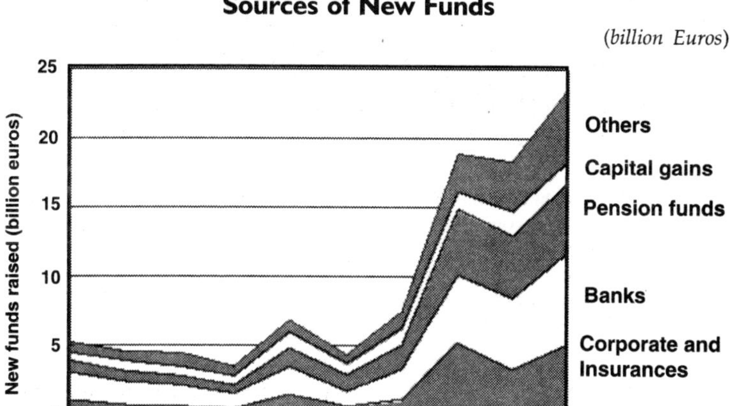

Note : New fund volumes have been deflated using consumer price indices (1995=100) converted into Euros using 12-month averages and then aggregated.

Source : New fund volumes and exchange rates are from EVCA 1991–2000; consumer price indices are from International Financial Statistics CD ROM IFS (2000).

firms in crisis, for the acquisition of an existing business by its own management and for the takeover of privately held firms.

The role of pension funds in Europe is a result of the importance of this source of funding in the British equity market. Since 1991, pension funds committed more capital for private equity investments than banks in the UK. (Figure 2.3)

FIG. 2.3

Private Equity Investments and Stages of Enterprises' Development

(Billion Euros)

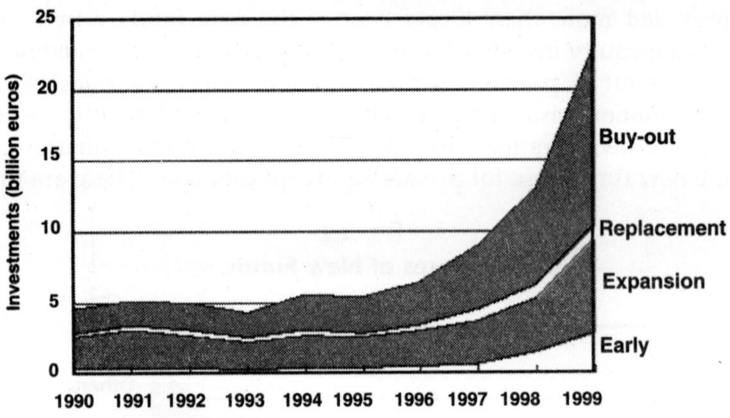

Note : Investment volumes have been deflated using consumer price indices (1995=100), converted into Euros using 12-month averages and then aggregated.

Source : Investment volumes and exchange rates are from EVCA 1991-2000; consumer price indices are from International Financial Statistics CD ROM IFS (2000).

European countries differ with respect to the stages of distribution of investments. Early stage investments of the private equity investors in the UK play a minor role measured as percentage of private equity investments: the seed and start-up investments together accounted for less than three per cent. For other European countries the shares are not only much higher but show also a divergent development over the observation period. In 1999, around one-fifth of the private equity went into the enterprises' early stages in France and the Netherlands; in Germany more than 30 per cent was invested in enterprises in the seed and start-up stage. Interestingly, some European countries considered here show a considerable upswing in the money invested in enterprises' early stages after 1997 while it is not so in UK.

From a study carried out by the Thomson Financial with EVCA in 2006, it was found that in Europe since 1980 to 2005, the net pooled IRR was 10.3 percent for the 1,063 equity funds with a 13.7 percent return for buy-out funds and 6.3 percent return for venture funds. As in previous years, the private equity market registered high-pooled returns then most public market equivalents. As a result, the private equity is gaining more importance than that of public market in Europe.

2.1.2 Summary of European VCF Experience

From the above paragraphs the following are the gist of European experiences on VCF:

- European venture capitalists consider themselves as intermediaries who often refer to venture capital as a prerequisite for productivity and employment growth to young enterprises in combination with management support for these enterprises. The role of venture capital in facilitating employment and productivity growth has made venture capital a major target of financial market policies by European Governments.
- The European VCF markets had passed through turmoil during 1960s and middle half of 1970s due to an unsupportive environment in entire Europe for VCF.
- During 1970s till late 1980s the Venture capital funds developed in Europe were mainly from banks and financial institutions, funded from their own limited resources and it takes a very long lifetime in European standards for an exit.
- During the gulf war period the prime focus for corporations operating in Europe were concentrated on re-structuring and on core activities rather than innovations and R&D. This leads to a dramatic fall in

the growth of VCF. Even in French, the Government has to intervene into the activities of VCF to save the possible looses.

- From 1992 onwards came the period of Internet business and Europe started thinking in that line. Very few local investors in Europe were fortunate to adapt the new concept and could sustain. But US VCF companies have en-cashed the opportunity to start up their business in Europe either in the form of joint ventures or floating European subsidiaries.
- The European VCF environment was often suffered from the concept of equity gap. Most of the studies revealed that venture capital is undersupplied in Germany and in UK.
- Most of the studies suggested that Governments may decide to address finance gaps by the application of different incentive policy instruments (e.g. tax-credits, loan guarantees, soft loans or equity) with the goal of establishing a new 'culture' of professional equity financing in Europe via an efficient early-stage VCF.
- The ability of German policy-makers to influence the establishment of a venture capital market was partly the result of the timing of their interventions in the mid-1990s when high technology investments were booming in a bullish market.
- In the mid-1990s, a substantial upswing took place in private equity as well as in more narrowly defined venture capital activity in Europe.
- Between 1990 and 1999, the seed and start-up investments in Europe grew annually by 20 per cent, between 1995 and 1999 even by 46 per cent. In 1995, 0.27 billion Euros went into enterprises' early stage, while in 1999 the respective amount was 2.7 billion Euros.
- The two most important sources of funds for the European private equity market are banks and pension funds.
- In Europe since 1980 to 2005, the net-pooled IRR was 10.3 percent for the 1,063 equity funds with a 13.7

percent return for buy-out funds and 6.3 percent return for venture funds.

- At present the private equity market is stronger than the public market equivalents in Europe.

2.2 THE US EXPERIENCE

Most of the US venture capitalist defines Venture capital is a form of intermediation particularly well suited to support the creation and growth of innovative, entrepreneurial companies. It specializes in financing and nurturing companies at an early stage of development ('start-ups') that operate in high-tech industries and later on the growth financing once the enterprise is established.

In the mid-1950s, the U.S. federal government wanted to speed the development of advanced technologies. In 1957, the Federal Reserve System conducted a study that concluded that a shortage of entrepreneurial financing was a chief obstacle to the development of what it called "entrepreneurial businesses." As a response to this a number of Small Business Investment Companies (SBIC) were established to "leverage" their private capital by borrowing from the federal government at below-market interest rates. Soon commercial banks were allowed to form SBICs and within four years, nearly 600 SBICs were in operation.

At the same time a number of venture capital firms were forming private partnerships outside the SBIC format. These partnerships added to the venture capitalist's toolkit, by offering a degree of flexibility that SBICs lacked. Within a decade, private venture capital partnerships became ahead of SBICs in total capital under management.

The 1960s saw a tremendous bull IPO market that allowed venture capital firms to demonstrate their ability to create companies and produce huge investment returns. For example, when Digital Equipment went public in 1968 it provided ARD with 101 percent annualized Return on Investment (ROI). The USD 70,000 Digital invested to start the company in 1959 had a market value of USD 37 m. As a result, venture capital became a hot market, particularly for wealthy individuals and families.

However, it was still considered too risky for institutional investors.

During 1970s, though, venture capital suffered a double-setback. First, a red-hot IPO market brought over 1,000 venture-backed companies to market in 1968, the public markets went into a seven-year slump. There were a lot of disappointed stock market investors and a lot of disappointed venture capital investors too. Then in 1974, after Congress legislation against the abuse of pension fund money, all high-risk investment of these funds was halted. As a result of poor public market and the pension fund legislation, venture capital fund raising hit rock bottom in 1975.

Things could only get better from there. Beginning in 1978, a series of legislative and regulatory changes gradually improved the climate for venture investing. First Congress slashed the capital gains tax rate to 28 percent from 49.5 percent. Then the Labor Department issued a clarification that eliminated the pension funds act as an obstacle to venture investing. At around the same time, there were a number of high-profile IPOs by venture-backed companies. These included Federal Express in 1978, and Apple Computer and Genetech Inc in 1981. This rekindled interest in venture capital on the part of wealthy families and institutional investors. Indeed, in the 1980s, the venture capital industry began its greatest period of growth. In 1980, venture firms raised and invested less than USD 600 million. That number soared to nearly USD 4 bn by 1987. The decade also marked the explosion in the buy-out business.

The late 1980s marked the transition of the primary source of venture capital funds from wealthy individuals and families to endowment, pension and other institutional funds. The surge in capital in the 1980s had predictable results. Returns on venture capital investments plunged. Many investors went into the funds anticipating returns of 30 percent or higher. That was probably an unrealistic expectation to begin with. The consensus today is that private equity investments generally should give the investor an internal rate of return something to the order of 15 percent to 25 percent, depending upon the degree of risk a firm takes.

However, by 1990, the average long-term return on venture capital funds fell below 8 percent, leading to yet another downturn in venture funding. Disappointed families and institutions withdrew from venture investing in phases during the 1989-91 period. The economic recovery and the IPO boom of 1991-94 had gone a long way towards reversing the trend in both private equity investment performance and partnership commitments.

In 1998, the venture capital industry in the United States continued its seventh straight year of growth. It raised USD 25 bn in committed capital for investments by venture firms, who invested over USD 16 bn into domestic growth companies in all sectors, but primarily focused on information technology.

This potential can be seen in the growth of sales figures for the US. From 1992 to 1998, venture-backed companies saw their sales grow, on average, by 66.5 per cent per annum as against five per cent for Fortune 500 firms. The export growth by venture-funded companies was 165 per cent. The top ten US sectors, measured by asset and sales growth, were technology-related.

Thus, venture capital is valuable not just because it makes risk capital available in the early stages of a project, but also because a venture capitalist brings expertise that leads to superior product development. The big focus of venture capital worldwide is, of course, technology. So in 1999, of USD 30 bn of venture capital invested in the US, technology firms received approximately 80 per cent. Additional to this huge supply of venture funds from formally organized venture capital firms, is an even larger pool of angel or seed/start-up funds provided by private investors. In 1999, according to estimates, approximately USD 90 bn of angel investment was available, thus making the total 'at-risk' investment in high technology ventures in a single year worth around USD 120 bn.

Pension funds have been the main capital providers to venture capital funds (limited partnerships), while corporations, and financial and insurance have played a minor role (Exhibit 2.1). Pension funds contributed between 35 and 60 per cent of the new funds raised between 1990 and 1998. In 1999, however, only 23 per cent of the capital was contributed by pension funds.

EXHIBIT 2.1

Sources of New Funds and its Allocation

	1990	1991	1992	1993	1994	1995	1996	1997	1998	1999
(1)	(2)	(3)	(4)	(5)	(6)	(7)	(8)	(9)	(10)	(11)
United States (New funds for venture capital, billion euros)	2.43	1.34	3.02	3.55	6.20	6.29	8.07	13.06	23.13	39.55
As percentage by type of limited partner									(Percent)	
Corporations	6.8	4.0	3.3	8.4	9.1	4.1	18.9	24.0	11.8	15.0
Endowments and Foundations	12.5	24.2	18.6	10.7	21.3	19.6	11.3	16.0	6.2	21.0
Foreign Investors	7.6	11.4	11.1	4.3	2.4	3.8	5.6	4.0	1.2	6.0
Individuals and Families	11.3	12.1	11.1	7.4	11.9	16.2	6.5	12.0	11.2	22.0
Financial and Insurances	9.4	5.4	14.4	10.4	9.5	19.2	2.9	6.0	10.2	13.0
Pension funds	52.5	42.3	41.7	59.1	45.8	37.0	54.8	38.0	59.4	23.0

Note : New funds raised have been deflated using consumer price indices (1995=100) and then converted into euros using 12-month averages.

Compiled from the original table source : European new funds raised and exchange rates are from EVCA 1991–2000, US new funds raised are from NVCA (2000), consumer price indices are from International Financial Statistics CD ROM IFS (2000).

The 1980 'Safe Harbor' Regulation further improved the conditions for venture capital committed by pension funds because it defined pension funds as limited partners, which reduced the risk exposure of venture capitalists. These acts had clearly a considerable impact for the upswing in venture capital activity at the beginning of the 1980s. Especially pension funds and their de-regulation seem to have played a significant role in the development of the US venture capital market.

This extraordinary boom during the 1990s is not the first significant change that the American market for venture capital has experienced since its humble beginnings in the 1930s. Two upswings of venture capital activity can be identified in the time series. The first upswing took place in the mid-1960s, the second at the beginning of the 1980s. Both upswings, however, in the US, new funds raised for private equity grew at a lower rate than new funds raised for venture capital are small compared to the increase in venture capital activity at the end of the 1990s. The first two upswings seemed to be influenced by public policies.[10]

The journal 'Venture Economics' had identified two reasons for the extraordinary boom in the investments in enterprises' early and expansion stages at the end of the 1990s (BVK, 2001).[11] Venture capital funds brought their passive investors high returns, resulting in a considerable re-investment of money; especially institutional investors reinvested large amounts of their funds. Secondly, the development of stock markets resulted in a restructuring of institutional investors' portfolios so as to invest more money in venture capital funds.[12] Thus, the US government also supports the creation of venture capital companies.

California, Texas, Massachusetts, Washington, and Pennsylvania topped the list of states by sales of venture capital backed firms headquartered in the State by 2003. Venture capital backed companies headquartered in California were responsible for USD 438 billion in sales in 2003. In Texas, venture backed sales reached nearly USD 190 billion in 2003 and exceeded USD 100 billion in Massachusetts. Other leading states measured by venture capital backed firms sales were Washington, at slightly more than USD 100 billion, and Pennsylvania, at USD 94 billion in 2003. (Exhibit 2.2)

EXHIBIT 2.2

State-wise Classification of Number of Sales by VC Backed Firms in US

Rank	*State*	*2000 Sales by VC Backed Firms*	*2003 Sales by VC Backed Firms*	*Percent Change*
1	California	$ 398 B	$ 186 B	10%
2	Texas	$ 176 B	$ 185 B	7%
3	Massachusetts	$ 96 B	$ 107 B	12%
4	Washington	$ 83 B	$ 102 B	22%
5	Pennsylvania	$ 74 B	$ 94 B	28%
6	Georgia	$ 74 B	$ 91 B	24%
7	New York	$ 75 B	$ 80 B	7%
8	Virginia	$ 48 B	$ 64 B	32%
9	Florida	$ 56 B	$ 61 B	8%
10	Tennessee	$ 51 B	$ 60 B	17%
11	Minnesota	$ 49 B	$ 57 B	15%
12	New Jersey	$ 45 B	$ 50 B	11%
13	Connecticut	$ 40 B	$ 49 B	24%
14	Illinois	$ 31 B	$ 34 B	10%
15	North Carolina	$ 24 B	$ 27 B	13%

Source : Global Impact 2004, Vol. 18, No. 3.

In the ensuing paragraph some research findings gives a detailed views about the state of VCF in US in recent times.

Among the important facts of venture capital finance in the US, the specialization and syndication as an investment strategy of venture capitalists must be emphasized. US venture capitalists tend to specialize in enterprises of particular industries or in enterprises that are in a particular development stage, Sahlman (1990[13]). Moreover, venture capitalists syndicate their investments, i.e., several venture capitalists finance a single enterprise and only one of them takes on the monitoring of the enterprise. This venture capitalist is called the lead venture capitalist. Both, specialization as well as syndication reacts rather sensitively to cyclical changes.

US venture capitalists build portfolios which are often concentrated on enterprises in specific stages or on enterprises in particular industries, so that the portfolios are not well-diversified, i.e., not all unsystematic risk is diversified away Norton *et. al.* (1993[14]). The degree of specialization appears to depend on the several factors. First, venture capitalists that invest money in the early stage of enterprises' development are on average more specialized on particular industries than venture capitalists that focus on later stages of enterprises' development, Norton *et. al.* (1993[15]), Gupta *et. al.* (1992[16]). Venture capitalists who manage large funds prefer greater industry diversity than venture capitalists managing small funds, Gupta *et. al.* (1992[17]). The specialization pattern of venture capitalists is also affected by the relationship between them and their passive investors. Corporate venture capitalists have a higher degree of specialization on industries than non-corporate venture capitalists, while SBICs have no preference regarding industry diversity, Gupta *et. al.* (1992[18]).

The degree of syndication seems to depend on uncertainty: the higher the uncertainty of an investment, the higher the degree of syndication is. For example, US venture capitalists prefer a higher degree of syndication when they finance enterprises' early stages of development although the investment amount per company is small compared to later-stage deals Bygrave (1987[19]). Spreading of financial risks does not seem to be the main reason for syndications, Bygrave (1987[20]). Syndication of investments mainly serves to share information, as the empirical study by Lerner (1994[21]) suggests. In the first financing stage, venture capitalists syndicate their investments with venture capitalists that have similar expertise, while in later stages of enterprises' development venture capitalists also syndicate their investments with venture capitalists that have less expertise.

2.2.1 The US Private Equity Market

The US market is one of the oldest markets for private equities. Although no specific record tells about its humble beginning but is considered as nearly eighty years old. However, till 60s such financing was made in very unorganized manner. But from 1990 onwards it bypassed the public equity market.

Private equity funds continued to outperform the public markets across all time horizons in the third quarter of 2005, according to Thomson Venture Economics and the National Venture Capital Association (NVCA). Long-term performance in both venture capital and buyouts remained steadfast, enjoying 20-year returns of 16.5 percent and 13.3 percent respectively. For the ten-year horizon, venture capital returned 26.5 percent; buyouts returned 8.7 percent. Short-term performance was considerably more volatile with one-year venture capital returns jumping from 7.8 percent in second quarter 2005 to 19.7 percent in third quarter 2005. For the same one-year horizon, buyout funds returned 32.5 percent in the third quarter compared to 26.9 percent in the second quarter.

Despite a lackluster IPO market for venture-backed companies, private equity funds continued to outperform the S&P 500 in the fourth quarter of 2005, according to Thomson Financial and the National Venture Capital Association (NVCA). Long-term performance in both venture capital and buyouts remained steadfast, enjoying 20-year returns of 16.5 percent and 13.3 percent respectively. For the ten-year horizon, venture capital returned 23.7 percent; buyouts returned 9.2 percent. Short-term performance showed more quarter-to-quarter stability with one-year venture capital returns slightly decreasing from 17.9 percent in third quarter 2005 to 15.6 in last quarter 2005. Buyout funds mirrored the venture capital market in the fourth quarter with a slight decrease in the one-year return from 35.2 percent in the third quarter to 31.3 percent in last quarter.

The venture-backed IPO market saw a volume and valuation drop off during the fourth quarter with 17 venture-backed companies going public. The venture-backed mergers and acquisitions market also saw a slight decline in the fourth quarter. Downward pressure was also placed on private equity performance as a result of a sharp correction in October 2005 after the Federal Reserve policy-makers disappointed investors who anticipated that there would be a pause in their short-term interest hike. An indication of this kind did not take place until 2006. Five-year performance for venture capital improved in the

EXHIBIT 2.3

Venture Economics' US Private Equity Performance Index* (PEPI)

Investment Horizon up to 3rd Qtr., 2005

(*Percent*)

CATEGORY / *Fund Type*	*1 Year*	*3 Years*	*5 Years*	*10 Years*	*20 Years*
Early/Seed VC	10.4	0.4	–13.2	46.8	20.2
Balanced VC	27.2	9.3	–5.6	20.8	14.6
Later Stage VC	13.1	6.1	–7.7	13.0	13.7
All Venture	19.7	4.9	9.3	26.5	16.5
Small Buyouts	48.3	8.9	2.4	7.2	26.3
Med Buyouts	34.2	8.6	0.2	10.2	17.9
Large Buyouts	25.0	15.6	1.8	9.2	12.8
Mega Buyouts	33.4	15.8	3.9	8.4	11.1
All Buyouts	32.5	14.7	3.1	8.7	13.3
Mezzanine	8.8	4.5	2.4	6.6	9.0
All Private Equity	27.0	11.3	–.8	12.4	14.3
NASDAQ	13.4	22.4	–10.1	7.5	12.3
S & P 500	10.2	14.7	–3.1	7.7	11.2

* The Private Equity Performance Index is based on the latest quarterly statistics from Thomson Venture Economics' Private Equity Performance Database analyzing the cashflows and returns for over 1750 US venture capital and private equity partnerships with a capitalization of USD 608 Billion. Sources are financial documents and schedules from Limited Partners investors and General Partners. All returns are calculated by Thomson Venture Economics from the underlying financial cash flows. Returns are net to investors after management fees and carried interest. Buyout funds sizes are defined as the following: Small: 0-250 m USD, Medium: 250-500 m USD, Large: 500-1000 m USD, Mega: USD1 bn +

Source : Thomson Venture Economics/National Venture Capital Association.

fourth quarter although still posted a negative return of -6.8 percent. This continued negative return had been due to the remaining accumulated losses taken by firms that made investments in the final stages of the Internet bubble era and the beginning of the subsequent recovery period. Five-year buyout returns remained in positive territory at 5.2 percent.

In the first quarter of 2007, venture capitalists invested USD 7.1 billion into 778 deals, the highest quarterly dollar amount since the fourth quarter of 2001, according to the MoneyTree Report by Price Waterhouse Coopers and the National Venture Capital Association based on Thomson Financial data. Deal volume actually declined in the quarter compared with the fourth quarter of 2006, indicating venture capitalists' willingness to put more dollars into each round.

The Life Sciences sector (Biotechnology and Medical Devices together) had an extremely strong quarter, with Biotechnology ranked as the number one industry for investment, while Medical Devices was at an all-time high. Later Stage investing also jumped in the quarter to the highest dollar level since the fourth quarter of 2000. First time financings remained relatively steady, increasing slightly over last quarter. Medical Device investing skyrocketed to an all-time high in the first quarter, with USD 1.08 billion going into 96 deals, a 60 percent increase in dollars over last quarter 2006. Biotechnology was the single largest industry sector with USD 1.5 billion going into 102 deals, unseating software, which was traditionally the largest sector. Life Sciences accounted for 36 percent of the quarter's dollars, an all-time high.

Software investments fell 10 percent from first quarter of 2006 to USD 1.1 billion into 193 deals in first quarter of 2007. The decrease can be attributed to lower deal volume. However, Software still had the highest deal level of all industries and was the second largest industry sector for dollar value in this quarter.

The Media and Entertainment sector increased 16 percent in dollars to USD 489 million into 72 deals. Telecommunications increased 27 percent in dollars over last quarter 2006 with USD 588 million going into 63 deals. Within the Telecom sector, Wireless Communications captured USD 356 million for the quarter.

Internet-specific companies captured USD 1.3 billion going into 167 deals, a 31 percent increase in investment dollars over last quarter 2006 and the highest quarterly level in five years. However, the number of Internet Specific deals decreased since the fourth quarter indicating more dollars being invested in each round. 'Internet-specific' is a discrete classification assigned to a company whose business model is fundamentally dependent on the Internet, regardless of the company's primary industry category such as Software or Telecommunications.

A new Clean Tech category, which crossed the traditional individual financing sector. Clean Tech category comprised of alternative energy, pollution and recycling, power supplies and conservation has been reported to be going forward. In the first quarter of 2007, venture capitalists invested USD 264 million into 23 deals in the Clean Tech category, a 41 percent increase in dollar value over the fourth quarter. For the full year 2006, Clean Tech investments were USD 1.5 billion or an average of USD 383 million per quarter.

Other major industry categories that experienced dollar increases in first quarter of 2007 include IT Services, Networking and Equipment, Retailing/Distribution, Industrial/Energy, Electronics/Instrumentation, and Computers/Peripherals. Other industries experiencing declines were Semiconductors and Consumer Products.

Investments in Later Stage companies increased significantly in the first quarter of 2007 with USD 3.0 billion dollars going into 245 deals. This was the highest dollar level in over six years. Average post-money valuations were USD 95.33 million for the 12-month period ending last quarter 2006.

Funding dollars for Seed and Early Stage companies declined 30 percent in first quarter to USD 1.1 billion in 259 companies, a 26 percent decline in deals. Average post-money valuations of Early Stage companies were USD 11.13 million for the 12 months ending last quarter 2006. Investments in Expansion Stage companies experienced a modest dollar increase in first quarter, rising nearly 9 percent to USD 2.9 billion invested into 274 deals. The average post-money valuation for an Expansion Stage company was USD 68.9 million for the full-year 2006. Overall for first quarter the number of deals was spread relatively evenly among the stages. Seed/Early Stage companies accounted for 33 percent of the deal volume; Expansion Stage for 35 percent; and Later Stage for 32 percent.

2.2.2 Overall US VCF Experience: At a Glance

From the above paragraphs the following are the gist of US experiences on VCF:

- The US venture capitalist views venture capital as a form of intermediation particularly well suited to support the creation and growth of innovative, entrepreneurial companies. It specializes in financing and nurturing companies at an early stage of development ('start-ups') that operate in high-tech industries and later on the growth financing once the enterprise is established.
- By 1957 a number of Small Business Investment Companies (SBIC) were established in US to "leverage" their private capital by borrowing from the Federal Government at below-market interest rates under the aegis of the Federal Reserve System. During that period only a number of venture capital firms were forming private partnerships outside the SBIC format.
- The 1960s saw a tremendous bull in US IPO market that allowed venture capital firms to demonstrate their ability to create companies and produce huge investment returns
- 1968, the public markets went into a seven-year slump. There were a lot of disappointed stock market investors and a lot of disappointed venture capital investors also. It is only in 1974, after Congress legislation against the abuse of pension fund money, all high-risk investment of these funds were halted. As a result of poor public market and the pension fund legislation, venture capital fund declined in 1975.
- 1978, a series of legislative and regulatory changes gradually improved the climate for VCF. The late 1980s marked the transition of the primary source of venture capital funds from wealthy individuals and families to endowment, pension and other institutional funds.
- By 1990, the average long-term return on venture capital funds fell below 8 percent, leading to yet another downturn in venture funding.
- From 1992 to 1998, venture-backed companies saw their turn over growth, on an average, by 66.5 per cent per annum as against five per cent for Fortune 500 companies.

- Pension funds contributed between 35 and 60 per cent of the new funds raised between 1990 and 1998. In 1999, however, only 23 per cent of the capital was contributed by pension funds.
- Venture capital funds brought their passive investors high returns, resulting in a considerable re-investment of money; especially institutional investors reinvested large amounts of their funds. Secondly, the development of stock markets resulted in a restructuring of institutional investors' portfolios so as to invest more money in venture capital funds. As a result, the US government also has supported the creation of venture capital companies.
- US venture capitalists seem to be specialized in particular industry category or in the development stage of enterprises.
- Venture capitalists syndicate their investments, i.e., several venture capitalists finance a single enterprise and only one of them takes on the monitoring of the enterprise. This venture capitalist is called the lead venture capitalist. Both, specialization as well as syndication reacts rather sensitively to cyclical changes.
- By 2005 Long-term performance in both venture capital and buyouts remained steady, enjoying 20-year returns of 16.5 percent and 13.3 percent respectively.
- In the first quarter of 2007, venture capitalists invested USD 7.1 billion into 778 deals, the highest quarterly investment since the fourth quarter of 2001.

2.3 THE ASIAN EXPERIENCE

A Japanese venture capitalist often expresses its view on VCF, as it is a means of financing fast-growing private companies.

The US and Continental success stories of Venture Capital financing has a good impact on the Asian countries like Japan, South Korea, Singapore, Hong Kong, Thailand and Malaysia as the venture capital market fosters in these countries because of the technological advancement. By 2005, Asian VCF has witnessed a good number of private equity. This 2005 may well rank with 1997 as a defining moment in the channels of Asian private equity. If the modern era of buyouts and control positions began with the 1997 financial crisis, then 2005 has seen the worlds' leading buyout and venture firms pouring into Asia. They are in Asia to open offices, hire staff, and launch Asian-related funds' region, which by and large, they had the access but had ignored until 2005. With Asian exits making headlines, fundraising hitting new highs, and Asian economies setting the pace for global expansion, Asia's attraction to global investors was tremendous and it has come with no surprise. New regulations in China and Japan hit the only temporary set backs as fund managers temporarily pulled back on investing while they waited for clarification by the authorities.

By 2003 the Asian VCF market has attain several milestones. An estimated USD 17.5 billion of private equity and venture capital was invested in the Asia Pacific region and has observed a whopping 92 percent increase in comparison to 2002. Japan led the region accounting for USD 7.3bn of the value of deals completed, followed by Korea with USD 3.3bn and Australia with USD 2.8bn. In contrast, only USD 3.32 billion of new funds were raised in 2003 (up only 10percent on 2002 levels). The pool of private equity capital under management rose to USD 97.6 billion in 2003 up from USD 88.6bn in 2002. By 2002, start-up and early stage investment was as low as USD 0.6 bn and USD 1.4 billion respectively and it was invested in expansion stages in 2003. Telecommunication section had the highest percentage of invested capital with USD 3.7bn or 21 percent followed by financial services with USD 2.3bn or 18.3 percent.

2.3.1 Investment Pattern

During 2005, overall private equity investment across Asia touched USD 8.6 billion at the end of second quarter, ahead of the same period's USD 6.2 billion in 2004. Regulatory changes in China and Japan had slowed down the investment activities there and impacted the overall numbers. Private equity investments into China fell to around USD 731 million by the end of second quarter 2005, down 38.4 percent from the USD 1.2 billion spent there in the same period of 2004. Japan, still Asia's largest private equity destination, had also seen investments plunge to USD 1.64 billion in second quarter 2005 from the USD 3.45 billion in second quarter 2004. With investment in other major regional economies, such as South Korea, at more or less stable levels, Japan's new tax laws and China's new regulations related to cross-border investments proved a temporary drag behind. The effects of these regulations seemed to have waned in the third quarter 2005 as investors, driven by the opportunities, returned back into the market.

As in the past, a large percentage (34.5 percent) of the capital went into buyouts, and a further 25.1 percent into turnaround or restructuring related transactions. Other magnets for private equity Capitals were expansion-stage and bridge transactions, accounting for 22.1 percent and 15.1 percent of the total respectively. Affinity Equity Partners printed the largest deal in the first half of 2005 with a USD 684 million consortium-led acquisition of an 80 percent stake in South Korean electronics chain Himart. Other significant deals included Advantage Partners' buyout of Japan's Daiei Inc and the ground breaking funding of Lenovo by a Texas Pacific Group Newbridge Capital General Atlantic consortium.

FIG. 2.4

Asian Venture Capital Pool 2006

US $ million

1996	1997	1998	1999	2000	2001	2002	2003	2004	2005	1H 2006
33,701	32,136	45,785	69,132	81,186	85,554	89,196	97,598	106,383	122,039	138,530

Source : AVCJ, 2007, Vol. 18, No. 4.

Buyout funds had another prosperous period from 2005 to first quarter of 2006, completing several profitable exits. Newbridge Capital took top honours in the trade sale category, selling Korea First Bank to Standard Chartered for just over USD 3.25 billion. The sale of Goldman Sachs and Morgan Stanley Private Equity's sale of their stake in China's Ping An Insurance cleared the USD 1 billion marks. Yahoo!'s USD 1 billion investment in alibaba.com constitute 35percent stake there. Figure 2.4 and 2.5 depicts the Asian venture capital pool and new fund raised during 2006 respectively.

FIG. 2.5
New Fund Raised in Asia : 2006

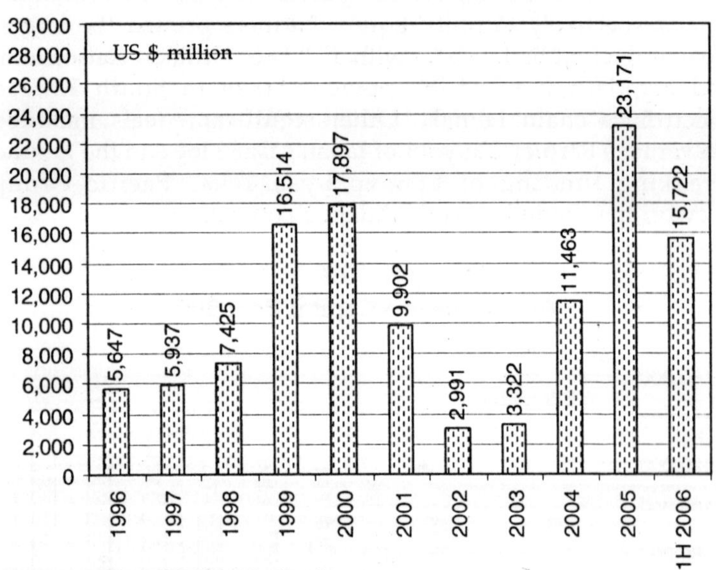

Source : AVCJ, 2007, Vol. 18, No. 4.

2.3.2 Private Equity in Asia

The private equity market in Asia although has a major contribution but due to absence of proper documentation, the present researcher focuses only in two of the oldest as well as promising private equity markets of Asia, i.e. Hong Kong and Thailand.

Hong Kong's Experience

Hong Kong rebounded dramatically from the downturn, which has reached its bottomline in the SARS crisis of spring 2003, have showed a strong economic recovery of over 8 percent growth for 2004 according to Asian Development Bank's (ADB) figures, compared to fewer than 2 percent annually for the preceding three years. Measures taken by the Government to restore confidence in the territory and buttress support for its appointees brought new economic activities and investments. The Closer Economic Partnership Agreement (CEPA) initiative facilitated cross-border partnerships, the relaxation of rules on mainland travel to—and investment into—Hong Kong brought a flood of capital and commerce. Hong Kong banks were allowed for the first time to offer personal banking and credit cards in Renminbi for mailand[22] customers. Speculation over a possible revaluation of the Hong Kong dollar, following the revaluation of the Renminbi during 2005, led to continuing capital inflows during the year. Most significant at all for private equity investors, the Hong Kong Stock Exchange became a destination of choice for mainland companies seeking to list outside China.

Thailand's Experience

Thailand began 2005 with the aftermath of the tsunami, which devastated so many maritime areas of Asia. This and the insurgency in Thailand's three Muslim southern provinces bordering Malaysia seemed to take the shine off the economic boom that had followed the election of Prime Minister Thaksin Shinawatra.

Both these factors hit Thailand's highly important tourism sector. The further impact of high oil prices and weakening OECD demand for Thai exports contributed to an overall slowdown in economic growth. Rising demand for imports also helped swing the national current account into deficit in 2005, although optimistic investors might argue that this shows that consumer demand—often a key factor in investments in Southeast Asia—was strong. Thaksin's re-election in February 2005 brought no turnround in either his government or the country's fortunes. An estimated USD 42.5 billion was earmarked for various infrastructure projects. However, concern over the rising budget deficit might delay some of these. There were no private equity exits in the first half of 2005.

After showing an upswing from USD 10 million in 2003 to USD 40 million in 2004, fund raising in Thailand cooled again, with no activity registering in the first half of 2005. Total capital under management remained at the same level since 2003, i.e.USD 645 million. During that period new investment in Thailand was not encouraging. After six deals in 2004 totaling USD 239 million, 2005 showed just one service deal, the USD 12 million acquisition of Mermaid Maritime Ltd. by Private Equity (Thailand) Co. Ltd. and UOB Venture Management. However, investment in Thailand tends to be both cyclical and fluctuating, and the small number of transactions can cause broad swings in statistical averages.

2.3.3 Overall Asian VCF experience: at a Glance

From the above paragraphs the following are the gist of Asian experiences on VCF:

- Japanese venture capitalist describes VCF, as a means of financing fast-growing private companies.
- Asian countries like Japan, South Korea, Singapore, Hong Kong, Thailand and Malaysia fosters the venture capital market due to its technological advancement.
- An estimated USD 17.5 billion of private equity and venture capital was invested in the Asia Pacific region in 2003-a whopping 92 percent increase in comparison to 2002.
- Japan led the region accounting for USD 7.3bn of the value of deals completed, followed by Korea with USD 3.3bn.
- In contrast, only USD 3.32 billion of new funds were raised in 2003 in Asia (up only 10 percent on 2002 levels).
- The pool of private equity capital under management rose to USD 97.6 billion in 2003 up from USD 88.6 bn in 2002.
- Start-up and early stage investment was USD 0.6 billion and USD 1.4 billion respectively in 2002 and it was invested in expansion stages' in 2003.

- Telecommunication section had the highest percentage of invested capital with USD 3.7 bn or 21 percent followed by financial services with USD 2.3 bn or 18.3 percent.
- Overall private equity investment across Asia touches USD 8.6 billion at the end of second quarter of 2005, ahead of the same period's USD 6.2 billion in 2004.
- By 2005 Asian VCF has witnessed a good number of private equity. This 2005 may well rank with 1997 as a defining moment in the channels of Asian private equity.
- By 2005, in Asia a large percentage (34.5 percent) of the capital went into buyouts, and a further 25.1 percent into turnaround or restructuring related transactions.
- After showing an upswing from USD 10 million in 2003 to USD 40 million in 2004, fund raising in Thailand got stagnated, with no activity registered in the first half of 2005.

2.4 OVERALL VCF DEVELOPMENT: GLOBAL EXPERIENCE

By 2000, the VCF through out the world has witnessed a sudden shift mainly due to the development of IT industry. The VCF is now not only looked from only a financial option but also for its social contributions. In US only venture capital funded companies were directly responsible for more than 10 million jobs and USD 1.8 trillion in sales in 2003. This corresponds to 9.4 percent of total U.S. private sector employment and 9.6 percent of company sales. This is impressive given that venture investment was less than two percent of total equity investment for most of the past 34 years.

From 2000 onwards the venture capital industry has made an enormous contribution to the high-technology industry. In turn, high technology has furthered national productivity. The three percent annual growth rate in productivity since 1996 in US stems from investments in a range of technology industries such as computers, software, and communications equipment. It has helped user industries like retailing, airlines, and manufacturing to be more productive. By 2000 some new

Fig. 2.6

The World View : Top 20 Countries in 2002—Based on Investment (2001 Rankings in Parentheses)

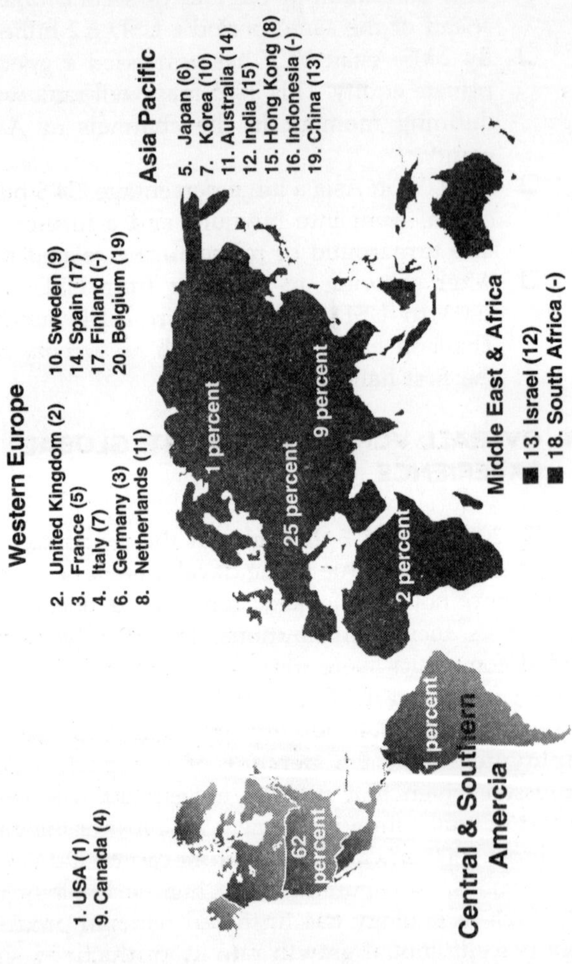

Source : AVCJ Report, 2003.

Fig. 2.7

The World View : Top 20 Countries—Based on Growth (CAGR 98-05)

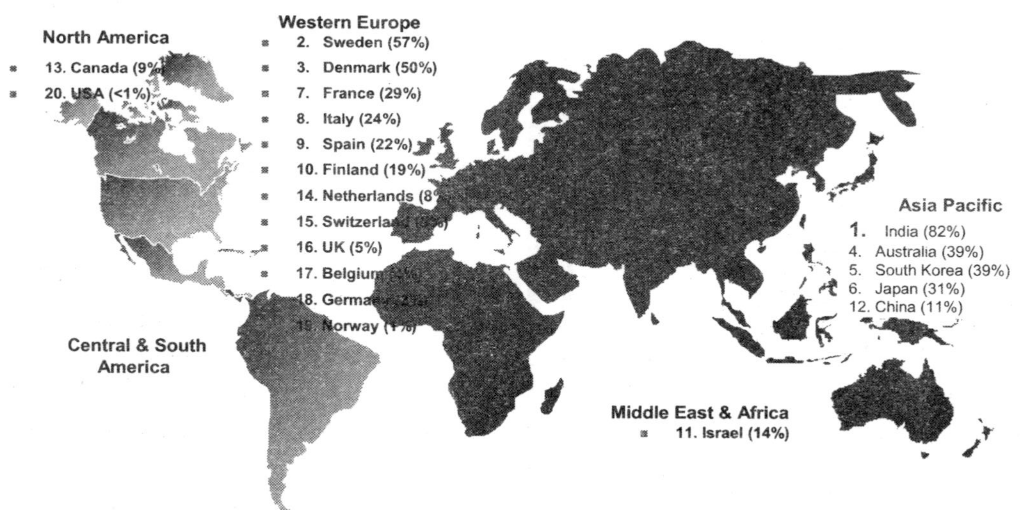

Note : Only Countries with investments of at least USD 0.225 billion in 2005 are shown.

Source : AVCJ Report, 2006.

countries has emerged in the field of VCF. India is a country where the VCF penetration was although taken place lately, but by 2002 it has attained the coveted list of top twenty countries based on investment criteria (Figure 2.6)

At the same time the growth of VCF is enormous during the period of 2000-05 in some of the developing countries like India, Denmark, Israel, etc. However, during this period the developed countries especially US, UK, Germany, etc. has witnessed a mixed growth pattern (Figure 2.7). This was mainly due to the fact that most of the VCF companies of these countries were concentrating more on financing companies/ firms originated in developing countries.

Figure 2.8 shows global trends in venture capital investment in the high-technology sector. Indeed, the data show that Israel is the worldwide leader in venture capital investment in high technology as a percent of GDP, followed by the United

FIG. 2.8

Venture Capital Investment* as a percent of GDP, Selected Industries (1999-2002)

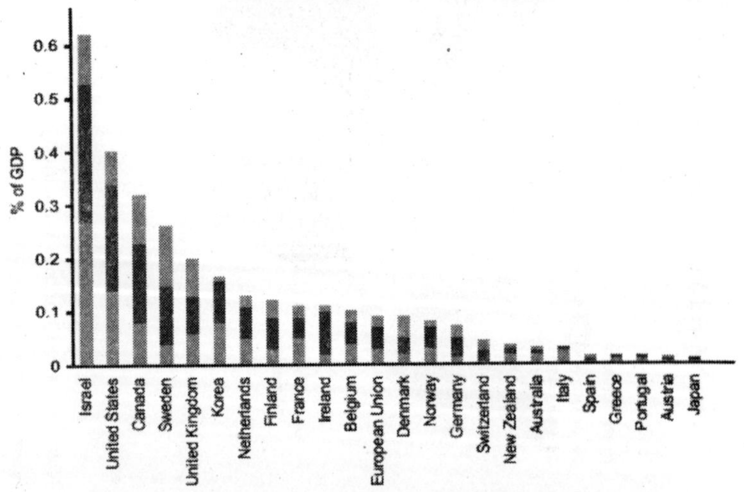

* The performance of India was not included in this database.

Source : OECD Venture Capital Database http://www.oecd.org/dataoecd/4/11/28881195.pdf

States, Canada, and Sweden. Also it is noteworthy to mention here that Korea, one of the least developed of the OECD countries, has an exceptional venture capital effort in high technology and health-related sectors. Interestingly, the share of venture capital investment in high-technology sectors continues to be small in many European Union countries, Japan, and Australia.

By 2006, it was observed that the United States maintains the oldest and most dominant position worldwide in venture capital. The lead of the United States in venture capital, combined with the widespread use of technology, has enabled an otherwise mature, wealthy economy to improve its income and standard of living over most other advanced economies. On the other hand, the UK and other European countries have started developing a unique mix of policy, entrepreneurship, and skilled research. Exhibit 2.4 highlights the position of the top ten countries in 2006 in terms of availability of venture capital measured by ease of availability for business development.

EXHIBIT 2.4

Availability of Venture Capital Measured by Ease of Availability for Business Development (2006)

Rank	*Country*
1	United States
2	Hong Kong
3	Finland
4	Taiwan
5	Singapore
6	Canada
7	United Kingdom
8	Ireland
9	Israel
10	Malaysia

Source : World Competitiveness Yearbook, 2006 available in www.global impact.com

Notes and References

1. Mason, C.M. and Harrison, R.T. (1995). Closing the Regional Equity Capital Gap: The Role of Informal Venture Capital, *Small Business Economics*, UK, Vol. 7, pp. 153-72.
2. Mason, C. M. and Harrison, R.T. (2003). 'Closing the regional equity gap? A critique of the department of trade and industry's regional venture capital funds initiative', *Regional Studies*, UK, Vol. 37, pp. 855-68.
3. MacMillan, H. (1931). Report of the Committee on Finance and Industry. Cmnd 3897, London: HMSO, p. 37.
4. Martin, R., Berndt, C. Klagge, B. Sunley, P.J. Herten S. & Sternberg, R. (2003). Regional Venture Capital Policy: UK and Germany Compared, Report for the Anglo-German Foundation for the Study of Industrial Society, pp. 24-48, Available at www.routledgepub.com/archive
5. Harding, R. (2000). Venture capital and regional development: towards a venture capital system', *Venture Capital*, Routledge Publication, UK, Vol. 2, pp. 287-311.
6. Martin, R., Berndt, C. Klagge, B. Sunley, P.J. Herten S. & Sternberg, R. (2003). Regional Venture Capital Policy: UK and Germany Compared, Report for the Anglo-German Foundation for the Study of Industrial Society, pp. 24-48. Available at www.routledgepub.com/archive
7. Mason, C.M. & Harrison, R.T. (1995). Closing the Regional Equity Capital Gap: The Role of Informal Venture Capital, *Small Business Economics*, UK, Vol. 7, pp. 153-72.
8. Harding, R. (2000). Venture capital and regional development: towards a venture capital 'system', *Venture Capital,* 2, 287-311.
9. Data obtained from various reports on venture capital financing in Europe published in *European Venture Capital Journal* (1998-2005), Vols. 14, 15 and 16; EVCA, London, UK.
10. Pfirrmann, O., U. Wupperfeld and J. Lerner (1997). Venture Capital and New Technology Based Firms: An US-German Comparison. Heidelberg: Physica-Verlag.
11. NVCA Report, Special Annual edn., 2003 available at www.nvca.org first accessed on July 23, 2004.
12. SBIR (Small Business Innovation Research Programme) is a highly competitive programme that encourages small business to explore their technological potential and provides the incentive to profit from its commercialization. By reserving a specific percentage of federal R&D funds for small business, SBIR protects the small business and enables it to compete on the same level as larger businesses. SBIR funds the critical start-up and development stages and it encourages the commercialization of the technology, product, or service, which, in turn, stimulates the US economy.
13. Sahlman, W.A. (1990). The Structure and Governance of Venture Capital Organizations. *Journal of Financial Economics*, Vol. 28, No. 2, pp. 102-24, Available at www.jfe.rochester.edu/jfenh.htm
14. Norton, E., and B.H. Tenenbaum (1993). Specialization *versus* Diversification as a Venture Capital Investment Strategy. *Journal of Business Venturing*, Elsevier, Netherland, Vol. 8, No. 5, pp. 234-54.

15. Norton, E., and B.H. Tenenbaum (1993). Specialization *versus* Diversification as a Venture Capital Investment Strategy. *Journal of Business Venturing*, Elsevier, Netherland, Vol. 8, No. 5, pp. 234-54.
16. Gupta, A.K., and H.J. Sapienza (1992). Determinants of Venture Capital Firms' Preferences Regarding the Industry Diversity and Geographic Scope of their Investments. *Journal of Business Venturing*, Elsevier, Netherland, Vol. 7, pp. 347-62.
17. Gupta, A.K., and H.J. Sapienza (1992). Determinants of Venture Capital Firms' Preferences Regarding the Industry Diversity and Geographic Scope of their Investments. *Journal of Business Venturing*, Elsevier, Netherland, Vol. 7, p. 360.
18. *Ibid.*, p. 361
19. Bygrave, W.D. (1987). Syndicated Investments by Venture Capital Firms: A Networking Perspective. *Journal of Business Venturing*, Elsevier, Netherland, Vol. 2, pp. 134-57.
20. *Ibid.*
21. Lerner, J. (1994). The Syndication of Venture Capital Investments. *Journal of the Financial Management Association*, Vol. 23, No. 3, p. 135, Available at www.jfma.com
22. Indigenous customers of Hong Kong.

Venture Capital Financing in India

In India, there is a progressive wave around venture capital financing. There is an aura of adventure, which burnishes success stories to a near legendary sheen. Perhaps the most famous legend of them all, in India is the case of Micro Land- a classic venture capital story. In 1989 technocrat Pradip Kar approached the Technology Development and Investment Corporation of India (TDICI) for Rs. 20 lacs loan to finance a company that sold the then esoteric concept of networking solutions. But he was refused, since the business was deemed to be service oriented not technology-oriented.

But Kar finally managed to start up after receiving funds from the SBI Capital fund under its equity support programme. Merely a year later SBI Caps' stake in Microland was sold to the TDICI at a premium of 100 Percent. To further sweeten the deal, the TDICI offered Kar the option to raise his stake once profitability and turnover targets were met. From these humble beginnings, Microland has morphed into as a net working giant, with a turn over of Rs. 150 crs. and PAT of Rs. 4 crs. in 1996-97.[1]

Examples like Micro Land have been few and far between in this country. But India's Venture Capital industry is slowly but surely, shifting gear. In the absence of an organized Venture Capital industry till 1998, individual investors (angel funds) and development financial institutions have played the role of venture capitalists in India. Entrepreneurs have largely depended upon private placements, public offerings and lending by the financial institutions.

A report (OECD, 2000[2]) identified venture capital as a critical component for the success of high-technology enterprises and recommended that all countries should consider strategies for encouraging the availability of venture capital. With such admiration and encouragement from the OECD[3] attempts were taken to create and develop venture capital industry in indigenous form. The possibility and ease of cross-national transference of financial institutions and specifically for the matter of VCF has been a subject of debate among scholars, policy-makers, and industrialists during the entire 20th century, if not earlier Kogut *et. al.*, (1998[4]). National economies have particular path-dependent trajectories, as to their national systems of innovation (NIS). The forces arrayed against transfer are numerous and include cultural factors, legal systems, entrenched institutions, and even absence of trained personnel in this context. The establishment of any institution in another environment can be a difficult trial-and-error learning process. Efforts in the 1980s by a number of European governments to create national venture capital industries also failed. Probably the only other country to develop a fully Silicon Valley-style venture capital industry is Israel. Taiwan, perhaps, is another country that appears to have developed a venture capital industry, though there has been little research on the dynamics of this process in Taiwan. Given the general difficulties in more wealthy and developed countries, it would seem that India would have discernible prospects for developing a viable venture capital financing system.

India is a significant case study for a number of reasons. First, in contrast to the United States, India had a history of state-directed institutional development that is similar, in certain ways, to such development in Japan and Korea, with the exception that ideologically the socialistic pattern of the Indian economy. Furthermore, the Government's powerful bureaucracy tightly controlled the economy, and the bureaucracy in some doses had unscrupulous practices. The then prevalent environment was not conducive for development of financial institutions having stable, transparent, and independent policies based on their own cost and benefit. India did have a number of strengths. It had an enormous number of small businesses and a public equity market. Wages were low, not only for physical labour, but also for technocrats and scientists, of which there was a surfeit.

India also boasted a homegrown software industry that began in the 1980s, and became visible upon the world scene in the mid-1990s. Experiencing rapid growth, some Indian software firms became significantly successful and were able to list on the NASDAQ. Finally, beginning in the 1980s, but especially in the 1990s, a number of Indian engineers who had immigrated to the United States became entrepreneurs and began their own high-technology firms. They were extremely successful, making them multimillionaires or even billionaires, and some of them then became venture capitalists or angel investors. So there was a group of potential transfer agents. For any transfer process, there has to be some match between the environment and the institution. In addition, there must be agents who will mobilize resources to facilitate the process, though these agents can be in the public or private sectors. Prior to 1985, the development of venture capital in India was very negligible. But the environment began to change after 1985, and continues to change till today. Even in the United States, venture capital is only a small component of the much larger NIS, and as such is dependent on many other institutions. Both in the United States and in India the development of venture capital has been a co-evolutionary process in certain aspect. This is particularly true in India, where it remains a small industry precariously dependent upon other institutions, particularly the government, and external actors such as international lending agencies, overseas investors, and successful Indian entrepreneurs in Silicon Valley. The growth of Indian venture capital must be examined within the context of the larger political and economic system in India. As was true in other countries, the Indian venture capital industry is the result of an iterative learning process, and it is still in its infancy. To be successful in this direction it is necessary not only for it to grow, but also for its institutional context to evolve.

3.1 THE VCF PERSPECTIVE

The earliest discussion of venture capital in India came in 1973, when the government appointed a commission to examine strategies for fostering small and medium-sized enterprises, Nasscom (1998[5]). Chitale, (1983[6]), in his book showed how the Indian financial systems' operation made it difficult to raise "risk capital" for new ventures and proposed various measures to liberalize and deregulate the financial market.

From its inception, the Indian venture capital industry has been affected by international and domestic developments; its current situation is the result of the evolution of what initially appeared to be unrelated historical events. The creation of a venture capital industry in India through transplantation required the existence of a minimal set of supportive conditions.[7] They need not necessarily be optimal, because, if the industry survived, it would likely set in motion a positive feedback process that would foster the emergence of successful new firms, encourage investment of more venture capital, and support the growth of other types of expertise associated with the venture capital industry. On the contrary, if the venture capital industry experienced any success, it could entrain a process of shaping its environment. In contrast to Israel and Taiwan, India would have to experience a hybrid of Interactions. If venture capital has to thrive, the environment surrounding it has to gradually change for its sustenance.

3.1.1 Mapping of Human Capital

Venture capital could begin with a suboptimal though minimally sustainable set of conditions; the venture capital industry could take root and shape its environment to a more optimal situation, while the institutions themselves would also need to change. Small and medium-sized enterprises have a long history and great importance to India. The leaders of the Independence movement were supporters of small businesses as an alternative to 'exploitation' by multinational firms. Yet, despite the emphasis upon small enterprises, the Indian economy was dualistic. However, the entrepreneurial propensity also has been demonstrated by the willingness of Indians emigrating in other countries to establish shops, restaurants, hotels and enterprises of all sorts. After Independence, the Indian government invested heavily in education, and Indian universities attracted excellent students. In the 1960s, the Ford Foundation worked with the Indian government to establish the Indian Institutes of Technology (IIT), which adopted MIT's undergraduate curriculum. Excellent Indian students were in demand by overseas university graduate programmes generally, and in engineering, particularly. After graduating from overseas programmes, many of these Indian students did not return to India. Many other Indian graduates remained in India, working in the large family conglomerates, the many Indian universities, and various top-level research institutes such as those for space research (Baskaran, 2000[8]). This meant that there remained in India a large pool of capable engineers and scientists that were underpaid (by global standards), and potentially mobile.

India has the second largest English speaking scientific and technical manpower in the world.[9] Some of its management (IIMs) and technology institutes (IITs) are known globally as centers of excellence. Every year, over 1,15,000 engineers graduated from government-run and private engineering colleges. Many also graduate with diploma courses in computers and other technical areas. Management institutes produce 40,000 plus management graduates annually and the number is increasing every year. Some of these candidates may be potential entrepreneurs.[10]

India also has a vast pool of existing and on-going scientific and technical research carried out by a large number of research laboratories, including defence laboratories as well as universities and technical institutes. A suitable venture capital environment—which includes incubation facilities—can help a great deal in identifying and actualizing some of these researches into commercial production.

3.1.2 Mapping of Social Capital

Social capital is a form of non-economic knowledge

separate from the foundation of human capital. Distinct from formal learning or instruction, it directly impacts the economic behaviours of individuals (Kelly, 1993[11]). Social capital emerges from the norms, networks, and relationship of the social structure in which an individual lives, potentially producing useful resources for business through the development of sets of obligations and expectations, information channels, and social norms that reinforce certain types of behaviours, Coleman (1988[12]).

Despite the strengths, India had many cultural rigidities and diversities to entrepreneurship and change, with an intrusive bureaucracy and extensive regulations. Until recently the job market was quite rigid. For well-educated Indians the ideal career path was to enter the government job with a lifetime position; enter the family business, which was then a lifetime position; or join one of the large conglomerates, which also effectively guaranteed lifetime employment. Another career path was to emigrate to join a job or to set-up their own enterprise abroad. In summation, the social institutions were not supportive to investment in entrepreneurship/business except in certain regions within the country.

With regard to South India there are a few notable deviations. Primarily, there have always been people pertaining to the indigenous population who were not only engaged with the learning of their sacred scripts but 'who were adept in Sanskrit learning as well', Stein (1999[13]). Hence, the foundations for a knowledge-based society have existed in South India ever since a period and, moreover, have been much more diffused. Secondly, the population of the South is said to be much more homogenous than in the North. For instance, political movements in favour of backward groups started much earlier in South India and led to a more equal pattern compared to the still traditionally dominated, hierarchically oriented North, Jaffrelot (2002[14]). Altogether, the Southern part of India seems to exhibit a more distinct regional culture of learning, not only in the sense of the regional development literature, Gertler (1997[15]) but also literally. Apparently, this attitude is a solid foundation for the absorptive capacity necessary in order to adapt to new technologies. The above were the views of some researchers who carried out their research on foundation of social capital in the context of southern part of India. However such views may not be analogous to the rest of India if appropriate research work is undertaken to perceive the foundations of social capital there, which is also not within the scope of this study. Thus, the observations of the present researcher are such that the diffusion of social capital that emerges from the basic texture of the society may vary from region to region and degree of diffusion of social capital may also vary accordingly.

3.2.3 Mapping of Financial Capital

India has a large, sophisticated financial system including private and public, formal and informal players. But within the structure of the formal financial system many are excluded to reap the benefit of it. In addition to formal financial institutions, informal institutions such as family and moneylenders are important sources of capital mostly for those who could not be included within the formal financial system. India has substantial capital resources, but it is found that the bulk of this capital has been parked in the banking system. In the formal financial system, lending is dominated by commercial banks for debt. The primary method for firms to raise capital is through the public equity markets, rather than through private placements.

The Banking System

Prior to independence, the banking system was entirely private and largely family-operated. In the pre-world war periods, the family-run banks often invested in new ventures. After Independence, the Reserve Bank of India (RBI) and the State Bank of India were nationalized, with the State Bank of India continuing to play the role of banker to the Government of India and the companies existing the then. Then, in 1969, the next 14 largest banks were nationalized. Another nationalization took place in the year 1980 when another 6 private sector banks were nationalized. Today State Bank of India including its 7 subsidiaries and 20 nationalized banks, there are altogether 28 public sector banks operating in India controlling over a substantial portion of financial assets. Such a huge lendable funds in the hands of public sector banks if can be percolated following innovative techniques to the excluded sections of the society it is expected that there will be a radical change in poverty elevation and technological development in the country. In the present study the poverty elevation part has been kept outside its scope. But so far as the technological development part is concerned the matter has been appropriately taken up in the relevant parts of the ensuing paragraphs.

The nationalized banking system became an instrument of social policy. During 1969–91, the financial position of the banks progressively weakened, due to loss-making branch expansions, ever-strengthening unions, overstaffing, and politicized loans. Until 1991, depositors were reluctant to use banks because although their savings were safe, the Government set deposit interest rates below the rate of inflation. By 1991, the entire bank system was unprofitable and nearing collapse.[16] The socialized banking system had other perverse effects. For example, although the bank managers were civil servants and very risk-averse, they could offer below-market interest rates. This created excessive demand for funds, but, quite naturally, bankers extended the loans to their safest customers. These were primarily the public sectors, which operated the largest steel, coal, electrical, oil, natural gas and other manufacturing industries. The other large bank borrowers were the giant family conglomerates and also professionally run corporate houses such as subsidiaries of multinationals and others. This increased the group's economic power, but did not lead to economically viable and effective capital deployment.

In the late 1990s, the Indian government became aware of the potential benefits of a healthy venture capital sector. Thus in 1999 a number of new regulations were promulgated. Some of the most significant of these related to liberalizing the regulations regarding the ability of various financial institutions to invest in venture capital. Perhaps the most important of these went into effect in April 1999 and allowed banks to invest up to 5 percent of their new funds annually in venture capital. Till 2001, however, they have not made any venture capital investments. This is not surprising since bank managers are rewarded for risk-averse behaviour. Lending to a risky, fast-growing firm could be unwise because the loan principal is at risk while the reward is only interest.[17]

Equity Markets

The first Indian stock market was recognized in May 1927 under the Bombay Securities Contracts Control Act, 1925. During the early part of the 20th century, Indian equity markets actively financed not only banking, but also the cotton and jute trades, Schrader (1997[18]). In 1989 there were 14 stock markets in India, though Bombay was by far the largest, World Bank (1989[19]). At present there are 23 stock exchanges in India and the National Stock Exchange of India Ltd., which is a tax paying company with a limited liability. The socialization of the economy and particularly banking after independence reinforced the strength of the stock markets as a source of capital, and by the 1960s, India had one of the most sophisticated stock markets in any developing country.

There were several reasons for the growth of the Indian stock market. Motivated by its egalitarian principles, the government supported the stock markets as an instrument for reducing the concentration of ownership in the hands of a few.

Second, the government industrial licensing policy instituted in 1961 meant that businesses had to apply for government permission to establish new ventures. Permissions were given only in the context of the Soviet style national plans for each sector. There was a strong element of favoritism in those who received permission in the form of a license. Most importantly, due to government central planning controls, shortages were endemic, and thus, permission to produce was a guarantee of profits. The distortion of these policies created by encouraging concentration were meant to be off-set by RBI stipulation that private sector borrowers could not own more than 40 percent of the firm's equity if they wished to receive bank finance. In 1973 the government required all foreign firms to decrease ownership in their Indian subsidiaries to 40 percent.[20] Faced with a choice between selling stakes privately and listing on the stock exchanges, most firms chose the latter and issued new stock, which led to a large increase in public ownership of such companies.

So, to raise money the private sector became reliant on stock markets. Investors, large and small, readily financed ventures since the shortages induced by the planning system guaranteed a ready market for anything produced. Curiously, the retention of 40 percent of the equity by the core investors meant that in reality they controlled the firm. The 40 percent regulation did not liberalize the markets as much as one might have expected. Because loans were also necessary for firms and this required collateral in fixed assets, new entrepreneurs were restricted to sectors with asset heavy projects. This limited the service sector, resulting in even greater concentration, and equity markets focused on financing low risk projects. Moreover, the public enthusiasm for firms operating within a licensed industry meant that it was difficult for other new firms to secure capital through listing on the stock exchanges. In 1991, as part of a large number of financial reforms, the Securities and Exchange Board of India (SEBI) was created to regulate the stock market. At the time, there were 6,229 companies listed on all the stock exchanges in India, RBI (1999[21]). The reforms and relaxation of regulations resulted in an increase in the number of listed companies to 9,877 by March 1999, and daily turnover on the stock exchanges rose to 107.5 billion rupees (US $ 2.46 billion) by December 1999.[22] One reform was the removal of a profitability criterion as a requirement of listing. To replace the profitability requirement, it was stipulated that a firm would be de-listed if it did not earn profits within three years of listing. This reform meant unprofitable firms could be listed, providing an exit mechanism for investors. Not surprisingly, there was a dramatic increase in the listings of firms, many of which could be considered as high technology. In terms of experience, India contrasted favorably with most developing countries, which had small, inefficient stock markets listing only established firms. Even in Europe, until the creation of new stock markets in the mid-1990s, it was extremely difficult to list small high technology firms, Posner (2000[23]). But, although these stock markets provided an exit opportunity, they did not provide the capital for firm establishment. However, in the context of VCF, the present scenario of the stock market has not stimulated the start up stage but it stimulated the later stages of it. Thus the stimulus through the stock market to start up new ventures was found to be discernible.

Other Institutional Sources of Funds

India has a strong mutual fund sector that began in 1964

with the formation of the Unit Trust of India (UTI), an open-ended mutual fund, promoted by a group of public sector financial institutions. Because UTI's investment portfolio was to consist of longer-term loans, it was meant to offer savers a return superior to bank rates. In keeping with the risk-averse Indian environment, initially UTI invested primarily in long-term corporate debt. But, UTI eventually became the country's largest public equity owner as well. This was because the government controlled interest rates in order to reduce the borrowing costs of the large manufacturing firms that it owned. These rates were usually set well below market rates, yet UTI and other institutional lenders were forced to lend at these rates. In response, firms started issuing debt that was partially convertible into equity in order to attract institutional funds. By 1985, the conversion of these securities led to UTI becoming the largest owner of publicly listed equity (UTI Annual Report, 1985). By 1991, the equity portion of the UTI portfolio had grown to 30 percent (UTI Annual Report, 1991). In 1992, in tandem with banking sector reform, permission to form privately owned mutual funds (including foreign-owned funds) was granted, leading to a gradual erosion in UTI's then-dominant market share. Until April 1999, mutual funds were not allowed to invest in venture capital companies. Since then, the mutual funds have been allowed to commit up to 5 percent of their funds as venture capital, either through direct investments or through investment in venture capital firms. But, the mutual funds instead of directly investing in any specific venture capital, either directly or indirectly but invested into venture capital funds only may be due to their risk adverse nature. Should the mutual funds decide to invest directly in firms, there would have arisen matters relating to operational issues regarding the capability of mutual funds to perform the venture capital function. The largest single source of funds for US venture capital funds since the 1980s has been public and private sector pension funds. In India, there are large pension funds but they are prohibited from investing in either equity or venture capital vehicles, but of late regarding this the matter has been entrusted to a separate body known as Pension Fund Regulatory and Development Authority of India. In summation, prior to the late 1980s, though India did have a vibrant stock market, the rigid and numerous regulations made it nearly impossible for the existing financial institutions to invest in venture capital firms or in startups.

Nearly all of these institutions were politicized, and the government bureaucrats operating them were risk-adverse. On the positive side, there was a stock market with investors amenable to purchasing the equity in fairly early stage companies. It was also possible to bootstrap a firm and/or secure funds from friends and family—if one was well connected. But, no financial intermediaries were comfortable with supporting small technology-based firms existed prior to the mid-1980s. It is however can be safely said that little capital was available for any entrepreneurial initiatives during those times. But to start up a technology-based enterprise with large scale was not possible under the prevalent situation then. An entrepreneur aiming to create a firm would have to depend upon own or familial capital to bootstrap the firm.

3.2 STRUCTURES OF VENTURE CAPITAL FUNDS IN INDIA

To understand the structures of venture capital funds in India requires special considerations of its regulatory and tax provisions. This endeavours to demystify the legal and regulatory concerns surrounding the VCF in India, which are stated as under.

3.2.1 Domestic Funds

For domestic venture funds (in which the funds are raised within India), the structure that is most commonly used is that of a domestic vehicle for the pooling of funds from the investors and a separate investment adviser to carry on the asset management activities. For the domestic vehicle, there are two options viz. a trust or a company. India at present does not have a limited partnership structure, which is a common choice in countries like the US.[24]

The 'trust' structure has been more commonly used since the company structure does have some limitations mostly arising from the provisions of the Companies Act, 1956 that may conflict with some of the basic underlying principles of venture capital investments. Some of these concerns are:

- *Difficulty in return of capital*: Redemption of securities by companies (i.e. buyback of securities) can be made only out of profits or proceeds of a fresh issue of securities. Furthermore, the buyback of securities by a company in any one financial year is restricted to a maximum of 25 percent of its total paid-up capital. This restriction restrains the ability of a venture capital company to return the capital to its investors if the investments made by it are sold at a loss.
- *Difficulty in distributing returns*: A company can declare dividends only if the company has profits. There are also statutory requirements whereby if the dividends declared are more than 10 percent of the par value (i.e. nominal value) of the shares, a certain portion of the distributable profits would have to be transferred to general reserve
- *Difficulty in termination*: At the time of termination of the fund, if the fund is structured as a company, winding up procedures are extremely time-consuming and also requires high court approval. This could make the winding up process quite cumbersome.

Though some of the above shortcomings of the 'company' structure can be addressed by carefully structuring the investment instruments, Indian venture capitalists have found the 'trust' structure executed under the Indian Trust Act to be more favourable as it offers them more flexibility.

3.2.2 Offshore Funds

Commonly there are two alternatives available to offshore investors participating in Indian venture capital investments. The offshore investors can either use an 'offshore structure' or a 'unified structure'.

Offshore Structure

Under this structure an investment vehicle, which could be a Limited Liability Corporation or a Limited Partnership organized in a jurisdiction outside India, makes investments directly into Indian portfolio companies. There would generally be an offshore manager for managing the assets of the fund and an investment advisor in India for identifying deals and to carry out preliminary due-diligence on prospective investment opportunities.

Unified Structure

This structure is generally used where domestic (i.e. Indian) investors are expected to participate in the fund. Under this structure, a trust or a company is organized in India. The domestic investors would directly contribute to the trust whereas overseas investors pool their investments in an offshore vehicle and this offshore vehicle invests in the domestic trust. The portfolio investments are made by the trust. The trust would generally have a domestic manager or an adviser. The offshore fund may also have its own offshore manager/adviser. This structure also enables the domestic manager to draw its share of carry directly from the trust.[25]

The offshore funds were gaining importance in Indian VCF from 2000 onwards. Warburg Pincus, the country's largest private equity investor, puts in $ 300 million (Rs. 1,380 crs.) in Bharati Tele-Ventures in 2001, which was worth $ 600 million by 2005 when they decide to exit; Citibank Private Equity's seven-year-old investment in software product company i-flex was also worth as much; Barings Private Equity had an investment of $ 16.5 million staggered investment in software services firm MphasiS during 2004 BFL (for a 35 percent stake) appreciate to about $ 183 million, and CDC Capital Partners walked away with a net gain of about Rs. 250 crore when it sold its stake in UTI Bank in December 2002 to British banking giants HSBC. In fact, CDC's best-performing fund among the 50 countries where it invests is in India.[26]

3.2.3 Non-Resident Indians (NRIs)

From 1950 onward, bright, well-educated Indian engineers attended US universities and remained there to work in high-technology firms. In the 1960s and 1970s, this was considered as 'brain drain'. It seems likely, however, that even if these engineers had returned to India, there would have been few opportunities for them. For this and other reasons, many Indians remained in the United States and secured employment in universities and corporations, including Silicon Valley electronics firms. Initially, these Indian engineers joined existing firms, but not surprisingly they were not immune to the attractions of entrepreneurship, especially in Silicon Valley. The first noteworthy group included Kanwal Rekhi, who co-founded Excelan, a data networking firm, with three other Indian engineers in 1981. Excelan later was purchased by Novell, leaving Rekhi and the other engineers with enormous capital gains. Another early entrepreneur was Vinod Khosla, who in 1982 had co-founded Daisy Systems, and was a driving force in the establishment of Sun Microsystems. After leaving Sun, he joined the prestigious venture capital firm, Kleiner, Perkins, Caufield and Byers. Yet another Indian engineer, Dalal (2000[27]), co -founded Metaphor in 1982, Claris in 1987, and in 1991 joined the top-tier venture capital fund, Mayfield Fund. Another successful early Indian entrepreneur was Suhas Patil, who confounded Cirrus Logic in 1984. These NRIs not only were successful entrepreneurs, but they soon began investing in yet other startups. Quite naturally, the NRIs remained in contact with family, friends, and classmates in India. Moreover, by the late 1980s, the success of the NRIs came to the attention of Indian policy-makers. Even after concerned about it, the brain drain continued, policy-makers recognized that it would be impossible to retain such highly skilled individuals if there were no opportunities for them in India. NRIs wished to assist India: they visited India and discussed their experiences in the United States, and expressed a willingness to invest in ventures that would come up in India. It was discovered by them quite soon that it was not so simple to transform their willingness to reality in India. But this initiated a process through which the NRIs were re-conceptualized from being "defectors" to potential source of knowledge, connections, and even capital, Saxenian, (1999[28]).

From the perspective of creating venture capital, India had a stock market that with minimal effort could handle public stock offerings from fledgling high-technology firms. There was also a growing IT industry, with some that experienced extremely fast growth. There was also a cadre of Indians, familiar with the operation of the US Silicon Valley, and there were sufficient skilled engineers in India to support start-ups. In other words, by 1990 the environmental preconditions for the successful establishment of a venture capital industry were in place.

3.3 VENTURE CAPITAL FUNDING IN INDIA

Traditionally, the role of venture capital was an extension of the developmental financial institutions like IDBI, ICICI, SIDBI, State Finance Corporations, etc. TDICI (now ICICI ventures) and Gujarat Venture were one of the first venture capital organizations in India. Both of these organizations were promoted by the financial institutions.[29]

However, it was realized that the concept of venture capital funding needed to be institutionalized and regulated. Besides this funding requires different skills in assessing the proposal. Thus dedicated funds were created to provide only venture capital funds. The sources of these funds are normally the financial institutions or foreign institutional investors or pension funds (overseas) and high net-worth individuals, etc. An attempt was also made to raise funds from the public to finance new ventures. Certain venture capital funds are industry specific (i.e. they fund enterprises only in certain industries such as pharmaceuticals, InfoTech or food processing, etc.) whereas others may have a much wider spectrum. Securities and Exchange Board of India (SEBI) has come out with guidelines to which a venture capital fund has to adhere to its norms in order to carry out its activities in India. Some of the important regulation and investment restrictions according to SEBI (Venture Regulations) 1996 have been enumerated below:

1. In case of minimum investment in venture capital fund by an investor should not be less then 5 lakh; the minimum corpus of the fund before it starts activities should be at least Rs. 5 crore.
2. A venture capital fund seeking to avail benefits under the Income Tax Act, 1961 will be required to disinvest its holdings within a period of one year from the listing of the venture capital units.

3. The venture capital fund is eligible to participate in the IPO through book building route as Qualified Institutional Buyer (QIB).
4. Automatic exemption may be granted from open offer requirements in case of transfer of shares from venture capital funds in Foreign Venture Capital Investors to promoters of a venture capital undertaking.

As regards restrictions in the aforesaid regulations of SEBI, following restrictions have been imposed:

1. The VCFs are to disclose their investment strategy at the time of their registrations with SEBI. At the time of registrations such VCFs should not have invested more then 25 percent of the corpus of the fund in any one venture capital unit at the same time the VCFs also are restrained from investing in associate companies. The VCFs should invest at least 75 percent of the investible funds in unlisted equity shares or equity linked instruments.
2. VCFs should not invest more then 25 percent of the investible funds as subscription to IPO of a venture capital unit whose shares are proposed to be listed subject to lock-in period of one year and debt or debt instrument of a venture capital unit in which the venture capital funds have already made an investment in the form of equity.

The above were in a nutshell some main regulations and restrictions only. The detailed SEBI guideline relating to the venture capital funds and venture capital units has been appended as an appendix at the end of this chapter.

There are a number of funds, which are currently operational in India and involved in funding start-up ventures. Most of them are not true venture funds, as they do not fund start-ups. They usually provide mezzanine or bridge funding and are better known as private equity players.

3.4 VENTURE CAPITAL GROWTH IN INDIA

The Indian VCF scenario has undergone a sea change over the last seven years or so. There has been a considerable interest, both domestic as well as international, in the VCF sector, which is evident from the fact that the total VCF committed to investments in India has increased exponentially. Exhibit 3.1 gives the statistics of growth of the venture capital industry in India.

EXHIBIT 3.1
Investments in VCF (Year-wise)

Year	*Rs. Million*	*U.S. $ Million*
1996	700	20
1997	3,200	80
1998	9,950	250
1999	21,875	500
2000	49,493	1160
2001	39,042	937
2002	26,698	590**
2003	37,345	774
2004	43,650	900
2005	87,850	1,750
2006	197,137	4,015
2008*	450,000	10,000

* Projected figures.
** Includes USD 241.8 Million for new commitments. (Indian Securities Market—A Review, Vol. VII, 2004, NSE, Mumbai).

Source : Original report compiled by the NASSCOM titled "Study on Indian Capital Industry" reproduced in IVCA Report 2007. Data for 2007 were not available in the report.

Though these numbers may not look substantial when compared to funds committed in other countries like the US and UK, they go a long way in demonstrating the rise of venture capital investments in India.

In India, the venture capital creation process has started taking off with all four stages receiving attention:

- Idea generation
- Start-up
- Growth ramp up
- Exit processes

It may be noted that during 1999, approximately 80 percent of the estimated US$ 30 billion worth of venture capital invested in United States, went to technology firms. India too, with its strengths in innovation and IT technology has attracted several VCF. In 2000 alone, 20 new venture capital funds have registered with SEBI, taking the total number to 30. In fact, VC or Angel investments in high tech firms in India have grown by over 5,000 percent from Rs. 70 crore to Rs. 2,200 crore between 1996 and 1999-00. And this figure is expected to grow to Rs. 45,000 crore by 2008.

An analysis of financing by investment stages indicates the following figures as depicted in Figure 3.1 below.

FIG 3.1

Analysis of Financing by Investment Stages

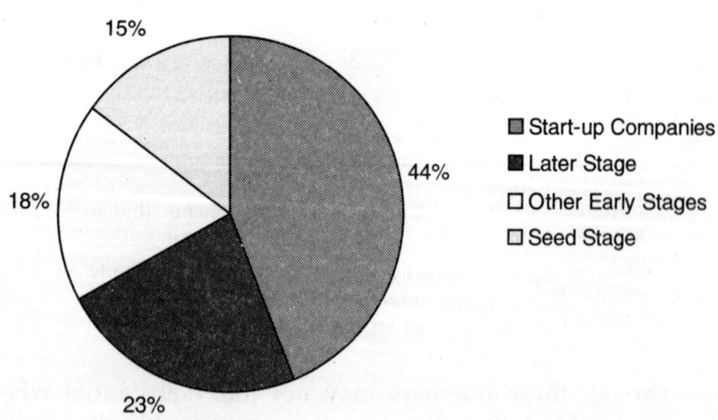

Source : IVCA Report 2003.

The major contributors to the venture funds in India by 2002 were FIIs with 51 percent, Financial Institutions in India with 23 percent, Multilateral Development Agencies with 9 percent, 11 percent by Individuals and Companies and around 5.95 percent by other types of Bank till FY 2002-03 (Figure 3.2). But by the end of FY 2005-06 it was found that there were further increased in stake by FIIs and FIs. However some new sectors like FDI, NRI, Nationalized banks etc also started playing a role in the contribution of VCF in the country (Exhibit 3.2). For Method of Financing, financing by Investment stage, financing by Industry and financing by states of India by the end of FY 2005-06 have been depicted in Exhibits 3.3, 3.4, 3.5 and 3.6 respectively.

FIG. 3.2

Major Contributors to the Funds

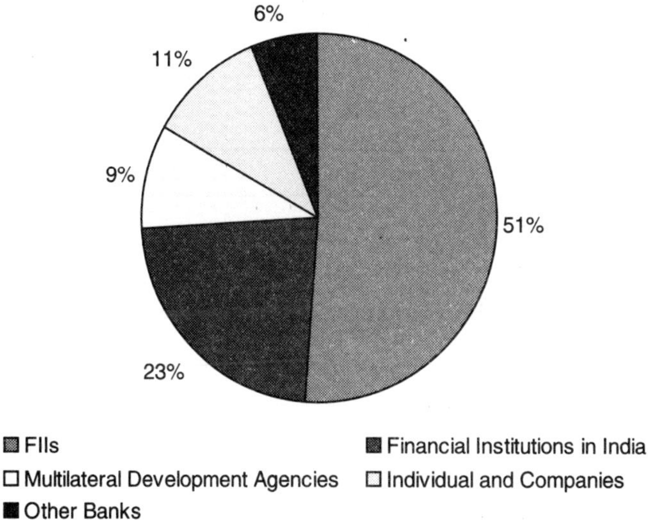

6%
11%
9%
51%
23%

FIIs
Financial Institutions in India
Multilateral Development Agencies
Individual and Companies
Other Banks

Source : IVCA Report 2003.

However it can be observed that the growth of venture capital in India by and large concentrated only in certain regions of the country and state like Assam or other north east region have never made any maiden entry into the pool. Reasons may

EXHIBIT 3.2
Contributors of Funds (FY 2005-06)

Contributors	*Rs. Million*	*Per cent*
Foreign Institutional Investors	103,418.07	52.46
All India Financial Institutions	48,160.57	24.43
Multilateral Development Agencies	16,441.23	8.34
Other Banks	11,867.65	6.02
Foreign Investors	4,396.16	2.23
Private Sector	3,173.91	1.61
Public Sector	2,503.64	1.27
Nationalized Banks	2,148.79	1.09
Non-Resident Indians	1,813.66	0.92
State Financial Institutions	1,655.95	0.84
Other Public	887.12	0.45
Insurance Companies	650.55	0.33
Mutual Funds	19.71	0.01
Total	197,137.00	100.00

Source : IVCA Report 2006.

EXHIBIT 3.3
Methods of Financing (2005-06)

Instruments	*Rs. Million*	*Per cent*
Equity Shares	124551.16	63.18
Redeemable Preference Shares	42463.31	21.54
Non-Convertible Debt	17210.06	8.73
Convertible Instruments	11433.95	5.8
Other Instruments	1478.53	0.75
Total	197137.00	100

Source : IVCA Report 2006.

EXHIBIT 3.4
Financing by Investment Stage (2005-06)

Investment Stages	*Rs. Million*	*Number*
Start-up	75164.88	5843
Later stage	65820.82	3030
Other early stage	35991.03	2440
Seed stage	18987.36	2105
Turnaround financing	1172.911	177
Total	197137	13595

Source : IVCA Report 2006.

EXHIBIT 3.5
Financing by Industry (2005-06)

Industry	*Rs. million*	*Number*
Industrial products, machinery	51239.86	4092
Computer Software	36113.84	1712
Consumer-related	27849.05	1141
Medical	12296.84	866
Food, food processing	9857.579	984
Other electronics	8605.423	807
Tel and Data Communications	7591.2	315
Biotechnology	7421.078	590
Energy-related	4919.525	374
Computer Hardware	4022.198	492
Miscellaneous	27220.41	2223
Total	197137	13595

Source : IVCA Report 2006.

EXHIBIT 3.6
Financing by States (2005-06)

Investment	*Rs. million*	*Number*
Maharashtra	50585.35	3168
Tamil Nadu	30181.67	2341
Andhra Pradesh	27047.20	1751
Gujarat	21724.50	964
Karnataka	20620.53	1830
West Bengal	6150.67	433
Haryana	5914.11	433
Delhi	5795.83	413
Uttar Pradesh	5578.98	571
Madhya Pradesh	4553.86	39
Kerala	2661.35	295
Goa	2069.94	315
Rajasthan	1715.09	216
Punjab	1655.95	118
Orissa	689.98	98
Dadra & Nagar Haveli	630.84	20
Himachal Pradesh	551.98	59
Pondicherry	433.70	39
Bihar	315.42	59
Overseas	8260.04	433
Total	197137.00	13595

Source : IVCA Report 2006, Vol. 12, No. 3.

be too many but the human attitude ultimately matters the most.[30]

3.5 PROBLEMS OF VCF IN INDIA

As per the present researcher the biggest impediment for balanced diffusion of VCF across the states was a mindset change from "collateral funding" to high risk high return funding. Most of the pioneers in the industry were people with credit background and exposure to manufacturing industries. Exposure to fast growing intellectual property business and services sector was almost negligible. All these combined to a slow start to the industry. The other issues that led to such a situation include has been highlighted briefly in the ensuing paragraphs.

3.5.1 License Regime and the IPO Boom

Till early 90s, under the license regime, only commodity centric businesses thrived in a deficit situation. To fund a cement plant, venture capital is not needed. What was needed was ability to get a license and then get the project funded by the banks and DFIs. In most cases, the promoters were well-established industrial houses, with no apparent need for funds. Most of these entities were capable of raising finances from conventional sources, including term loans from institutions and equity markets.

3.5.2 Scalability

The Indian software segment has recorded an impressive growth over the last few years and earns large revenues from its export earnings, yet India's share in the global market is less than 5 per cent. Within the software industry, the value chain ranges from body shopping at the bottom to strategic consulting at the top. Higher value addition and profitability as well as significant market presence take place at the higher end of the value chain.[31] If the industry has to grow further and survive the flux it would only be through innovation. For any venture idea to succeed there should be a product that has a growing market with a scalable business model. The IT industry (which is most suited for venture funding because of its "ideas" nature) in India till recently had a service centric business model. Products developed for Indian markets is lacking in scale.

3.5.3 Mindsets

Venture capital as an activity was virtually non-existent in India till early 1990s. Most venture capital companies want to provide capital on a secured debt basis, to established businesses with profitable operating histories. Most of the venture capital units were offshoots of financial institutions and banks and as a result the lending mindset continued. True venture capital is capital that is used to help in launching products and ideas of tomorrow. In abroad, this problem is solved by the presence of 'angel investors'. They are typically wealthy individuals who not only provide venture finance but also help entrepreneurs to shape their business and make their venture successful.

3.5.4 Returns, Taxes and Regulations

There is a multiplicity of regulators like SEBI and RBI. Domestic venture funds are set up under the Indian Trusts Act of 1882 as per SEBI guidelines (see Appendix 1), while offshore funds routed through Mauritius follow RBI guidelines.[32] Abroad, such funds are made under the Limited Partnership Act, which brings advantages in terms of taxation. The Government however does not allow pension funds and insurance companies to invest in venture capitals as in USA where corporate contributions to venture funds are large.

3.5.5 Exit

The exit routes available to the venture capitalists in India were restricted to the IPO route. Before deregulation, pricing was dependent on the erstwhile CCI regulations. In general, all issues were under priced. Even now SEBI guidelines make it difficult for pricing issues for an easy exit. Given the failure of the OTCEI and the revised guidelines, small companies could not hope for a BSE/NSE listing.[33] With the dull market for mergers and acquisitions, strategic sale was also not available.

3.5.6 Valuation

The recent phenomenon is valuation mismatches. It may be largely due to the software boom, most promoters have sky-high valuation expectations. Given this, it is difficult for deals to reach financial closure, as promoters do not agree to a valuation. This coupled with the fancy for software stocks in the bourses means that most companies are proponing their IPOs. Consequently, the number and quality of deals available to the venture funds gets reduced.

3.6 GROWTH PROSPECTS IN INDIA

India certainly is in need of a large pool of risk capital both from home and abroad. Examples of the US, Taiwan and Israel clearly show that this can happen. But this is dependent on the right regulatory, legal, tax and institutional environment; the risk-taking capacities among the budding entrepreneurs; start-up access to R&D flowing out of national and state level laboratories; support from universities; and infrastructure support, such as telecoms, technology parks, etc.

Steps are being taken at governmental level to improve infrastructure and R&D. Certain NRI organisations are taking initiatives to create a corpus of US $ 150m to strengthen the infrastructure of IITs. More focused attempts will be required in all these directions.

Recent phenomena partly ignited by success stories of Indians in the US and other places abroad, provide the indications of a growing number of young, technically qualified entrepreneurs in India. Already there are some success stories in India. At the same time, an increasing number of savvy, senior management personnel have been leaving established multinationals and promoted Indian companies to start new ventures. The quality of enterprise in human capital in India is tends to be on an ascending curve.

The environment is ripe for creating the right regulatory and policy environment for sustaining the momentum for high-technology entrepreneurship. Indians abroad have gone through the value chain of technology to reach higher levels. At home in India, this is still to happen. By bringing venture capital and other supporting infrastructure, this can certainly become a reality in India as well.

India is rightly poised for a big leap. What is needed is a vibrant venture capital sector, which can leverage innovation, promote technology and harness the ongoing knowledge explosion. This can happen by creating the right environment and the mindset needed to understand global forces.

The Indian government has reiterated its commitment to the Indian software-driven IT industry by creating a National Venture Capital Fund for the Software and IT Industry (NFSIT). NFSIT, set-up in association with various financial institutions and the industry, operates under the umbrella of the Small Industries Development Bank of India (SIDBI). The objective of the fund is to encourage entrepreneurship in the areas of software, services, dot.com and other IT-related sectors in which India has inherent as well as acquired competency.[34] The fund would expected to be a key component in addressing the rapidly growing demand for venture capital in India. The fund will be looking at supporting entrepreneurship in high growth sectors.

The venture capital industry is emerging in India as a result of internal and external factors. Resource decisions are the most important decisions entrepreneurs make, like where to obtain resources, which to acquire and how they will be used (Hart, 1995[35]). Several studies found that prior to start up or ownership experience did not influence the use of personal sources or loans, but did influence other bootstrapping techniques—however in an unexpected direction (See Chapter 1). Entrepreneurs without startup ownership experience were more likely to have used credit and retained earrings; however with this experience were less likely to use those financing options. It may be that lack of start-up experience limits some entrepreneurs to the use of easily attainable credit, such as personal credit cards and trade credit, and internally generated funds. It is widely noted that education and experience are key to IT entrepreneurial success and that venture capitalist consider human capital factors as primary funding decisions (Smart 1999[36]). However, many studies conducted at different level reveals that there is a significant effect of human capital was found on the odds of entrepreneurs to found such business. It is a hard reality that many Indian entrepreneurs have acquired professional degrees and the rate is always booming, but there is a lack of capitalizing the same when it comes to promote such businesses.

Many State Governments of India have already set-up venture capital funds for the upcoming sector in partnership with local state financial institutions and financial institutions like SIDBI. These include Andhra Pradesh, Karnataka, Delhi, Kerala and Tamil Nadu. Clearly there is little point in spending public money to regulate high-risk private investment. With this new found flexibility, the walks between the various subjects of venture capital financing seed capital, start up financing and private equity are crumbling. Now the research observation would be to identify how the India's fledgling venture capital industry will redefine itself and in what best possible way it will shape the solutions to one's financing needs.

With so much of changes happening around venture capital financing in India yet, the fruitful result of exploring the advantages of such financing has not been equally distributed among the states in India. It is a fact that certain states like Karnataka and Andhra Pradesh are far more advanced in mobilizing the venture capital funds rather than the rest of the country thanks to the information and technology advancement.

The picture of venture capital financing is more glomming specially in Assam. Although it has been recognized several times that any business running down in the North Eastern region is a risky proposition may be due to its geographical location, environment, the infrastructure bottlenecks and likewise, but there are hardly any venture capital environment being developed around this place.

Notes and References

1. Mahanta, V. (1997), "Shifting Paradigm of Venture Capital"; *Business Today*, Vol. 5, No. 19, October.
2. OECD (2000). A New Economy? The Changing Role of Innovation and Information Technology in Growth. Paris: OECD Publication, available at www.oecd.org
3. On path Dependency, Refer Arthur (1994) and David (1986). For NIS, refer Lundvall (1992) and Nelson (1993).
4. Kogut, B. and Parkinson, D. (1998). Adoption of the Multidivisional Structure: Analyzing History for the Start. *Industrial and Corporate Change*, Oxford University Press, UK, Vol. 7, pp. 249–73.
5. Nasscom, (1998). Enabling a Quantum Leap in Successful Indian Venture Creation, New Delhi: Nasscom.
6. Chitale, V.P. (1983). Risk Capital for Industry. New Delhi: Allied Publishers, pp. 182-209.
7. Dossani, R. and Kenney, M. (2002); Creating an Environment for Venture Capital in India; *World Development*, USA, Vol. 30, No. 2, pp. 227-53.
8. Baskaran, A. (2000). Duality in National Innovation Systems: The Case of India. *Science and Public Policy*, USA, Vol. 27, No. 5, pp. 367-74.
9. *Ibid.*
10. Mishra, A.K., (1995) 'Venture Capital Financing'. New Delhi, Shipra Publications. p. 22.

11. Kelly, M., (1993), Towanda's triumph: social and culture capital in the transition to adulthood in the urban ghetto. International Journal of Urban and Regional Research, Vol.18, March, pp. 88-111 available at http://www.blackwellpublishing.com/journal.asp?ref=0309-1317.
12. Coleman, J., (1988), Social Capital in the Creation of Human Capital. *American Journal of Sociology*, NY, Vol. 94, pp. S95-S120.
13. Stein, B. (1999), Peasant State and Society in Medieval South India, New Delhi: Oxford University Press, pp. 78-103.
14. Jaffrelot, C. (2002), The subordinate caste revolution, in A. Ayres & P. Oldenburg (eds.), India Briefing: Quickening the Pace of Change, Armonk, NY: M.E. Sharpe, pp. 121-58.
15. Gertler, M. (1997), The Invention of Regional Culture, in R. Lee & J. Wills (eds.), Geographies of Economies, London *et. al.* : Arnold, UK, pp. 47-58.
16. According to a 1991 RBI report, the gross profit (before provisions on bank assets and taxes) had come down to 1% of assets (a healthy norm would be about 1% for profits after provisions and taxes). Moreover, approximately 25% of the total loans were bad.
17. It is true that in the United States, banks have never been an important source of venture capital, even through their SBIC subsidiaries. For the most part, a bank's core competencies are in evaluating and taking loans. The problem with loans to small startups is that the capital is at high risk, so any interest rate would have to be usurious. Moreover, since the new firm is often losing money in its early days, paying interest and principal would drain money from the firm during the period when it most requires the money for investment.
18. Schrader, H. (1997). Changing Financial Landscapes in India and Indonesia, New York: St. Martin's Press, pp. 218-36.
19. World Bank (1989), India Industrial Technology Development Project Staff Appraisals Report. Washington, DC: World Bank, available at www.worldbank.org.
20. Baskaran, A. (2000). Duality in Nnational Innovation Systems: The Case of India. *Science and Public Policy*, UK, Vol. 27, No. 5, pp. 367-74.
21. Reserve Bank of India (RBI) (1999). Report on Currency and Finance. New Delhi, RBI, p. 16.
22. Dossani R. and Kenney M. (2002); "Creating an Environment for Venture Capital in India"; *World Development*, Vol. 30, No. 2, pp. 227-50.
23. Posner, E. (2000). Is there a Revolution in European Venture Capital? Berkeley Roundtable on the International Economy Conference Paper Number 4, University of California, Berkeley, CA.
24. Quindlen, R., "Confession of a Venture Capitalist", Warner Books, p. 73.
25. Verma, J.C.; "Venture Capital Financing in India", Sage Publication, p. 34.
26. Sridharan, R., "The Year of the VC", "*Business Today*", Vol. 13, No. 2, p. 47.
27. Dalal, Y. (2000). Email Communication to Martin Kenney, August 14. available in note on paper of Dossani R. & Kenney M.; "Creating an Environment for Venture Capital in India"; *World Development*, Vol. 30, No. 2, pp. 227-53, 2002.
28. Saxenian, A.L. (1998). Regional Advantage. Cambridge: Harvard University Press.

29. Pandey, I.M., "Venture Capital—The Indian Experience", PHI, p. 16.
30. Dy. Gen. Manager, IDBI's note on researcher's quarry.
31. Singh, J.K., "Regulatory Framework of Venture Capital Financing in India", *The Journal of Accounting & Finance*, Vol. 16, No. 2 Apr.-Sept. 2002, p. 53.
32. Singh, J.K., "Regulatory Framework of Venture Capital Financing in India", *The Journal of Accounting & Finance*, Vol. 16, No. 2 Apr.-Sept. 2002, p. 53.
33. Singh, J.K., "Regulatory Framework of Venture Capital Financing in India", *The Journal of Accounting & Finance*, Vol. 16, No. 2, Apr.-Sept. 2002, p. 54.
34. Verma, J.C., 'A study on Venture Capital in the Promotion of Industrial Growth in India,' Senior Fellowship of Indian Council of Social Sciences Research, New Delhi, 1995.
35. Hart, M., 1995, Founding Resource Choices: Influences and Effects. Doctoral Dissertation. Harvard Graduate School of Business.
36. Smart, G.H., 1999, Management Assessment Methods in Venture Capital: An Empirical Analysis of Human Capital Valuation. "*Venture Capital*", 1, 59-83.
37. Online official site www.sebi.net.in originated from SEBI, Mumbai.

APPENDIX I

*SEBI Regulations**

- ✓ A venture capital fund means a fund established in the form of a trust or a company including a body corporate and registered under these regulations which:
  - (i) has a dedicated pool of capital,
  - (ii) raised in a manner specified in the regulations, and
  - (iii) invests in venture capital undertaking in accordance with the regulations.
- ✓ Venture capital undertaking means a domestic company:
  - (i) whose shares are not listed on a recognized stock exchange in India;
  - (ii) which is engaged in the business for providing services, production or manufacture of article or things or does not include such activities or sectors which are specified in the negative list by the Board with the approval of the Central Government by notification in the Official Gazette in this behalf.
- ✓ Negative List
  1. Real Estate
  2. Non-banking financial services
  3. Gold Financing
  4. Activities not permitted under industrial policy of Government of India.
  5. Any other activity, which may be specified by the Board in consultation with Government of India from time to time.
- ✓ Associate in relation to venture capital fund means a person :
  - (i) who, directly or indirectly, by himself, or in combination with relatives, exercises control over the venture capital fund; or

* Online official site www.sebi.net.in originated from SEBI, Mumbai.

(ii) in respect of whom the venture capital fund, directly or indirectly, by itself, or in combination with other persons, exercises control; or

(iii) whose director, is also a director, of the venture capital fund.

- ✓ Equity linked instruments includes instruments convertible into equity shares or share warrants, preference shares, debentures compulsorily convertible into equity.
- ✓ Investible Funds means corpus of the fund net of expenditure for administration and management of the fund.
- ✓ Unit means beneficial interest of the investors in the scheme or fund floated by trust or any other securities issued by a company including a body corporate.
- ✓ Application for grant of certificate

Any company or trust or body corporate proposing to carry on any activity as a venture capital fund must apply to SEBI for grant of a certificate of carrying out venture capital activity in India. An application for grant of certificate must be made in Form A and must be accompanied by a non-refundable application fee of Rs. 25,000 payable by bank draft in favor of the Securities and Exchange Board of India at Mumbai. Registration fee for grant of certificate is Rs. 500,000.

Eligibility Criteria

For the purpose of grant of certificate by SEBI, the following conditions must be satisfied :

A. If the application is made by a company :

1. The main object of the company as per its Memorandum of Association must be the carrying on of the activity of venture capital fund.
2. It is prohibited by its Memorandum and Articles of Association from making an invitation to the public subscribe to its securities.
3. None of its directors or its principal officer or employee is involved in any litigation concerned

with the securities market which may have an adverse bearing on the business of the applicant. The directors or the principal officer or employee must not have been at anytime convicted for an offense involving moral turpitude or any economic offense and is a fit and proper person to act as director or principal officer or employee of the company.

B. If the application is made by a trust:

1. The instrument of trust (Trust Deed) is in the form of a deed and has been duly registered under the provisions of the Indian Registration Act, 1908.
2. The main object of the trust is to carry on the activity of a venture capital fund.
3. None of its trustees or directors of the trustee company, if any, is involved in any litigation connected with the securities market which may have an adverse bearing in the business of the venture capital fund.
4. The directors of its trustee company or the trustees have not at anytime being convicted of an offense involving moral turpitude or any economic offense.

In both cases, the applicant must not have already applied for certificate from SEBI or its certificate must not have been suspended by SEBI or cancelled by SEBI and the applicant must be a fit and proper person.

Furnishing of Information and Clarification

SEBI may require the applicant to furnish such further information as it considers necessary for processing the application. An application, which is not complete in all respects, shall be rejected by SEBI. However, before rejecting any application, the applicant will be given an opportunity to make representation before SEBI and to remove any defect in the application within 30 days of the date of receipt of communication from SEBI regarding the defect. SEBI may extend the period of 30 days for upto another 90 days on being satisfied that it is necessary and is equitable to do so.

Procedure for Grant of Certificate

If SEBI is satisfied that the applicant is eligible for grant of certificate, it shall send intimation to the applicant of its eligibility. On receipt of intimation, the applicant must pay to SEBI, registration fee of Rs. 500,000 and on the receipt of such fees, SEBI shall grant a certificate of registration in Form B.

Conditions of Certificate

The certificate granted shall be subject to the following conditions:

1. The venture capital fund shall abide by the provisions of the SEBI Act and these regulations.
2. The venture capital fund shall not carry on any other activity other than that of a venture capital fund.
3. The venture capital fund shall inform SEBI in writing of any information or details previously submitted to SEBI which have changed after grant of the certificate.
4. If the information or details submitted are found to be false or are misleading in any particular manner, suitable penal action can be taken.

Procedure where Certificate is not Granted

After considering any application, if SEBI is of the opinion that the certificate cannot be granted under law, it may reject the application after giving the applicant a reasonable opportunity of making its representation. The decision of SEBI to reject the application shall be communicated to the applicant within 30 days.

Effect of Refusal to Grant Certificate

Any applicant whose application is rejected cannot carry out any activity as a venture capital fund.

Investment Conditions and Restrictions

A venture capital fund may raise money from any source, whether Indian, foreign or non resident Indian by way of issue of units. No venture capital fund shall accept any investment from any investor less than Rs. 500,000. However, this condition is not applicable to :

a. employees or the principal officer or directors of the venture capital fund, or directors of the trustee company or trustees where the venture capital fund has been established as a trust, and
b. the employees of the fund manager or asset management company.

For the purpose of these regulations, fund raised means actual money raised from investors for subscribing to the securities of the venture capital fund and includes money that is raised from the author of the trust (in case the venture capital fund has been established as a trust) but does not include the paid up capital of the trustee company, if any.

Each scheme launched or fund set-up by a venture capital fund shall have firm commitment from the investors for contribution of an amount of at least Rupees five crores before the start of operations by the venture capital fund.

All investment made or to be made by a venture capital fund shall be subject to the following conditions, namely:

a. venture capital fund shall disclose the investment strategy at the time of application for registration;
b. venture capital fund shall not invest more than 25 percent corpus of the fund in one venture capital undertaking;
c. shall not invest in the associated companies; and
d. venture capital fund shall make investment in the venture capital undertaking as enumerated below:
    (i) at least 75 percent of the investible funds shall be invested in unlisted equity shares or equity linked instruments. However, if the venture capital fund seeks to avail of benefits under the relevant provisions of the Income Tax Act applicable to a venture capital fund, it shall be required to disinvest from such investments within a period of one year from the date on which the shares of the venture capital undertaking are listed in a

recognized Stock Exchange.

(ii) Not more than 25 percent of the investible funds may be invested by way of:

a. subscription to initial public offer of a venture capital undertaking whose shares are proposed to be listed subject to lock-in period of one year; and

b. debt or debt instrument of a venture capital undertaking in which the venture capital fund has already made an investment by way of equity.

Prohibition on Listing

No venture capital fund shall be entitled to get its securities or units listed on any recognized stock exchange upto the expiry of three years from the date of issue of securities or units by the venture capital fund.

General Obligations and Responsibilities

No venture capital fund shall issue any documents or advertisement inviting offers from the public for the subscription of the purchase of any of its securities or units.

Private Placement

A venture capital fund may raise money only through private placement of its securities or units. The venture capital fund before issuing any securities or units must file with SEBI a placement memorandum.

Placement Memorandum or Subscription Agreement

The venture capital fund must :

a. issue a placement memorandum which shall contain details of the terms and conditions subject to which monies are proposed to be raised from investors; or

b. enter into contribution or subscription agreement with the investors which shall specify the terms and conditions subject to which monies are proposed to be raised.

The Venture Capital Fund must file with the Board for information, the copy of the placement memorandum or the copy of the contribution or subscription agreement entered with the investors along with a report of money actually collected from the investor.

Maintenance of Books and Records

Every venture capital fund must maintain for a period of 8 years books of accounts, records and documents which must give a true and fair picture of state of affairs of the venture capital fund.

Power to Call for Information

SEBI may at anytime call for any information from the venture capital fund in respect to any matter relating to its activity as a venture capital fund. Such information must be submitted within the time specified by days to SEBI.

Submission of Reports to SEBI

SEBI may at anytime call upon the venture capital fund to file such report as it deems fit with regards to the activity carried out by venture capital fund.

Winding-up

A scheme of venture capital fund set-up as a trust shall be wound up:

1. When the period of the scheme as mentioned in the placement memorandum is over; or
2. If, in the opinion of the trustees or the trustee company, it is in the interest of the investors that be wound-up; or
3. If 75 percent of the investors in the scheme pass a resolution at a meeting of unit holders of the scheme that the scheme be wound up; or
4. If SEBI so directs, in the interest of investors.

The venture capital fund set-up as a company shall be wound up according to provision of the Companies Act, 1956.

A venture capital fund set-up as a body corporate shall be wound up in accordance with the provisions of the statute under which it is constituted.

The trustees or trustee company of the venture capital fund set-up as a trust or the Board of Directors in the case of the venture capital fund is set-up as a company (including body corporate) shall intimate the Board and investors of the circumstances leading to the winding up of the Fund or Scheme.

Effect of Winding up

On and from the date of intimation of the winding up, no further investments shall be made on behalf of the scheme to be wound up. Within three months from the date of intimation, the assets of the scheme shall be liquidated and the proceeds accruing to the investors in the scheme distributed to them after satisfying all liabilities.

Inspection and Investigation

SEBI may appoint one or more person, *suo-moto* or upon receipt of information or complaint, as inspecting or investigating officer for inspection or investigation of the books of accounts, records and documents relating to the venture capital fund for any of the following reason :

1. To ensure that the books of accounts records and documents are being maintained by the venture capital fund in the manner specified in these regulations.
2. To inspect or investigate into complaints received from investors, clients or any other person on any matter having a bearing on the activity of the venture capital fund.
3. To ascertain that the provision of the SEBI Act and these regulations are being complied with by the venture capital fund.
4. To inspect or investigate *suo moto* into the affairs of the venture capital fund in the interest of the securities market and the interest of investors.

Notice before Inspection or Investigation

Before ordering an inspection or investigation, SEBI shall give not less than 10 days notice to the venture capital fund.

However, where SEBI is satisfied that in the interest of the investors, no such notice need be given, it may by order in writing not give such notice.

Obligation of Venture Capital Fund on Inspection or Investigation

It shall be the duty of every officer of the Venture Capital Fund in respect of whom an inspection or investigation has been ordered and any other associate person who is in possession of relevant information pertaining to conduct and affairs of such Venture Capital Fund including fund manager or asset management company, if any, to produce to the Investigating or Inspecting Officer such books, accounts and other documents in his custody or control and furnish him with such statements and information as the said Officer may require for the purposes of the investigation or inspection.

It shall be the duty of every officer of the Venture Capital Fund and any other associate person who is in possession of relevant information pertaining to conduct and affairs of the Venture Capital Fund to give to the Inspecting or Investigating Officer all such assistance and shall extend all such co-operation as may be required in connection with the inspection or investigations and shall furnish such information sought by the inspecting or investigating officer in connection with the inspection or investigation.

The Investigating or Inspecting Officer shall, for the purposes of inspection or investigation, have power to examine on oath and record the statement of any employees, directors or person responsible for or connected with the activities of venture capital fund or any other associate person having relevant information pertaining to such Venture Capital Fund.

The Inspecting or Investigating Officer shall, for the purposes of inspection or investigation, have power to obtain authenticated copies of documents, books, accounts of Venture Capital Fund, from any person having control or custody of such documents, books or accounts.

The inspecting or investigating officer in the course of inspection or investigation shall be entitled to examine or record the statement of any director, trustee, officer or employee of the venture capital fund.

It shall be the duty of the director, trustee, officer or employee to reasonably assist the inspecting or investigating officer in connection with the inspection or investigation.

Submission of the Report to SEBI

The inspecting or investigating officer shall as soon as possible on completion of the inspection submit his inspection or investigation report to SEBI. He may also submit an interim report if so required.

SEBI shall after consideration of inspection or investigation report or the interim report communicate the finding of the inspecting officer to the venture capital fund and give it an opportunity to make a representation. On receipt of the reply, if any, from the venture capital fund, SEBI may call upon the venture capital fund to take such measures as the board may befit in the interest of the securities market or for due compliance with the provisions of the SEBI Act.

The Board may after consideration of the investigation or inspection report and after giving reasonable opportunity of hearing to the venture capital fund or its trustees, directors issue such direction as it deems fit in the interest of securities market or the investors including directors in the nature of:

a. requiring a venture capital fund not to launch new schemes or raise money from investors for a particular period;
b. prohibiting the person concerned from disposing of any of the properties of the fund or scheme acquired in violation of these regulations;
c. requiring the person connected to dispose of the assets of the fund or scheme in a manner as may be specified in the directions;
d. requiring the person concerned to refund any money or the assets to the concerned investors along with the requisite interest or otherwise, collected under the scheme; and
e. prohibiting the person concerned from operating in the capital market or from accessing the capital market for a specified period.

Procedure for Action in Case of Default

Suspension of Certificate

SEBI may suspend, without prejudice to issue of directions or measure as above, the certificate granted to a venture capital fund if the venture capital fund contravenes any of the provisions of the SEBI Act or of the regulations made there under or fails to furnish any information relating to its activity as a venture capital fund as required by SEBI or furnishes to SEBI false or misleading information or does not submit periodical returns or reports as required by SEBI or does not co-operate with any enquiry inspection or investigation conducted by SEBI or fails to redress the complaints of investors or fails to give a satisfactory reply to SEBI in this behalf.

Cancellation of Certificate

SEBI may cancel the certificate granted to a venture capital fund where the venture capital fund is guilty of fraud or as been convicted of an offence involving moral turpitude or where the venture capital fund has been guilty of repeated default under these regulations.

No order of suspension or cancellation shall be made by except after holding an enquiry in accordance with the following procedure:

> For the purpose of holding an enquiry, SEBI may appoint one or more enquiry officers. The enquiry officer shall issue to venture capital fund at its registered office or principal place of business a notice stating the grounds on which the action is proposed to be taken and show cause why such action need not be taken within a period of 14 days from the date of receipt of notice.

The venture capital fund may within 14 days from the date of receipt of such notice, furnish to the enquiry officer its reply and make its representation before him. A venture capital fund may appear through any person duly authorized by it. The enquiry officer shall after taking into account all relevant facts and circumstances, submit a report to SEBI and recommend penal action, if any, to be taken against the venture capital fund as also the grounds on which such action is justified.

On receipt of the report from the enquiry officer, SEBI shall consider the same and may issue to the venture capital fund a show cause notice as to why such penal action as proposed by the enquiry officer or such appropriate action should not be taken against it. The venture capital fund, within 14 days from the date of receipt of such show cause notice, sends a reply to SEBI. After considering the reply, if any, of the venture capital fund, SEBI shall pass such an order as it deems fit.

On and from the date of suspension of certificate, the venture capital fund shall cease to carryon any activity as a venture capital fund during the period of suspension and shall be subject to such directions of SEBI with regards to any records, documents, securities as may be in its custody or control relating into its activity as a venture capital fund as SEBI specifies. On and from the date of cancellation of a certificate, the venture capital fund, with immediate effect, shall cease to carry on any activity of the venture capital fund and shall be subject to such direction of SEBI with regard to transfer of records, documents and securities that may be in its custody or control relating to the activities of the venture capital fund as SEBI may specify.

The order of suspension or cancellation of certificate may be published by SEBI in at least two newspapers.

Action against Intermediaries

The Board may initiate action for suspension or cancellation of registration of an intermediary holding a certificate of registration who fails to exercise due diligence in the performance of its functions or fails to comply with its obligations under these regulations. However, no such certificate of registration shall be suspended or cancelled unless the procedure specified in the regulations applicable to such intermediary is complied with.

Appeal to the Central Government

Any person aggrieved by an order of the Board under these regulations may prefer an appeal to the Securities Appellate Tribunal.

Income Tax Benefits

In order to encourage the development of venture capital funds, the Income Tax Act, 1961 exempts the income of a venture capital fund from income tax.

Income of a Venture Capital fund [section 10(23FB)] (on and from Financial Year 1999-2000)

Any income of a Venture Capital Fund (VCF) or a Venture Capital Company (VCC) set-up to raise funds for investment in a Venture Capital Undertaking (VCU) is exempt.

VCC means a company which has been granted a certificate of registration by SEBI and which fulfils the conditions laid down by SEBI with the approval of the Central Government.

VCF means a fund operating under a trust deed registered under the Registration Act, 1908, which has been granted a certificate of registration by SEBI and which fulfils the conditions laid down by SEBI with the approval of the Central Government.

VCU means a domestic company whose shares are not listed in a recognized stock exchange in India and which is engaged in the business for providing services, production or manufacture of an article or thing but does not include activities or sectors which are specified by SEBI with approval of the Central Government.

3.2.1 Foreign Venture Capital Regulations*

SEBI has made regulations in order to regulate venture capital investment in India by foreign venture capital funds. These regulations are known as Securities and Exchange Board of India (Foreign Venture Capital Investor) Regulations, 2000.

Definitions

In these regulations, unless the context otherwise requires:

1. Equity linked instruments includes instruments convertible into equity shares or share warrants, preference shares, debentures compulsorily convertible into equity.

---

* Online official site www.sebi.net.in originated from SEBI, Mumbai.

2. Foreign Venture Capital Investor means an investor incorporated and established outside India, which proposes to make investment in venture capital fund(s) or venture capital undertakings in India and is registered under these Regulations.
3. Investible funds means the fund committed for investments in India net of expenditure for administration and management of the fund.
4. Venture Capital Fund means a Fund established in the form of a trust, a company including a body corporate and registered under Securities and Exchange Board of India (Venture Capital Fund) Regulations, 1996, which
   (i) has a dedicated pool of capital;
   (ii) raised in the manner specified under the Regulations; and
   (iii) invests in venture capital undertaking in accordance with these Regulations.
4. Venture Capital Undertaking means a domestic company :
   (i) whose shares are not listed in a recognized stock exchange in India; and
   (ii) which is engaged in the business of providing services, production or manufacture of articles or things, but does not include such activities or sectors which are specified in the negative list by the Board, with the approval of Central Government, by notification in the Official Gazette in this behalf.

Registration of Foreign Venture Capital Investors as CAPITAL INVESTORS

Application for grant of certificate

For the purposes of seeking registration under these regulations, the applicant must make an application to the Board in Form A along with the prescribed application fee.

Eligibility Criteria

For the purpose of the grant of a certificate to an applicant as a Foreign Venture Capital Investor, the Board shall consider the following conditions for eligibility, namely :

a. the applicants track record, professional competence, financial soundness, experience, general reputation of fairness and integrity;
b. whether the applicant has been granted necessary approval by the Reserve Bank of India for making investments in India; or
c. whether the applicant is an investment company, investment trust, investment partnership, pension fund, mutual fund, endowment fund, university fund, charitable institution or any other entity incorporated outside India; or
d. whether the applicant is an asset management company, investment manager or investment management company or any other investment vehicle incorporated outside India; or
e. whether the applicant is authorized to invest in venture capital fund or carry on activity as a venture capital fund; or
f. whether the applicant is regulated by an appropriate foreign regulatory authority or is an income tax payer; or submits a certificate from its banker of its or its promoter's track record where the applicant is neither a regulated entity nor an income tax payer.
g. the applicant has not been refused a certificate by the Board.
h. whether the applicant is a fit and proper person.

Furnishing of Information, Clarification

The Board may require the applicant to furnish such further information, as it may consider necessary.

Consideration of Application

An application which is not complete in all respects shall be rejected by the Board. However, before rejecting any such application, the applicant shall be given an opportunity to remove, within thirty days of the date of receipt of communication, the objections indicated by the Board.

The Board may, on being satisfied that it is necessary to extend the period specified above may extend such period not beyond ninety days.

Procedure for Grant of Certificate

If the Board is satisfied that the applicant is eligible for the grant of certificate, it shall send an intimation to the applicant. On receipt of intimation, the applicant shall pay to the Board, the prescribed registration fee. The Board shall on receipt of the registration fee grant a certificate of registration in Form B.

Conditions of Certificate

The certificate granted to the foreign venture capital fund shall be *inter-alia,* subject to the following conditions, namely:

a. it shall abide by the provisions of the Act, and these regulations;
b. it shall appoint a domestic custodian for purpose of custody of securities;
c. it shall enter into arrangement with a designated bank for the purpose of operating a special non-resident rupee or foreign currency account; and
d. it shall forthwith inform the Board in writing if any information or particulars previously submitted to the Board are found to be false or misleading in any material particular or if there is any change in the information already submitted.

Procedure where Certificate is not Granted

On considering an application, if the Board is of the opinion that a certificate should not be granted, it may reject the application after giving the applicant a reasonable opportunity of being heard. The decision of the Board to reject the application shall be communicated to the applicant.

Effect of Refusal to Grant Certificate

Any applicant whose application has been rejected shall not carry on any activity as a Foreign Venture Capital Investor.

Investment Conditions and Restrictions

Investment Criteria for a Foreign Venture Capital Investor.

All investments to be made by a foreign venture capital investors shall be subject to the following conditions:

a. it shall disclose to the Board its investment strategy;
b. while it can invest its total funds committed in one venture capital fund it shall however not invest more than 25 percent of the funds committed for investments to India in one Venture Capital Undertaking; and
c. it shall make investments in the Venture Capital Undertaking as enumerated below :
   - at least 75 percent of the investible funds shall be invested in unlisted equity shares or equity linked instruments,
   - not more than 25 percent of the investible funds may be invested by way of :
     - subscription to initial public offer of a venture capital undertaking whose shares are proposed to be listed subject to lock-in period of one year; and
     - debt or debt instrument of a venture capital undertaking in which the venture capital fund has already made an investment by way of equity.

General Obligations and Responsibilities

Maintenance of Books and Records

Every Foreign Venture Capital Investor shall maintain for a period of eight years, books of accounts, records and documents which shall give a true and fair picture of the state of affairs of the Foreign Venture Capital Investor.

Every Foreign Venture Capital Investor shall intimate to the Board, in writing, the place where the books, records and documents are being maintained.

Power to Call for Information

The Board may at any time call for any information from a Foreign Venture Capital Investor with respect to any matter relating to its activity as a Foreign Venture Capital Investor.

Submission of Reports to the Board

Where any information is called for, it shall be furnished within the time specified by the Board.

Appointment of Designated Bank

The Foreign Venture Capital Investor or a global custodian acting on behalf of the foreign venture capital investor must enter into an agreement with the domestic custodian to act as a custodian of securities for Foreign Venture Capital Investor.

The Foreign Venture Capital Investor shall ensure that domestic custodian takes steps for:

(a) monitoring of investment of Foreign Venture Capital Investors in India;
(b) furnishing of periodic reports to the Board; and
(c) furnishing such information as may be called for by the Board.

The Foreign Venture Capital Investor must appoint a branch of a bank approved by Reserve Bank of India as designated bank for opening of foreign currency denominated accounts or special non-resident rupee account.

Inspection and Investigations

Board's Right to Inspect or Investigate

The Board may, *suo-moto* or upon receipt of information or complaint, cause an inspection or investigation to be made in respect of conduct and affairs of any foreign venture capital investor by an Officer whom the Board considers fit for any of the following reasons namely:

a. to ensure that the books of account, records and documents are being maintained by the foreign venture capital investor in the manner specified in these regulations;
b. to inspect or investigate into complaints received from investors, clients or any other person, on any matter having a bearing on the activities of the foreign venture capital investor;

c. to ascertain whether the provisions of the Act and these regulations are being complied with by the foreign venture capital investor; and
d. to inspect or investigate *suo-moto* into the affairs of a foreign venture capital investor in the interest of the securities market or in the interest of investors.

Obligation of Foreign Venture Capital Investor on investigation or inspection by Board

It shall be the duty of every Foreign Venture Capital Investor in respect of whom an inspection or investigation has been ordered and any other associated person who is in possession of the relevant information pertaining to conduct and affairs of such Foreign Venture Capital Investor (including asset management company or fund manager), to produce to the Inspecting or Investigating Officer, such books, accounts and other documents in his custody or control and furnish to him with such statements and information as the said Officer may require for the purposes of the inspection or investigation.

It is the duty of Foreign Venture Capital Investor and any other associated person who is in possession of the relevant information (pertaining to conduct and affairs of the Foreign Venture Capital Investor) to give to the Inspecting or Investigating Officer all such assistance and he must extend all such co-operation as may be required in connection with the inspections or investigations and must furnish such information sought by the Inspecting or Investigating Officer in connection with the inspections or investigations.

The Inspecting or Investigating Officer, (for the purposes of inspection or investigation), has the power to examine on oath and record the statement of any person responsible for or connected with activities of Foreign Venture Capital Investor or any other associated person having relevant information pertaining to such Foreign Venture Capital Investor.

The Inspecting or Investigating Officer, (for the purposes of inspection or investigation), has the power to get authenticated copies of documents, books, accounts of Foreign Venture Capital Investor, from any person having control or custody of such documents, books or accounts.

Submission of the Report

The Inspecting or Investigating Officer shall on completion of inspection or investigations, submit a report to the Board.

Board's right to issue any direction to Foreign Venture Capital Investor.

The Board may after consideration of the inspection or investigation report and after giving a reasonable opportunity of hearing to the Foreign Venture Capital Investor, require it to take such measure or issue such directions as it deems fit in the interest of capital market and investors, including directions in the nature of:

a. requiring the person concerned to dispose of the securities or disinvest in a manner as may be specified in the directions;
b. requiring the person concerned not to further invest for a particular period; and
c. prohibiting the person concerned from operating in the capital market in India for a specified period

Procedure for Action in Case of Default

Board's Right to Suspend or Cancel Certificate of Registration

The Board may after consideration of the investigation report, initiate action for suspension or cancellation of the registration of such Foreign Venture Capital Investor. However, no such certificate of registration shall be suspended or cancelled unless the procedure given below is complied with.

Suspension of Certificate

The Board may suspend the certificate where the Foreign Venture Capital Investor:

a. contravenes any of the provisions of the Act or these regulations;
b. fails to furnish any information relating to its activity as a Foreign Venture Capital Investor as required by the Board;
c. furnishes to the Board information which is false or misleading in any material particular;

d. does not submit periodic returns or reports as required by the Board; and
e. does not co-operate in any enquiry or inspection conducted by the Board;

Cancellation of Certificate

The Board may cancel the certificate granted to a Foreign Venture Capital Investor :

a. when the Foreign Venture Capital Investor is guilty of fraud or has been convicted of an offence involving moral turpitude;
b. the Foreign Venture Capital Investor has been guilty of repeated defaults of the nature mentioned above;
c. the Foreign Venture Capital Investor does not continue to meet the eligibility criteria laid down in these regulations; and
d. contravenes any of the provisions of the Act or these regulations.

Manner of Making Order of Cancellation or Suspension

No order of penalty or cancellation of certificate shall be imposed on the Foreign Venture Capital Investor except after holding an enquiry in accordance with the prescribed procedure.

Manner of holding enquiry before suspension or cancellation.

For the purpose of holding an enquiry, the Board may appoint one or more enquiry officers. The enquiry officer shall issue to the Foreign Venture Capital Investors, at its registered office or its principal place of business or its agent or representative in India, a notice setting out the grounds on which action is proposed to be taken against it and call upon it to show cause against such action within a period of fourteen days from the date of receipt of the notice.

· The Foreign Venture Capital Investor may, within fourteen days from the date of receipt of such notice, furnish to the enquiry officer a written reply, together with copies of documentary or other evidence relied on by it or sought by the Board from the Foreign Venture Capital Investor.

The enquiry officer shall give a reasonable opportunity of hearing to the Foreign Venture Capital Investor to enable him to make submissions in support of its reply.

Before the enquiry officer, the Foreign Venture Capital Investor may appear through any person duly authorized by the Foreign Venture Capital Investor. However, no lawyer or advocate shall be permitted to represent the Foreign Venture Capital Investors at the enquiry. Where a lawyer or an advocate has been appointed by the Board as a presenting officer, it shall be lawful for the Foreign Venture Capital Investor to present its case through a lawyer or advocate.

The enquiry officer may, if he considers it necessary, ask the Board to appoint a presenting officer to present its case

The enquiry officer shall, after taking into account all relevant facts and submissions made by the Foreign Venture Capital Investor, submit a report to the Board and recommend the penal action, if any, to be taken against the Foreign Venture Capital Investor as also the grounds on which the proposed action is justified.

Show-cause Notice and Order

On receipt of the report from the enquiry officer, the Board shall consider the same and may issue to the Foreign Venture Capital Investor a show-cause notice as to why the penal action as proposed by the enquiry officer or such appropriate action should not be taken against it.

The Foreign Venture Capital Investor shall, within fourteen days of the date of the receipt of the show-cause notice, send a reply to the Board.

The Board, after considering the reply, if any, of the Foreign Venture Capital Investor, shall, as soon as possible pass such order as it deems fit.

Effect of Suspension and Cancellation of Certificate

On and from the date of the suspension of the certificate, the Foreign Venture Capital Investor shall cease to carry on any activity as a Foreign Venture Capital Investor during the period of suspension, and shall be subject to such directions of the Board with regard to any records, documents or securities that may be in its custody or control, relating to its activities as Foreign Venture Capital Investor, as the Board may specify.

On and from the date of cancellation of the certificate, the Foreign Venture Capital Investor shall, with immediate effect, cease to carry on any activity as a Foreign Venture Capital Investor, and shall be subject to such directions of the Board with regard to the transfer of records, documents or securities that may be in its custody or control, relating to its activities as Foreign Venture Capital Investor, as the Board may specify.

Publication of Order of Suspension or Cancellation

The order of suspension or cancellation of certificate passed may be published by the Board in two newspapers.

Action against Intermediary

The Board may initiate action for suspension or cancellation of registration of an intermediary holding a certificate of registration who fails to exercise due diligence in the performance of its functions or fails to comply with its obligations under these regulations. However, no such certificate of registration shall be suspended or cancelled unless the procedure specified in the regulations applicable to such intermediary is complied with.

Appeal to Securities and Exchange Board of India

Any person aggrieved by an order of the Board under these regulations may prefer an appeal to the Securities Appellate Tribunal.

The above tax rates may be reduced under Double Taxation Avoidance Treaty (Tax Treaty) between India and the foreign country in which the investors are residing.

There is no specific tax exemption available for the income earned by a FVCI. However, the way the Section 10(23FB) is worded, there is a possibility that even the FVCI would be entitled to the benefits available to domestic VCFs mentioned above. In the event that the FVCI avails of the exemption under Section 10(23FB), the investors in a FVCI would become liable to tax on the income earned by the FVCI as per the provisions of Section 115U.

As per the provisions of Section 90(2) of the ITA, a non-resident investor investing from a country with which India has a tax treaty, would have an option to be taxed as per the provisions of the tax treaty or ITA, whichever is more beneficial. In light of this, the FVCI investing through a tax treaty jurisdiction may be in a position to elect to take tax benefits available under the tax treaty in which case the Sections 10(23FB) and Section 115U of the ITA should not be applicable. For example, if the FVCI is incorporated in Mauritius, the Indian capital gains tax on the income earned by the FVCI on its investments in India can be eliminated under the India-Mauritius Tax Treaty provided the FVCI does not have a "permanent establishment" in India. The investors in FVCI may also not be taxable in India.

On account of its favourable tax treaty with India, Mauritius has become a favourite jurisdiction for investing into India. As a matter of fact, Mauritius has become the largest investor into India. In order to structure the FVCI through Mauritius and in order to be eligible to avail the benefit under the India-Mauritius Tax Treaty, careful structuring is extremely crucial. There have been instances in the past where the use of Mauritius as a conduit for investing into India has been looked upon unfavourably by the Indian tax authorities. In the case of NatWest, the Authority for Advance Rulings (AAR) had denied a ruling on the grounds that use of Mauritius was merely for tax avoidance and the AAR need not rule on an application which is prima facie for avoidance of tax. However, careful structuring of an investment can reduce the risk of denial of Tax Treaty benefits. There has been a ruling in case of AIG followed by DLJ, wherein the AAR granted the benefits of India-Mauritius Tax Treaty and observed that if there was a commercial justification for setting up an SPV and then if the same was established in Mauritius, that per se should not result in denial of a ruling and benefits under the India-Mauritius Tax Treaty. In addition to the commercial justification, it is also important to ensure that the structure does not expose the FVCI to a "permanent establishment" (PE) in India. Under the India-Mauritius Tax Treaty, if the FVCI were held to have a PE in India, the income attributable to such PE would be subject to tax in India. There is a fair amount of subjectivity involved in the determination of a PE and hence very careful thought has to be given while finalizing structure, especially to the management of the FVCI.

APPENDIX 2
Investment Criteria of Indian FIs

Name of the Financial Institutions	*Total Fund Size*	*Types of Financing*	*Investment Preference*	*Industry Focus*
(1)	*(2)*	*(3)*	*(4)*	*(5)*
2i Capital (India) Pvt. Ltd.	NA	1. Early/Stage/Growth 2. Development/Expansion	1. Less than 10 Million	1. IT 2. Computer Software 3. Computer Hardware 4. IT Enabled Services 5. Biotech
Acer Technology Ventures Advisory (India) Pvt. Ltd.	Rs. 260 Million	1. Early Stage/Growth 2. Development/Expansion	1. Less than 10 Million	1. IT 2. Computer Software 3. Computer Hardware
Baring Private Equity Partners (India) Limited	Rs. 2000 Million	1. Development/Expansion 2. MBO	1. Above 200 Million	1. IT 2. Computer Hardware 3. Computer Software 4. IT Enabled Services
Canbank Venture Capital Fund Ltd.	CVCF I—Rs. 164.25 Million CVCF II—Rs.105 Million CVCF III—Rs. 300 Million	1. Start-up 2. Early Stage/Growth 3. Development/Expansion	1. 10-25 Million 2. 25-50 Million	1. IT 2. Computer Hardware 3. Computer Software 4. IT Enabled Services 5. Biotech 6. Industries with promising growth potential

Chrys Capital Fund II, LLC	Rs. 126.7 Million	1. Start-up 2. Early Stage/Growth 3. Development/Expansion 4. Mezzanine	1. 2-5 Million 2. 5-10 Million	1. Biotech 2. Computer Hardware 3. Computer Software 4. IT 5. IT Enabled Outsourcing Services
ChrysCapital Fund I, LLC	Rs. 63.9 Million	1. Development/Expansion	1. 2-5 Million 2. 5-10 Million	1. Computer Hardware 2. Computer Software 3. IT 4. IT Enabled Outsourcing Services
Frontline Ventures	Rs. 50 Million	1. Early Stage/Growth 2. Development/Expansion 3. Mezzanine	1. 50-100 Million 2. 100-200 Million	1. Computer Hardware 2. Computer Software 3. IT 4. IT Enabled Services 5. Media/Retail
HSBC Pvt. Equity Management Ltd. India Liaison Off.	US $ 59.60 Million			
ICF Ventures	Rs. 750 Million	1. Start-up 2. Early Stage/Growth 3. Development/Expansion	1. 50-100 Million	1. IT 2. Computer Hardware 3. Computer Software 4. Biotech 5. Consumer 6. Media

(Contd.)

APPENDIX (*Contd.*)

(1)	*(2)*	*(3)*	*(4)*	*(5)*
IFCI Venture Capital Funds Ltd.	Rs. 80 Million	1. Seed 2. Start-up 3. Early Stage/Growth 4. Development/Expansion 5. Mezzanine	1. 10-25 Million	1. IT 2. Computer Hardware 3. Computer Software 4. IT Enabled Services 5. Biotech 6. Pharma
iLabs Venture Capital Fund	18 Crores	Equity	NA	Technology
IL&FS Venture Corporation Ltd.	Rs. 2270 Million	1. Seed 2. Start-up 3. Early Stage/Growth 4. Development/Expansion 5. Mezzanine 6. MBO	1. 50-100 Million	1. IT 2. Computer Hardware 3. Computer Software 4. IT Enabled Services 5. Telecommunications 6. Biotech 7. Life Sciences 8. Retail 9. Auto Ancillary 10. Engineering
IndAsia Fund Advisors Pvt. Ltd.	Rs. 534 Million	1. Start-up 2. Early Stage/Growth 3. Development/Expansion 4. MBO	1. 100-200 Million 2. Above 200 Million	1. IT 2. Computer Hardware 3. Computer Software 4. IT Enabled Services 5. Biotech 6. Media/ Entertainment

				7. Distribution/ Logistics 8. Communications 9. Life Sciences (including Pharmaceuticals) 10. Companies changing their business paradigm
Industrial Venture Capital Ltd.	7 CR (USD)	1. Seed 2. Start-up 3. Mezzanine	10 TO 25 (USD)	1. IT/Software/ Hardware 2. Hi Tech Printing 3. Construction 4. Textile
Infinity Technology Investments Pvt. Ltd.	Rs.1500 Million	1. Seed 2. Start-up 3. Early Stage/Growth	1. Less than 10 Million	1. IT 2. Computer Software 3. Computer Hardware 4. ITES
Jump start-up Fund Advisors Pvt. Ltd.	Rs. 2000 Million	1. Start-up 2. Early Stage/Growth	1. 10-25 Million	1. IT 2. Computer Hardware 3. Computer Software 4. IT Enabled Services
Karnataka Information Technology Venture Capital Fund	15 CR (USD)	1. Dev/Expansion 2. Mezzanine	25-150 LACS (USD)	1. IT/Software/ Hardware

(Contd.)

APPENDIX (*Contd.*)

(1)	(2)	(3)	(4)	(5)
Kerala Venture Capital Fund	20 CR (USD)	1. Start-up 2. Early State/Growth 3. Dev/Exp.	25-150 LACS (USD)	1. IT/Software/ Hardware 2. ITES 3. Bio-Tech 4. Tourism
Rajasthan Assest Management Co. Pvt. Ltd.	16 CR (USD)	1. Early Stage/Growth 2. Dev/Expansion	10 TO 25 (USD)	1. IT/Software/ Hardware 2. ITES
Sicom Capital Management Ltd.	Rs. 240 Million	1. Early Stage/Growth	1. 10-25 Million	1. Computer Hardware 2. Computer Software 3. IT
SIDBI Venture Capital Limited	Rs. 1000 Million	1. Early Stage/Growth 2. Development/Expansion	1. 50-100 Million	1. IT 2. Computer Hardware 3. Computer Software 4. IT Enabled Services
Walden International	Rs. 2100 Million	1. Seed 2. Start-up 3. Early Stage/Growth 4. Development/Expansion	1. Above 200 Million	1. IT 2. Computer Hardware 3. Computer Software 4. IT Enabled Services 5. Biotech
Waygate Capital		1. Mezzanine 2. MBO	1. 100-200 Million	1. IT 2. Computer Hardware 3. Computer Software 4. IT Enabled Services 5. Media/ Entertainment

Source : IVCA Report (2005).

CHAPTER 4

Venture Capital Growth in Unorganized Environment

From the last chapter it has been observed that there are substantial regional differences between the different states of India in respect of VCF growth. The picture of venture capital financing is not very encouraging especially in Assam. It is a fact though not sounds in sweet that the state of Assam, till today, could not find any place in the coveted list of Indian states promoting VCF in the country. It has been a recognized fact that to start up business ventures in Assam is difficult and risky due to its geographical location, various socio-economic environmental factors, the infrastructural bottlenecks, etc. Although risk aversiveness should not be the characteristic of VCF but it is astonishing that a very poor response from the FIs in this part of the country in the direction of VCF. Moreover, the Government initiative in this direction to develop an environment to harness VCF possibilities is also discernible.

As stated in the first chapter, we have considered Assam as a representitive of an unorganized environment for VCF due to its discernible growth. In order to get experiences of an organized environment for VCF we have considered Karnataka as representative state due to its fastest growth in VCF in global standard. The lack of research samples including or focusing on business owners; required the study to draw on contiguous bodies of literature for hypothesizing the influences of human, social and financial capital. (Figure 4.1). So, from the review of different literature and statistical data, it can be inferred that with higher human capital and social capital Karnataka is exploring the Venture capital market extensively then that of Assam. It can further be believed that entrepreneurs with more diverse social networks[1] are more likely to secure venture financing than entrepreneurs with less diverse social networks.

FIG. 4.1

Showing Diffusion of Human and Social Capital and its Impact on Financial Capital

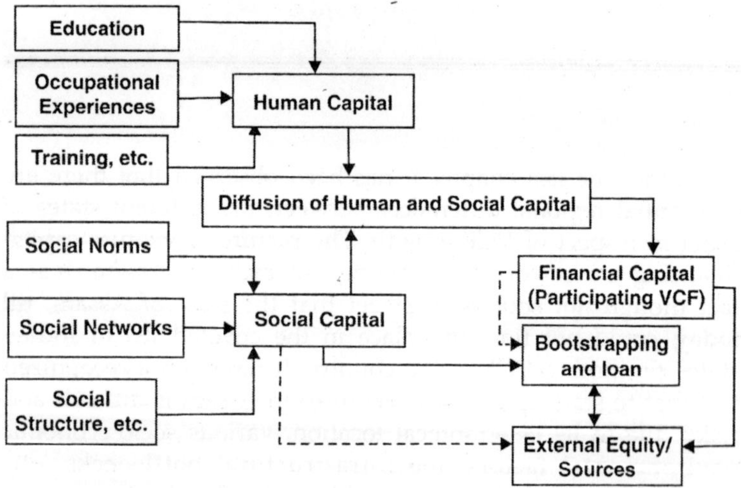

Note : Slaughted lines indicate initial capital contributions in monetary terms only.

It is also observed that entrepreneurs having both Social and Human Capital are more likely to use financing from financial institutions rather than from any private angels. At the same time the financial institutions are happy to finance those entrepreneurs as the other risk factors apart from business risk reduces substantially. Ever since it was understood that the creation of Human Capital and Social Capital is not a difficult task if the attitudes of all the concern bodies are positive, there is a potentiality ahead for the Venture Capital Financing growth in the state of Assam.

Assam is rich in natural resources and has a conducive climatic condition for various agro-based industrial ventures. It is worthy to quote: Hunter who wrote in 1879 in "The Statistical Account of Assam" that 'Silk cultivation in the region was capable of in-definitive development, provided that capital and enterprise were enlisted in the speculation'; Sir George Watt, Superintendent of Indian Museum who did extensive survey referred in 1890 in his monumental volumes of the 'Dictionary of Economic Products of India' that 'Assam is preeminently a Rhea (Riha) province of India, though doubtless to this category must be added the northern tract of Burma which are practically an extension eastward of the Rhea area until it becomes conterminous with that of the districts of northern and North East Bengal." He further referred that 'No more congenial climate than Assam exists, probably in India for the cultivation of this (Ramie) plant, for it grows to the greatest perfection possible where it received the requisite care and cultivation'. Intensive screening of the flora of the northeast has resulted in retrieving 7,000 primitive cultivars of various crop plants from the region with valuable results.[2]

Even after having such rich resources, Assam has witnessed awfully poor development of venture capital growth. Therefore, a millionaire question would be as to why the growth is very negligible in Assam. But, to identify the problems of Venture Capital growth in Assam, it was found prudent to grasp reasons of high growth of Venture Capital Financing in some of the states of India where Venture Capital Financing has taken place in large numbers. Maharashtra is the leading state in terms of Venture Capital movement followed by Gujarat, Tamil Nadu and Karnataka.[3] From the forgone chapters it emerges that Karnataka has over the years developed in venturing into this type of capital, and for that reason the present study has made an attempt to reveal the factors responsible for the growth of VCF in Karnataka to suggest some methodology of VCF for the state of Assam. The study could have been more broad based had the experiences of Maharashtra, Gujarat and Tamil Nadu been used for developing a more comprehensive methodology for VCF in Assam. But due to time and economic constraints, the work has been limited to Karnataka only. This apart, Karnataka happens to be the state where it has been observed that, before the information technology (IT) revolution since 1995 onwards, there were negligible diffusion of venture capital funding.[4] Predominantly having an agro-based economy, Karnataka has shifted their focus from Agriculture to IT and IT enabled services during the first generation of reforms and has started enjoying the benefits during the second-generation reforms starting from 1995 onwards. So far, it has also been observed that the other top positioned states in terms of VCF penetration differ in characteristics as compared to Assam. May be in those states the mindset of the people has been found to be of entrepreneurial character by tradition or culture, which attribute has been found to be very poor among the people of Assam. However, to make a comprehensive comment on the psyche of the people of a particular region is outside the scope of this book. Thus to reiterate, the book has attempted to gather the experiences of Karnataka in the direction of VCF development to suggest a comprehensive methodology of VCF development in Assam as because Assam is still an agrarian economy like pre-1995 Karnataka.

4.1 MAPPING OF FACILITIES IN KARNATAKA

Infrastructural Facilities

A glimpse over the infrastructure facilities of Karnataka shows some of the infrastructural advantages as depicted in Exhibit 4.1.

The government incentives offered in the state also has certain inputs for growth of venture capital there:

Industrial Policy of Karnataka

A glimpse over the Industrial Policy of Karnataka reveals some interesting development targeting towards the industrial development in the state. The main objectives of Industrial Policy 1996 are to active participation of Industry in development of infrastructure. It also emphasis on development

EXHIBIT 4.1

Infrastructure of Karnataka

Railway track length	3,089 km
Road length	1,37,500 km
National Highway length	2,587 km
Domestic airport	Bangalore, Belgaum, Bellary, Hubli, Mangalore, Mysore
International airport	Bangalore
Ports	New Mangalore, Port Karwar
Industrial Zones and Parks	23
Export Processing zone	1

of potential growth centers, thrust for growth in the export of value added goods, encouragement of utilization of Non-conventional energy sources and co-generation, and encouragement for improvement in productivity, R & D and quality upgradation, etc. The State has been classified into three zones:

Zone-I : Developed Areas	:	Bangalore South and North Talukas and Bangalore Urban Agglomeration areas as per 1991 census
Zone-II : Developing Areas	:	All the remaining parts of State -173 talukas
Zone-III : Growth Centers	:	Growth Centers at Dharwad, Hassan and Raichur, Proposed Mini Growth Centres at Bijapur, Malur-Kolar District, Chitradurga, Chikmagalur, Nippani, Gadag and Bellary, and Ancillary Complex at Thoranagallum Ballary District and such other areas as may be so declared by Government in Commerce and Industries Department from time to time.

4.1.1 Macro-Economic Factors

As per the above classifications, the incentives offered[5] by the central/state during the last decade are:

- Capital investment subsidy of 25% of fixed capital upto Rs. 2.5 million, for Tiny & Small Scale Industries in Zone-II.
- Capital investment subsidy of 30% of fixed capital up to Rs. 3 million, for Tiny & Small Scale Industries in Zone-III.
- Additional 10% investment subsidy for installing renewable energy equipment, upto Rs. 05 million.
- Additional 5% investment subsidy up to Rs. 0.5 million for tiny and SSI in Zone-II and III for thrust sector projects.
- Additional investment subsidy 5% of capital investment up to Rs. 0.1 million for thrust and SSI units all zones established by special category entrepreneurs.
- Industrial estates promoted in Private/Co-operative sector (in Zone-II and III) shall be allowed an investment subsidy @ 20% upto Rs. 2 million for project cost upto Rs. 50 million.
- Sales tax exemption or deferral for investment in small, medium, and large scale units.
- Five-year exemption from electricity tax on captive generation for self-consumption.
- Special incentive package, on case-to-case basis, for projects over Rs. 1000 million.
- All new, tiny, and SSI units in Zone-II and III exempted from stamp duty.
- Subsidy for SSIs of 25% of fixed capital or Rs. 2.5 million (Zone-II); and 30% or Rs. 3 million (Zone-III) which ever are higher.
- Additional 5% subsidy of upto Rs. 0.5 million for 100% export oriented units.
- Exemption from planned power cuts for 100% export oriented units.

4.1.2 State Identified Priority Sectors

The Government of Karnataka has identified some

priority sectors where one can venture. These are: Electronics, Telecommunication, Informatics (software), Leather and Leather Products, Pharmaceuticals, Agro Food Processing, Sugar Industry, Bio-technology industries, Automobile industries.

As it is also felt that the manufacturing processes could be an area where Venture Capital Financing has a role to play, the automobile industries can also gear up to avail such facilities.

4.2 MAPPING OF FACILITIES IN ASSAM

By far the strongest and best-substantiated conclusion from economic research on the North Eastern region is the urgent need to stimulate job-creating growth in a region with the fastest growing population. Assam's population quadrupled since 1950, and is expected to double soon.[6] Unemployment rates for the non-oil producing economies of Assam are average 20%, among the highest in the country. Unemployment for those less than 25 years of age is over 40%, with serious economic/social exclusion and brain drain* implications. Yet if it is looked into the infrastructural facilities in Assam, we found certain similarities with Karnataka. The infrastructural facilities available in Assam are highlighted in Exhibit 4.2.

EXHIBIT 4.2
Infrastructure of Assam

Railway track length	2,467 km.
Road length	68,913 km.
National Highway length	2,296 km.
Domestic airport (functional)	Dibrugarh, Guwahati, Jorhat, Lakhimpur, Silchar, Tezpur
International airport	Guwahati
Sea Ports	None
Industrial Zones and Parks	3
Export Processing Zone	1

4.2.1 Macro Economic Factors

It has been observed that the central/state government from time to time provides some special packages in terms of

Industrial upliftment for the state. Some of these incentives[7] offered in the last decade are:

- Development Subsidy of up to 10% of fixed capital up to Rs. 0.3 million per unit, for all sector of industrial units where fixed investment does no exceed Rs. 50 million (1992).
- Special state capital subsidy of 30% of cost of main plant and machinery, upto Rs. 3 million, for industries, till the Central Capital Investment (1992).
- Subsidy scheme is re-introduced (1998).
- Additional state capital subsidy of 5% of fixed capital investment fo pioneer units, subject to a ceiling of Rs. 1 million (1995).
- Assam Finance Tax on industries lowered from 12% to 4%.
- 50% subsidy on power consumption of up to 1MW (Max. Rs. 0.5 million), 30% between 1 MW (Max. Rs. 1.5 million) and 20% above 5 MW (Max Rs. 3 million).
- Subsidy on manpower development to compensate for cost of training.
- Equity participation in medium and large-scale units and SSIs by AIDC and ASIC respectively.

So, from the above observation it emerges that there are hardly any differences enjoyed by both the states in terms of infrastructures and Government policies related to industrial development. At the same time, looking at the priority sectors of Karnataka, it can also be noted that in Assam also, there are certain sectors being identified by the Government to offer priorities like: Coal & Hydro-Electric Power, Bio Technology, Plastic Processing, Rapid Transport System, Textiles, Urban Infrastructure Development.

Therefore, the research investigation here is to identify the reason of deterrence to the formation of venture capital in Assam. In the ensuing parts of this chapter, an attempt has been made to identify the basic reasons of poor growth of venture capital financing here. Also at the same time, an effort has been made to uncover the reason of lack of entrepreneurial zeal, adverse attitude towards venture capital financing, absence or otherwise of innovative ideas (in the form of new technology), other factors governing the growth and development of human and social capital, and the absence of investing environment in Assam.

4.3 DEVELOPMENT OF SOCIAL AND HUMAN CAPITAL

This section focuses on the impact of Social and Human Capital on venture capital to be considered as a source of funding for young high-technology enterprises in the Karnataka, while the next section will focuses on the Assam. The differences between equity investors acting in a single state market are of special interest, since their likely heterogeneity is important when interpreting aggregated data on investments or on new funds raised, because this heterogeneity may imply significant differences in the quality of capital offered.

The Karnataka equity market has experienced strong growth in terms of invested Venture capital and raised funds since 1997.[8] Two causes of this extraordinary upswing can be identified. First, the establishment of the IT zone which has considerably affected the Karnataki culture of owning shares in general and venture capital activities in particular. Second, the Karnataka government has supported VCF participations substantially. In particular, the government program entitled *Subarna Karnataka* (2000) has had a considerable impact on the development of investments in young high-technology enterprises.

The IT revolution has affected the development of Karnataka for equity positively, since it has offered a new exit channel for equity investors. This exit channel is important for equity investors because it helps them to build a record of accomplishment for high-technology investments that is in turn important for raising new funds. The development of the equity market, however, has not been solely due to the stimulus provided by the establishment of the IT Zone. The early success stories of publicly offered firms in 1997, for example, Bharati Telecom (now merged with Airtel), an upstart telecom services provider, contributed considerably to the upswing on the equity market.

From various literatures, it has been found that the common approach towards entrepreneurship development has multiple dimensions. It is basically the approach that often creates miracles. "Entrepreneurs are the Essence of the digital economy. Their ideas are constantly setting and breaking the boundaries of the fastest moving business in the history of capitalism. Some are serial successes. Most fail. But their dynamism, even when they crash and burn is the spur that keeps wary established businesses on their toes"; Herring (1977[9]). Doing business in the old economy was little difficult, particularly in India. Usually the people belonging to business families and a negligible few with extreme tenacity and entrepreneurial ability could succeed in this direction. Intelligent young graduates usually would settle for jobs in good companies. The introduction of Internet and the consequential digital economy has made it much easier for young entrepreneurs to challenge the established businesses. This activity has been at a high pace at Bangalore, the Silicon Valley of India.

Despite all the efforts made by the Government as well as the private venture capital financing institutions in India to promote the technological development, but the success cannot be rated very highly in India. Most of the Indian companies that made classic early stage entry in technology-oriented innovative companies have experienced a number of difficulties such as early loss incurred, compelled them exit off their business. On the other hand those who succeeded in the early stage had to experience growing pains of continuation. It has been observed that there were until recently poor incentives available to those who strictly followed venture capital norms. Moreover, no further incentives were provided by other agencies that are empowered to do so even for narrowly defined venture capital investments on the plea of its riskiness especially for innovative technology-based entities. Under such circumstances, the growth of technology-based sector through venture capital financing route in India has not been properly matching with some of the Asian countries.[10] It is worth mentioning here that countries like Taiwan, Vietnam, China, Japan, Korea, etc. are provided with incentives in the form of tax rebates to both VCF and the recipient of the venture capital fund. Apart from this the

Governments of these countries also stimulate VCF by diverting the pension fund for its growth.

The IT revolution in Karnataka began with the multinational TI (Texas Instruments) in 1984. Today, the IT industry has 75,000 professionals in Bangalore only. Almost 40% of the business concentrated in extremely high-tech areas like Integrated Circuit Design (IC), Systems Software and Communications Software.

Karnataka has the best research centers and educational institutions. The Indian Institute of Science (IISc) has a distinguished faculty in several high technology fields. The Indian Space Research Organisation (ISRO) develops the best quality software in mission critical applications. The Indian Institute of Management, Bangalore (IIMB) provides premier strategic advice to entrepreneurs. The Indian Institute of Information Technology, Bangalore (IIIT-B) offers post-graduation courses in Information Technology. Bangalore also boasts of several research institutions like LRDE, Centre for Artificial Intelligence and Robotics, etc.

Many ideas do not materialize because of the lack of proper business plan supporting the idea. Many young professionals with exciting ideas do not get exposed to creating the business plan supporting their ideas. Most of the Financial Institutions of this region focuses on the various processes for building an effective business plan and to present the same business plan for the prospective venture capitalists. The successful business plan will describe the product, the customer, the distribution channel, the cost of design, the market, the breakeven and the exit strategy.

Strategic relations play a very important role for success in growing competitive environment. The start-up companies need to develop strategic relations with various stakeholders, customers, players, shareholders, investors, professionals and other employees. An organization should develop abilities to network with other successful players effectively such as the entry strategy, the product service design, sales, marketing, choosing the distribution channel, after sales service, etc. This has been observed that the aforesaid network created by the organizations exist in Karnataka. Karnataki ventures are in a process of building brand equity in both product and service sector. It is extremely difficult to introduce a new brand and even more difficult to sustain it. In the recent years, many dot com companies were able to build the brand by heavy advertising. A few of them spent over 10-20 times their revenue and built their brands. While that was possible in the bullish IPO market, the heavy advertising in a normal market cannot be sustained. Building brand equity for the product or service requires innovative methods, understanding the competitor's products and articulates the Unique Selling Proposition (USP) of the brand.

On the other hand, research on the value of expertise, refining domain specific experience over time, shows a very significant relationship to improved performance in a broad range of settings Ericsson *et al.*, (1996[11]). Experience as an investor is likely to facilitate their deal flow, their ability of insightful due diligence, and smoothen various transactional details. Investors who are able to continue investing over time require being reasonably successful to raise new investment funds.

Most Karnataki IT companies primarily depend on bank financing. The public sector banks still possess a traditional bent of mind in financing with collaterals, which happens to be a lengthy and cumbersome process. In addition, the old rules have not recognized the new requirements of the IT companies that do not have a need for large real assets. The IT companies however require the soft assets, royalties for the use of software, agreements that allow usage of code, etc. which has been identified properly by the financial institutions operating in the state.

Karnataka now has a number of venture capital funds. Many banks and financial institutions have also set-up their venture capital funds in the state. SEBI, the securities market regulator has brought in lot of simplifications in the venture capital funding. A number of Silicon Valley players are also in Bangalore and have started venture capital operations in a big way. Many multinationals are aggressively investing in technology start-ups and a few fund ideas of their own employees, which is sufficient enough for creation of adequate Human and Social Capital for development of Venture Capital there.

4.4 ROLE OF FINANCIAL INSTITUTIONS' (FIS') IN DEVELOPING VENTURE CAPITAL FINANCING IN KARNATAKA

Basically, since 1995, some of the financial institutions have started operating in Karnataka for financing venture capital. This was of course an outcome of second-generation reforms. However, the momentum received only from 2000 to 2003 when the Karnataka is flooded with financial institutions offering venture capital financing. Until the third quarter of 2006, there were in total 160 small or big projects being funded by these financial institutions under review having a financial involvement of around INR 267.3 Crores.

A glimpse over the pattern of funding by these Financial institutions shows that around 91.67% investment are in equity participation and approximately 8.33% of investment is in bridge financing. The pattern gives an idea that almost all the Financial institutions believes only in equity participation and at times only they go ahead with bridge financing. This definitely provides an input that the financial institutions are fully convinced with the proposals as well as the entrepreneurial qualities. A participation in the management requires not only the financial capital but also the human and social capital. It can be derived that the societal values being given priorities by the financial institutions, as they want to create the venture capital financing environment in the state. Exhibit 4.3 depicts the financing stages in which the financial institutions are at present involved in:

EXHIBIT 4.3

Funding Stages by Financial Institutions in Karnataka

Financing Stages	*No. of Projects*	*In Percentage (%)*
Seed Financing	27	16.88
Growth Stage	130	81.25
Convertible financing	01	0.62
Exit stage	02	1.25
Total	160	100

Source : Field Survey.

From the Exhibit 4.3 it is found that most of the investment is in the growth stage and some of them even reached the exit stage. This defiantly gives an idea that the process, which has shifted its gear from 2000 onwards, now in the mid stage of growth and some of the investments, which were carried out before 2000, has attained the maturity stage. Further for many financial institutions, within 2007 to 2010 most of their earlier investments will attain their exit stage. However, it can be inferred that the seed financing percentage is not that high, as it was expect to be. On this, the financial institutions have different view as they said that the seed financing is quite satisfactory if it is compared to 2000-03 period. At the same time they were expressing their concern about the SEBI Regulations[12] regarding real estate investments, because of which they have to forgo many proposals right at the entry level.

4.4.1 Identifying Priority Sectors by FIs' of Karnataka

The Financial Institutions offering Venture capital in the region have identified some of the priority sectors where they are interested to invest in. These are:

> IT, Pharmaceuticals, Electronics, Bio-technology industries, Telecommunication, Informatics (software), Leather & Leather Products, Agro Food Processing, Engineering designs, Legal and Health BQs; IT enabled BPOs, etc.

4.4.2 Financial Institutions on Setting Criteria for Venture Capital Financing

Exhibit 4.4 depicts the financial institutions ranking on the criteria laid down by them to select a proposal for venture capital financing. From the exhibit it is found that emphasis is given on analysis of business plan followed by analysis of entrepreneurial skills by most of the financial institutions. This definitely results in putting more thrust in the human capital as well as the financial capital. However, it is noteworthy to mention here that the exit routs were given lowest preference, as the FIs were of the view that if the business plan is good and the entrepreneur is efficient the exit route is not a big problem for them. Innovative skills and analysis of management and organizational pattern also plays a crucial criterion for selecting a venture capital financing proposal. Such attributes can be derived from the social capital, as the conventional route is not dearer for the financial institutions for venture capital financing. However, from the exhibit it can be observed that such attributes were given second choice after human capital. The financial analysis and projection is another criterion where all the financial institutions are putting prudent considerations while analyzing a proposal for venture capital financing.

EXHIBIT 4.4
Financial Institutions' Ranking on Venture Capital Financing Criteria

Criteria/Parameter	*Financial institutions' Ranking (%)*						
	(1)	*(2)*	*(3)*	*(4)*	*(5)*	*(6)*	*(7)*
Innovative Skill/ Innovative Idea Generation	8.33	16.67	33.33	41.67	—	—	—
Entrepreneurial Skill	25	66.67	—	8.33	—	—	—
Analysis of Management and Organizational Pattern	—	—	66.67	8.33	8.33	8.33	8.34
Analysis of Business Plan	66.67	25	8.33	—	—	—	—
Financial Analysis and Projection	50	25	16.67	8.33	—	—	—
Analysis of Reference Information	—	—	—	25	8.33	58.33	8.34
Exit Routes	—	—	—	16.67	83.33	—	—

Note : Ranking has been done considering highest priority as 1 and least priority as per the attributes made available as 7.

Source : Complied from the Questionnaire.

Further, when it was enquired about the criteria laid down by the financial institutions for analyzing the entrepreneurial quality, the following views were found:

Exhibit 4.5
Financial Institutions' Ranking on Analyzing Entrepreneurial Quality

Criteria/Parameter	*Financial institutions' Ranking (%)*						
	(1)	*(2)*	*(3)*	*(4)*	*(5)*	*(6)*	*(7)*
Entrepreneur's qualification.	8.33	25	58.33	—	8.34	—	—
Professional skills (Including Experience)	75	—	16.67	—	8.33	—	—
Mental Attributes	—	—	—	91.67	8.33	—	—
Behavioural Attributes	—	—	—	8.33	91.67	—	—
Risk Bearing Capacity	8.33	75	16.67	—	—	—	—
Focus on Proposed Project	8.33	66.67	16.67	8.33	—	—	—
Entrepreneurial Generation and Family Background	—	—	—	—	8.33	91.67	—

Note : Ranking has been done considering highest priority as 1 and least priority as per the attributes made available as 7

Source : Complied from the Questionnaire.

It can be perceived from the exhibit 4.5 that professional skill of the entrepreneurs is the key to success in the venture capital financing as conceived by most of the financial institutions. Risk bearing capacity and focus on the proposed projects are the two criteria where most of the financial institutions have a careful evaluation while interpreting the entrepreneurial skills. All these three attributes constitute the human capital and as such it can be interpreted that the financial institutions are keen in putting importance on human capital as a major reason for venture capital financing. Although the entrepreneurial qualification has not been considered as the major criterion for judging the entrepreneurial skills as expressed by the financial institutions but the presence of this has not been totally ignored by them. Mental attributes and the behavioral attributes that can be generated from the social capital, receives less importance from the financial institutions operating in Karnataka. However, a further enquiry depicts a different picture as most of the financial institutions are of the view that since the social atmosphere of Karnataka is very conducive, less importance has been given on those attributes; which can easily be acquired from the social environment for judging the entrepreneurial skills. So far regarding the entrepreneurial generation and family background attribute, the financial institutions were found least interested to consider such attribute in adjudicating the entrepreneurial skills.

4.5 VCF IN ASSAM

The scenario of venture capital financing is very gloomy in Assam. Though it has been a matter of discussion in many academic and professional forums that, running business in Assam is risky due to various reasons including absence of sustainable peace, yet this is still pre-mature to recognize this phenomenon as true. Despite this, the venture capital financing environment is not being developed around this place.

4.5.1 Views of Financial Institutions about Assam

As there is no such financial institution who offers exclusive venture capital in Assam, the researcher approached the COOs of branches/head offices of Financial Institutions who has their parent organization operating in Assam in conventional financing and offers venture capital financing elsewhere in India through their subsidiaries or through a specific purpose vehicle (SPV). When it was enquired whether they have any plan to introduce venture capital financing in the state, 83.33% of COOs had a clear view that they do not have any such plan at present. Only 16.67% revealed that they are planning to introduce venture capital financing in Assam but when is quite uncertain. However, it seems that almost no respondents were quite sure as to when they may go for financing venture capital in the state.

Accordingly, on a further enquiry as to the reasons for not introducing venture capital financing in the state, 50% of them were of the opinion that they have not yet opened up their subsidiaries or any SPV in the state for such financing. 33.33% put the ball in their respective head offices' court by stating that it's all about head offices' decision and they do not have any comment in this regard. 16.67% of the COOs have stated that they have not yet created a separate fund exclusively for venture capital financing, as they have not yet received any proposal from the demand side. It seems that almost all the Financial Institutions are directly or indirectly referring the matter to the discretion of the respective head offices.

Further, when it was enquired about the overall reasons for not venturing into the venture capital financing in the state, the financial institutions were of different opinions. 33.33% were of the opinion that Assam is quite premature for Venture Capital Financing and another 33.33% of them believe that Assam is quite under-prepared for Venture Capital Financing and requires the creation of environment for Venture Capital Financing. On the other hand, 16.67% of them were of the opinion that entrepreneurial climate is missing in Assam and another 16.67% says that the youth are not properly motivated. Clearly, from the views of the Financial Institutions it can be inferred that the formation of Social Capital in the state requires prudent consideration to have an impact of introduction of venture capital in the state.

By looking at the above responses, it seems that the financial institutions are uncertain about introducing Venture Capital Financing in Assam as because the environment is not conducive for such financing according to them. When it was enquired that whether they believe that the geographical remoteness of the place could be a factor for such reluctances, it was found that only 33.33% believe that it could be a major factor for them whereas, 66.67% believe that it is not at all a major factor. So, it can be argued that the geographical remoteness is not a major factor in the state considering the fact that infrastructure-wise the state is not much lagging behind.

Further, it was also found that 83.33% of the COOs are of the opinion that lack of adequate economic platform in Assam could be a reason for poor venture capital financing formation in the state. Almost all the COOs of the financial institutions were of the arbitrary opinion that there is a lack of ventured entrepreneurs in the state. It is mainly because that there is substantial brain drainage occurred in the state since 1990. Such brain drainage leads to dearth of skilled entrepreneurs, which is an essential for Venture Capital Financing. According to them;

the old course curricula, lesser thrust on developing entrepreneurial skill, poor role of district industrial centers, information asymmetry etc. are some of the reasons which lead to shortage of skilled entrepreneurs. In the context of information asymmetry, it is noteworthy to mention that the basic supply-demand gap for venture capital formation is a reason for lack of development of venture capital Kogut *et al* (1998)[13] and it is observed that this may be one of the reasons for poor venture capital formation in the state.

When the respondents were questioned with the present social platform in Assam, whether it is adequate enough for Venture Capital Financing, all the financial institutions were of the opinion that the present social system of Assam is not conducive. 50% of the COOs were of the opinion that for the conventional type of loans only, the repayment is very poor and it has somewhat becoming a culture in the region. On the other hand, rest 50% believes that since the entrepreneurial activities are receiving second status than a job in the state, a major portion of the youths are therefore, less interested to become an entrepreneur. Thus, it leads to perceive that the social capital formation in the state is negligible.

Another factor when highlighted to the COOs regarding the socio-economic risk and the business risk for their observation, it was stated by them that regarding the business risk, they are ready to fund the projects even though the business risk is high. However, in case of other risks, they were found quite defensive and were looking for minimization of such risks by the Government. This leads to an understating that the acquisition of financial capital is not a big difficulty in the state. However, some common conditions should be ensured like reduction of information asymmetry; insistence of financial honesty, co-operation and co-ordination.

Exhibit 4.6 depicts the financial institutions' ranking on the criteria on which they would like to focus while selecting a proposal for venture capital financing.

From the Exhibit 4.6, it emerges that all the financial institutions would like to give top priority to analyze the business plan and also to financial analysis and projections. However, regarding the other parameters it seems that they are having mixed priorities, which, of course, can be understood

EXHIBIT 4.6
Financial Institutions Ranking on Venture Capital Financing Criteria

Criteria/Parameter	*Financial institutions' Ranking (%)*						
	(1)	(2)	(3)	(4)	(5)	(6)	(7)
Innovative Skill/ Innovative Idea Generation	16.66	16.67	16.67	50	—	—	—
Entrepreneurial Skill	—	50	33.33	16.67	—	—	—
Analysis of Management and Organizational Pattern	—	—	16.67	33.33	50	—	—
Analysis of Business Plan	100	—	—	—	—	—	—
Financial Analysis and Projection	16.67	83.33	—	—	—	—	—
Analysis of Reference Information	—	—	33.33	33.33	16.67	16.67	—
Exit Routes	—	—	—	33.33	16.67	50	—

Note : Ranking has been done considering highest priority as 1 and least priority as per the attributes made available as 7.
Source : Complied from the Questionnaire.

from the fact that they are relatively fresher, having less exposure to finance venture capital financing in the state. This can further be realized from the opinions received from the officials of these financial institutions as the researcher found that they are even confused between the very concept of venture capital financing and conventional loan financing.

On enquiry about the proposed criteria to be laid down by these financial institutions for analyzing the entrepreneurial quality for financing venture capital, the following views were depicted in Exhibit 4.7 given on the next page.

From the Exhibit 4.7, it has been observed that the focus on proposed projects receives top priority while analyzing the entrepreneurial quality, hence leading to an understanding that priority is on financial capital. However, the social and human capital has received less importance. Some of the Financial

EXHIBIT 4.7

Financial Institutions Ranking on Judging Entrepreneurial Quality

Criteria/Parameter	*Financial institutions' Ranking (%)*						
	(1)	*(2)*	*(3)*	*(4)*	*(5)*	*(6)*	*(7)*
Entrepreneur's qualification	—	50	50	—	—	—	—
Professional skills (Including Experience)	—	50	50	—	—	—	—
Mental Attributes	—	—	16.67	83.33	—	—	—
Behavioural Attributes	—	66.67	—	16.67	16.66	—	—
Risk Bearing Capacity	50	50	—	—	—	—	—
Focus on Proposed Project	100	—	—	—	—	—	—
Entrepreneurial Generation and Family Background	—	—	—	—	100	—	—

Note : Ranking has been done considering highest priority as 1 and least priority as per the attributes made available as 7

Source : Complied from the Questionnaire.

Institutions put some thrust on the behavioural attributes and some put thrust on risk bearing capacity. Though almost all the Financial Institutions were of the opinion that entrepreneurial generation do not play an important role while analyzing the entrepreneurial quality but still they wanted to put some weightage on this attribute; so that the risk arising from the social and human capital can be minimized.

4.6 VIEWS EXPRESSED BY VENTURE CAPITAL FIRMS OF KARNATAKA ON ASSAM

When the researcher approach the Venture Capital Financing firms of Karnataka and enquired about their views on venture capital financing in Assam, some interesting aspects has been revealed. Almost all the financial institutions were of the opinion that the socio-economic environment of Assam is not conducive enough for starting venture capital financing.

66.67% of them believe that there is a lack of entrepreneurial prospects in Assam. Again 50% of them were of the opinion that there are often some social risk factors associated with any investment in Assam and 33.33% believe that there is a poor support from the government side to develop an atmosphere for venture capital financing. According to them, the government as a social institution should be exposed for the formation of social capital. So, in this respect if the responses by the financial institutions in Assam are compared, then one can infer that the head offices of these financial institutions are at present not interested to put their heads for introducing the VCF in Assam due to lack of entrepreneurial prospects, social risk factors, poor support from the government, etc.

When it was enquired whether the geographical remoteness could be a reason for poor growth of venture capital financing in the state, 75% financial institutions believed that it is not a major problem now-a-days. Only 16.66% believed that it is one of the vital problems and rest 8.34% believed that it may be a problem but could not be treated as a serious problem. Thus, comparing the responses from both the states, inferences can be drawn on the bottom line that geographical remoteness is not a big problem for the state to go for formation of venture capital.

Referring to the required economic platform for Venture Capital growth, 66.67% respondents were of the view that it is somewhat missing in Assam. Another 16.67% believed that the Governments' role in creating such platform is much to be desired in Assam and the rest financial institutions were of the view that industrial exposer is less in the state. By comparison, it is clear that the Financial Institutions were of unanimous opinion that Assam requires a good economic platform for venture capital growth and the present platform is inadequate for venture capital formation.

Again, 58.33% of the financial institutions hold the opinion that there is a lack of entrepreneurs seeking venture capital financing in Assam and almost 75% of them believed that honesty is measured in terms of financial discipline and it is missing among a portion of the youths in Assam. This problem has manifold implications. It affects both the Human Capital and Social Capital formation in the state. Further, the trust and co-operation between the provider and receiver has been affected. These institutions have developed such ideas from their experiences of financing conventional loans and as a result; the mutual trust got lost on the crossroad. Thus, if it is compared, the responses between both the states it appears that there is a shortage of entrepreneurial skills in the state.

Regarding the overall view on venture capital financing in Assam, the financial institutions are almost unanimous in stating that the social atmosphere in the state is not conducive enough to have venture capital financing in the state. They believed that a portion of the youths of this region is not financially disciplined enough to create the environment required for venture capital financing. They believed that for a venture capital financing, at first it should be a win-win situation for both the party and to have such a situation the entrepreneurs should come up with good proposals, create an environment of trust, co-operation and profitability and at the same time the intervention of the state machineries should be there to ensure social harmony.

From the analysis, it was found that Human Capital effects on venture capital financing were different in Assam from anticipated, considering the responses of Karnataka. It is widely noted that previous experience and education are key to entrepreneurial success Cooper *et al.* (1988[14]). However, in case of Assam, only one type of human capital, i.e. entrepreneurial education, has been considered for VCF. In Karnataka, the Financial Institutions' focus is on professional skills and entrepreneurial qualification as it receives equal importance for venture capital financing.

Social capital seems no direct effect on increasing the use of equity or loans in the financial strategy but it influences certain bootstrapping[15] techniques in Assam. Interestingly, most of those relationships were in a negative direction till the period of the present study. Entrepreneurs who did not use foundational and professional advisors were more likely to use personal sources (savings, family and friends) to finance their businesses than entrepreneurs who used these types of advisors. It may be that the use of advisors provided greater knowledge of and access to other forms of financing.[16] In Karnataka also the importance on social capital was not given due weightage by the financial institutions but for the reason that the social atmosphere of Karnataka is very conducive, and as such less importance has been given on the social attributes; which can easily be acquired from the social environment for judging the entrepreneurial skills.

From the above findings, it can be inferred that as a compensating strategy that entrepreneurs can adopt, is to have a wide range of contacts in their social networks. Research also showed that when networks contain people from a verity of work backgrounds, especially those beyond the immediate work group, they tended to be more powerful Blau *et. al.* (1982)[17] Network diversity enhances the chances of accessing a wide array of resources. Nevertheless, the likelihood that the contacts will deliver value or resources depends on the strength of the tie, or the nature of the relationships between the network members. Individuals draw both instrumental resources like materials and physical resources, as well as expressive resources such as friendship, mutual trust, from their network contacts, Brush *et. al.* (2001).[18] In case of Karnataka, it seems that the financial institutions were keen in financing VCF as the presence of human capital is there among the entrepreneurs. Apart from education and training, human capital derives from work environment, Carter *et. al.* (1997).[19] In Karnataka such environment is created not only from the efforts of people of the state but also by the government. There is a positive relationship between prior work experience and venture survival and success (Bruderl *et. al.* 1992)[20] and it can be proved in Karnataka, specially in IT enabled businesses financed through the route of venture capital. However, in Assam due to the information asymmetry, brain drainage, as well as absence of social network, the entrepreneurial development in the state is not encouraging. The governmental effort receives lesser success due to creation of a negative environment for developing entrepreneurial skills among the youths. A disciplined approach is necessary for venture capital financing, which is missing in the state. Thus, by looking at all the phenomena, the first hypothesis of the study can be accepted that Venture Capital growth in Assam is poor due to lack of diffusion of Social and Human capital.

Research studies show that bootstrapping and loan financing provide a foundation for gaining experience and legitimacy that position ventures to secure equity financing (Ben Daniel *et. al.* 2000).[21] From the present study it was observed that in Karnataka, almost all the Financial institutions were doing equity financing and for that they consider only the presence of Human and Social capital. However, in Assam, the experience of loan financing gives a very gloomy picture to the financial institutions, so the researcher was told that the majority of the repayment scenario for the conventional loans in the state is awfully poor. Under the circumstances, an equity financing, according to them could turn out to be a daydream. It can also be inferred that since the human as well as social capital formulation in the state is very low, the financial institutions are not interested to go for venture capital financing. Therefore, the second hypothesis of the study can be accepted that Financial Institutions operating in Assam; at present are unwilling to release venture capital.

Thus, it can be inferred that in comparison to Karnataka or any other leading states of India in terms of VCF growth, Assam is suffering from poor diffusion of venture capital, which is at present mainly due to poor Human and Social Capital formation in the state. As a result, it has also reflected in terms of releasing the venture capital by the financial institutions operating in the state. However, the state still enjoys certain potentialities, which if well utilized than the growth of venture capital in the state is possible in near future.

Notes and References

1. Social networks include friendship, referral groups and other family members, institutions, etc., it allow entrepreneurs to gain access to opportunities and resources, save time, and tap into advice and moral support that may otherwise be unavailable.
2. Chowdhuri, S.N., "India's North-East Industrial Resources and Opportunities", Devi Prasad Bagrodia, Laser King, Tinsukia, 1996, p. 311.
3. Verma, J.C., "Venture Capital Financing in India" , Response Books, New Delhi; 1999 2nd edn., p. 97.
4. Mittal, R., "Karnataka Boom", *Business World*, Vol. 25, Issue 3, 2005.

5. KIDC Publications, 2006, published under the ministry of Industries, Govt. of Karnataka, (Subarna Karnataka Jayanti edn.)
6. Yogi, A.K., 2001, "Development of the North-East Region", Spectrum Publications, Guwahati, 2nd pub. p. 23.
a. Has a serious implication on development of sunrise industries using VCF, highlighted in the subsequent chapters.
7. North-Eastern Industrial Policy, 2003, DI&CC Publication, Dibrugarh; Published under the ministry of Industry, Government of Assam.
8. Mittal, R., "Karnataka Boom", *Business World*, Vol. 25, issue 3, 2005.
9. Herring, R. (1977) 'Venture Capital Finance: A Security Design Approach,' *The Review of Finance*, UK, Vol. 8, No. 1, pp. 75-108.
10. Singh, J.K.; "Regulatory framework of venture capital financing in India", *The journal of Accounting and Finance*, Vol. 16, No. 2 Apr.-Sept. 2002, p. 53.
11. Ericsson, K.A. and Lehmann, A.C. (1996) Expert and exceptional Performance: Evidence on maximal adaptations on task constraints, *Annual Review of Psychology*, 47, pp. 273-305.
12. See SEBI Regulation as amended upto-date available at www.sebi.net.in
13. Kogut, B. and Parkinson, D. (1998). Adoption of the multidivisional structure: analyzing history for the start. *Industrial and Corporate Change*, 7, 249-73.
14. Cooper, A.C., Gimeno-Gascon, F.J. and Woo, C.Y., (1988), Survival failure: a longitudinal Study. Frontiers of Entrepreneurship Research, Wellesley, M.A: Babson College, pp. 225-37.
15. Application of Bootstrapping technique, which is a combination of debt and participative financing, allows the enterprise in a better position to receive equity investments in the later stage of the development.
16. Coleman, S., (2000), Access to Capital and Terms of Credit: A Comparison of Men and Women-owned Small Business. *Journal of Small Business Management*, UK, Vol. 38, pp. 48-52.
17. Blau, J.R. and Alba, R.D. (1982), "Empowering nets of Participation". *Administrative Science Quarterly*, USA, Vol. 27, pp. 363-79.
18. Brush, C.G., (1992), Research on Women Business Owners: Past Trends, a New Perspective and Future Directions, Entrepreneurship Theory and Practice, Baylor University, Waco, Vol. 16, pp. 5-30.
19. Carter, N.M., Williams, M. and Reynolds, P.D. 1997, Discontinuance among new firms in Retail: The Influence of Initial Resources, Strategy and gender, *Journal of Business Venturing*, Elsevier, Netherlands, Vol. 12, pp. 125-46.
20. Bruderl, J. Preisendorfer, P. and Zeigler, R., (1992), Survival Chances of Newly Founded Business Organizations. *American Sociological Review*, USA, Vol. 57, pp. 227-42.
21. Ben Denial, D., Reyes, J. and d'Angelo, M., 2000, "Concentration in the Venture Capital Industry". *Journal of Private Equity*, USA, Summer, pp. 7-13.

Potentiality of VCF in Unorganized Environment

Observation from the forgone chapter has brought forward certain issues of VCF in Assam. Though some of the problems associated with poor diffusion of Venture Capital in Assam were unrevealed, yet, it is understandable from various available literatures that Assam does posses certain advantages for industrial growth, which need to be capitalized for a better growth of VCF in the state. It is worthy to reiterate that in Chapter 4 a comparison of various macro-economic factors in both the states of Assam and Karnataka has been pursued. These factors are usually responsible for industrial growth in any part of the country. Inspite of discernible differences in macro-economic factors as compared to Karnataka, the State of Assam has been placed at 28th position in Perceptual Rank, 16th position in Factual Rank, overall 26th rank in 1997, 26th in 1999 and 20th in 2003[1] in terms investment-friendly states of India is really depicts a gloomy picture about the industrial growth of the state. However, if it is evaluated from the business potentiality and that too for growing up of a considerable venture capital market, Assam can provide many opportunities.

The state of Assam is situated in a strategic location where it can access to the vast domestic and South Asian market. The potentiality galloping large with the opening up of Nathula border and will turn out to be more lucrative when the Stillwell road will open road link between India, Myanmar and China. The state of Assam has a large and rapidly growing consumer market; as constitute the market for branded consumer goods—estimated to be growing at 8% per annum. Demand for several consumer products is growing at over 12% per annum.[2]

The State has a compendium of skilled manpower and professional managers in certain specific areas* and that too are available at competitive cost. It is the pool of scientists, technicians and managers in certain specific areas. The state is potential for R&D infrastructure and technical and marketing services for biotech sector. It is one of the largest agro-based sectors in the world in terms of tea production. There is a rich source of natural resources in the state. It has a long history of market economy infrastructure and the foreign brand names are freely used.

The state suffers from slow but moderate financial sector. Considering this, the State as well as the Central Government often offers well-balanced package of fiscal incentives. During the last decade, the State Policy environment has provided freedom of entry, investment, location, choice of technology, production, import and export. The state government has offered free and full repatriation of capital, technical fee, royalty and dividends. Foreign investment is welcomed in the state though approval is required; it is automatic in sixty categories of Industries (till 2005). As a part of several incentives that can be enjoyed by establishing any enterprise in the state, the enterprises are exempted from any income tax on profits derived from export of goods. There is a complete exemption from customs' duty on industrial inputs and corporate tax holiday for five years for 100 per cent export-oriented units and units in export processing zone in the state. The corporate tax applicable to the foreign companies of a country, with which

* It includes Tea and Tea allied areas, Petroleum and Petroleum-based, coal and coal-based, handicrafts, sericulture, horticulture, natural gas and gas-based, bell metal, paper, etc.

agreement for avoidance of double taxation exists, can be one, which is lower between the rates prevailing in any one of the two countries and the treaty rate which is at par with rest of the country.

In order to give a boost to investment in North-East Region, the North-East Industrial Policy 2007 provides for an enhanced capital investment subsidy @ 30% of Plant and Machinery subject to a maximum of INR 1.5 crore. This represents a five-fold increase in the ceiling for capital investment subsidy, which is currently INR 30 lakh only. The Policy has also a provision to consider medium and large projects that have a significant potential for employment generation, to be given subsidy upto INR 30 crores subject to the approval of an Empowered Committee.

Another important feature of the Policy is that incentives are being extended to service sectors and selected sectors such as biotechnology industry and power generating industry in addition to manufacturing sector. In order to ensure that genuine industries come up in the region, the Policy disallows concessions to goods in respect of which only peripheral activities take place. In order to have proper coordination and monitoring, setting up of a High Level Committee and an Advisory Committee along with an Over Sight Committee has been proposed.

The Policy allows continuation of benefits of excise duty and income tax exemption, interest subsidy and comprehensive insurance. The NEIIPP, 2007 is full of attractive package of incentives and is expected to go a long way towards increasing the pace and level of industrialization in the North-Eastern Region. The previous policy has been amended to make it more attractive for investors, mainly automobile and ancillary industries whose presence in the region is negligible. Power, a scarce commodity in all the seven states of the north-east is another focus area in the new industrial policy. With the anticipated growth in industries, the need for more hydel power projects has become imperative. According to P.K. Sharma, Deputy Director, Industry and Commerce, Government of Assam, "We also expect Assam's hydel projects to function efficiently as the condition (of power in the region) is miserable."[3] Two major ongoing hydroelectric power projects in

Assam are the 2×50 mw Karbi Langpi project and the 6×250 mw Tipaimukh project. At the same time, the Assam government, in its industrial policy, has granted several exemptions such as entry tax on capital goods, works contract tax during construction; and VAT on feedstock and products for 15 years from the date of commencement of production. It is expected that nearly 500 plastic processing industries to come up throughout the north-east region due to GAIL's multi-crore Assam Gas Cracker Project (named as Brahmaputra Polymer and Gas Cracker Limited), which has finally taken off.

However, there is a need to redefine the business environment in the state to create the platform for venture capital formation. Looking at the problems of low formation of venture capital financing in the state, it can be observed that there is a low formation of Human, Social; and Financial Capital. One of such reasons is the lower industrial growth in the state. However, it can be argued here that low formation of aforesaid capitals and lower industrial growth are supplementing to each other and it has an impact on low VCF penetration in the state. While mapping the potentialities of the state, it is essential to review the investment climate which is somewhat missing at present as stated by the FIs, in foregone chapter.

5.1 INVESTMENT CLIMATE

Investment destination, involves consideration of several factors like government attitudes and policy support, proximity to markets, and physical and social infrastructure. Most industrial investments in India usually take time to come to the mainstream of investment. Such timing-gap arises from investor unfriendly, ambiguous and non-transparent policies and procedures—which are significantly different across the states in India. Another factor to be considered with prudent consideration would be the relative growth rates of different sectors in the Gross Domestic Products (GDP) of the states.

The entrepreneur should not only take into account the ease of entry and growth, but also exit while assessing business climate in any particular region. Different states have different attitudes towards closure of business units, which may not be necessarily related with labour-related issues. Thus, based on these criteria the government's attitude through policy support should be made conducive to create the investment climate in the states.

5.2 LINKING HUMAN AND SOCIAL CAPITAL TO VENTURE CAPITAL FINANCING

Though the growth of Venture Capital Financing in the state is in the premature stage, the potentiality of growth of such financing cannot be ruled out. The emergence of Venture Capital Funds is relatively a new phenomenon in India, largely because innovation-driven new projects are rare in the context of marginal R&D investments in the country.[4] However, in Assam, one emerging area of potential for increased R&D investment, which has been necessitated by the post-2005 patent scenario in the country at large, is the pharmaceutical sector.[5] For venture capital funds to sustain in Assam especially in the pharmaceutical sector, the experiences of VCF companies in developed and other developing countries are a necessity. It is observed that in order to be a successful, the VCF companies should have risk-taking and not risk-averse attitude and be able to identify projects and products at a very early research and/or development phase, which have high potential for commercial success. Many of the academic institutions, universities and regional laboratories in Assam, where bulk of the R&D spending is deployed are funded by both the State and the Central Government. The inventions or innovations as the outcome of such investment in R&D are found to be incapable of commercial applications through setting up industrial units, which ought to be essentially a lucrative area of investment through VCF. The VCF Companies should take pro-active steps to track such projects and support them to enable to sustain their development and commercialization. However, the initiative from the demand side cannot be undermined.

Considering the large population of the country and conversely the low per capita consumption of Ayurvedic drugs in India, the potentiality is enormous in this sector to commercialize new inventions in Ayurvedic medicines to increase per capita consumption and at the same time the development of pharmaceutical sector of Assam. The same logic as inserted above also applies in the area of Homeopathic drugs. In addition, India, by virtue of its technological ability to produce cost-effective, drugs in bulk, and formulations matching in quality with rest of the World, also paves the opportunity of being a major exporter of these items, particularly the generic products to tap the South-Asian markets.

It is therefore reasonable to assume that in volume terms, by 2010; India would produce around 15% of global requirements of bulk drugs and drug intermediates as indicated in the study conducted by Business India with ORG-Marg reported in September, 2005 issue. Such a growth calls for large investments in production capacity, of the order of perhaps, around INR 50 billion during this period.

The finances required for setting up world-size manufacturing capacities, have to come from large financial institutions (for term loans) and banks (for working capital loans), these apart the major portion through equity. VCF, on the other hand is directed largely to projects, which are in the innovation phase with substantial potential for commercial success. Identifying such projects in an early phase (in the embryonic or growth phase) in the life cycle of the project and supporting it are the critical challenges, to the VCF companies to face.

Assessing the inherent risks associated with innovation and betting on the major success of at least a small percentage of the projects supported by the venture capital funds calls for proper understanding of the state-of-the-art of the technology and the innovative potential for major breakthroughs in the area, in the coming years. Assam has a pool of resources to draw from, for scouting innovative projects in the pharmaceuticals sector. The biggest and largely untapped sources are the regional laboratories, which can get support from few independent Institutions, such as the Indian Institute of Science, Tata Institute of Fundamental Research, a few Central and State universities, and Indian Institutes of Technologies. In Assam, Laboratories like RRL Jorhat, Toklai Tea Research and Experimentation Center, Regional Research and

Training Center on Indian Traditional Treatment, Golaghat, Central and State Universities, IIT Gauhati, and ITI centers have been working in certain areas that could be relevant to biological and other research with the potential to lead to marketable products. The scientists in these laboratories are now concentrating more on application-oriented or product-oriented research and development.

There are several phases involved in the invention and development of new drugs. They are: selection of a candidate[*] preparation, by synthesis or extraction of natural material, extensive pre-clinical evaluation involving the use of multiple screening models, toxicity in animal species, drug behaviour studies in animals and humans (pharmacokinetics), and various phases of clinical evaluation. Only a successful culmination of all these activities, which would take 10 to 15 years and an investment of over USD 800 million (by western standards and costs), will result in the launch of a New Molecular Entity (NME), emphasing the risk and high cost involved.[6]

From a SWOT analysis, the Strength in Assam in drug discovery and development are in identifying candidates for development, conventional in-vitro and in-vivo screening and clinical research, particularly from Phase two (2) onwards.[7] For all the other activities, collaboration with leading R&D based national and international companies would be the appropriate model for Assam. Establishing such synergy will lead to a win-win situation and cost and time-effective drug discovery and development. Even though VCF companies and organisations in Assam have not yet involved in providing financial support for early stage R&D projects, in the state context, it would be worthwhile for these companies to act as a negotiator for technology and product development collaborations, between R&D organizations with national and international Companies. Some of the leading Companies in India, such as Ranbaxy (with Bayer) and Dr. Reddy's Laboratories (with Novo-Nordisk and Novartis), Torrent (with Novartis), Dabur (with Abbotts), etc. have already entered into agreements following this model. This model has as an essential pre-requisite; valid patent for the

[*] In Pharmaceutical Science, candidate means a problem, a case or a base.

invention and the ability to convert the Patent Portfolio into tradable commodities.

VCF companies may take a total inventory with the support of the concerned agencies to identify activities relevant to healthcare, which in turn will lead to novel and innovative products. In the present climate, meaningful dialogue with the concerned parties can lead to a win-win situation. Venture Capitalists, in Assam, however, have to in addition to financing, assist in technology development and management support. These naturally followed by equity capital financing, apart from loans, which will help commercialization of R&D outputs.

One of the problems which Indian companies face, particularly in the Small and Medium Enterprises (SMEs), is in the area of using the Intellectual Property Protection system as a forerunner for negotiations for licensing with third party companies. Many SMEs have the capability to create innovations, which will be useful for new processes and products for both bulk drugs and formulations. Additionally, they could command R&D capabilities in discovery research by setting up laboratories for synthesizing new molecules or extracting natural products with potentially useful therapeutic properties.

For screening purposes, it is possible to carry out primary screening in their own laboratories or outsource them from contract research groups. Assuming that they do come up with patentable new candidate molecules, they still lack expertise and resources for patenting them in the market. VCF companies can indeed assist these SMEs by providing technical expertise for evaluating the worth of the invention and drafting, filing and prosecution of the patent application and providing the necessary funds for these activities. By appropriate contractual arrangements, the VCF company could also assist in finding the right collaboration partner who ultimately will develop and market the product in the relevant markets, under agreed and guaranteed returns to the SME as well as to it.

The leading Indian companies, however, have the capability to engage in new drug research for global diseases as well as for diseases, which are endemic to Developing countries. The former comprises Coronary Heart Diseases, Diabetes, Viral and Bacterial Infections, Inflammatory Disorders, Old Age and

Degenerative Diseases and Cancer, while the latter are communicable diseases of protozoal or parasitic origins. While the former require international collaboration with R&D-based Multi-National Corporations (MNCs) for total discovery and development, in view of the high costs and competitive nature of activities needed, the latter, being less attractive commercially would need support from governments and international organizations and funding agencies.

Whether venture capital can be channeled with expected returns on their investments in the latter areas, is the scope for further study. In terms of sheer numbers of people who require products for diseases primarily endemic to developing countries, the markets are large. The present scenario of low affordability and buying power of these people and the healthcare systems of these countries is changing, and hence such projects may become viable for VCF companies during the coming years. Moreover, the cost of production of Ayurvedic and Homeopathic medicines are comparatively lower than the other drugs and as the ingredients required can be explored locally in the state, Assam may turn out to be just the right place for growth of VCF in such industries.

Support from Venture Capital sources are most needed, where the innovator, whether an Organisation or an individual has not adequate finance or infrastructural backing to take the innovation to its logical target, i.e. the market place. In order to successfully take up for support a project of that nature, the VCF company needs to have competence to assess the innovative potential of the researchers and their approaches, the current and the future markets, the quantum of investments required and most importantly the inherent financial risk that the company needs to take.

In Assam, the concept of supporting entrepreneurs and innovators with Venture Capital funds has not yet developed. Even though development funds have been available from various Financial Institutions and Development Banks, they are largely to support proven technologies whether indigenously developed or imported. Supports by funding "Home grown technologies" are available through government and other sources; they still follow the pre-condition of having established technology but not in technology in process. Even today, most of the VCF Companies whether attached to large financial institutions such as IDBI or ICICI or to State and Central Governments vary in supporting very early stage projects, which are at R&D stage, primarily due to the fear of failure.

At the national level, CSIR, ICMR, ICAR, etc, are all agencies which not only run R&D Institutes, but also fund research projects in out-house research. Among the laboratories in Assam, some of them have research projects, which have a bearing on health care related projects and products. They may carry out excellent basic research in biological and chemical sciences, which if properly directed and developed may lead to application and product-oriented research. The VCF companies should work in close collaboration with these laboratories, so that innovations of great potential commercial interest can be identified and supported through negotiating with potential licensees and collaborators. For proper development, the Licensees may require not only financial inputs, but also technological, management and marketing support.

Similar approach should be adopted for collaborations with university research units. For individual inventors and entrepreneurs in the small and medium sector, since their work is poorly documented and less known, VCF Companies as highlighted earlier also should take pro-active role by working with these groups from an early stage, guiding them in their product development-oriented approach and once the product is protected by patents, promoting it for licensing or other commercialization processes.

Even in case of health care products, VCF companies have a potential market in Assam due to the contributions by these laboratories and institutions. Health care products fall under four major categories. They are:

- Prophylactics (Vaccines)
- Diagnostics (Laboratory)
- Therapeutics
- Medical Devices.

All the four categories are potentially very rewarding areas for VCF support and projects under each of these should be individually and independently evaluated for their commercial potential. The nature and modalities of support will vary depending on the innovator, nature of the project, estimated gestation period for completion, potential markets, and competition from the established products in the market.

Within the above areas, the state-of-the-art disciplines that would warrant support would be:

- Biotechnology based products (r-DNA proteins for any of the above categories);
- New molecules or natural products extracts;
- Chiral Molecules from established or new racemates;
- Novel and innovative Drug Delivery Systems; and
- Traditional Systems of Medicine-based products.

A state-scouting of the various R&D projects being undertaken by the various groups in the state could be a starting point followed by critical appraisals of their potential, prioritization for support and a detailed analysis of investments requirements, timeframe for levels of progress, continuous evaluation of competitive activity in the area, expected returns etc are some of the sequential approaches to be adopted by VCF Companies. Such a pro-active step alone will ensure that the results of indigenous R&D are gainfully converted into commercially viable projects and products.

Patents like "Process for the preparation of 1, 2, 3, 4-tetra hydro-B carboline derivative"; "An improved process for the preparation of Secondary Phenethyl alcohol from acetophenone"; "A process for the extraction of the essential oil(s) from Cymbopogon species"; "A Process for the preparation of high melting point microcrystalline wax",[8] etc. filed in India by the researchers of RRL, Jorhat could turn out to be good commercially viable projects for VCF in Assam. Another area, which can be explored by the VCF in the state, is the IT and IT enabled industry. Customized services along with Enterprise Resource Planning (ERP) can go a long way to develop the formation of such capital in the state. The Information Technology Policy of Assam 2000 had laid down several provisions about the role of the Government regarding creation of an IT environment in the state. According to the policy the Industry & Commerce Department would function as nodal department for implementation of the IT policy, which would co-ordinate with all the other departments of the Government of Assam in order to ensure that the detailed objectives and goals of the IT Policy are achieved. (Appendix 1)

At the present time and in the prevailing environment, most of the academic research groups are not duly informed and equipped to identify areas of commercial interests from existing projects or for designing new projects. Moreover, the VCF Companies also have not put thrust to evaluate grass root R&D during the early phases of innovation, which have the potential of being converted into technically and commercially viable projects. The ability to weigh the balance between risks and returns inherent in any Venture funding is an important component of the investment decision by the investor. At the same time, the VCF Companies are expected to assess the odds against major success in at least some of the projects. After all, the successful ones have to cover the costs involved in promoting the large proportion of failures, which are inevitable in this business.

5.3 LINKING FINANCIAL CAPITAL TO VENTURE CAPITAL FINANCING

Assam has witnessed a series of setbacks in terms of developing a conducive financial market and perhaps the state is in the limelight not because of its development but for its regression of development. Over the years, new projects, studies are being carried out to find out ways of harnessing the potential for growth and development. Out of many constraints, the one that affect all the sectors equally and which can be removed without major overhaul is the problem of availability, adequacy and timeliness of financial provision for industries. Both equity and debt capital are being considered here because studies have revealed that bootstrapping and loan financing provide a foundation for gaining experience and legitimacy that position ventures to secure equity financing (Ben Daniel *et. al.*, 2000).[9] Factors like infrastructure, social instability, and governance need revamping in a big way to ensure growth of VCF companies to penetrate into. In this context, a specific directive from the Government to the nationalized banks or to the all India financial institutions (AIFI) to increase their lending may be theoretically right, unless the social impediments which are rampant at the present moment is totally eradicated. Subject to the eradication of the social impediments presently encountered by the state, the nationalized banks and other FIs may be directed by the government to include financing the viable projects in this state under the priority sector lending.

From the macro point of view, if it is looked into 40% of the GDP of Assam is contributed by the agricultural sector comparing to overall 26% (2005) from agricultural sector to the national GDP.[10] At the same time the state planning of Assam or any other state are prepared and executed according to the broader guidelines of the planning commission of India. Thus it has been argued by the present researcher that some amount of relaxation is expected of the planning commission of India to be awarded to the state planning commission of Assam considering its rural and agrarian economy. Even when differences are recognized as being industrially backward, the backward areas of the developed regions or state may garner all the benefits. However, in recent past, in January, 2000, the then Honourable Prime Minister, Shri A.B. Vajpayee announced a financial package of INR 10,271 crores for the development of the NE which is a beginning of special assistance to the NE on regular basis. There is now a non-lapsable pool at the Centre, earmarking unspent budgeted funds of the Central Ministries for the NE that also ensures availability of funds for the region.

It is an accepted fact that India has started a race towards development amongst states some of which are handicapped. Liberalization is a double-edged sword, punishing the inefficient members and rewarding the efficient ones. It is generally agreed that the present handicap that Assam is facing is not a result whole of it is not its own doing. However, the inefficiencies observed in many aspects are not to be overlooked because of this. The then Union Minister Arun Shourie did rightly point out the same thing when he was told that the Centre had neglected the North-East by keeping most of the important sectors under the Union list.[11] According to him, enough sectors in the state list empower the state governments to uplift their people. Improving the availability of financial assistance to the people who are willing to set-up business ventures can be an important agenda for the state governments in the North-East. It is also an agenda for the financial institutions that criticize the government and the first generation entrepreneurs but not doing much in this direction.

Sarma,[12] who propagated to have a separate financial institute interconnected with the Government of Assam and other FIs to address the problems of the important sectors in this state. Upholding his views the present researcher is more specific to propagate a similar kind of FI addressing the needs of venture capital financing to tap the growth of untrodden sectors, which have been excluded so far. In other words, the proposed FI especially for Assam shall look into the technology development aspects right from the initial stage to the final stage in various research laboratories or institutions in this state and take up the viable ones for venture capital financing.

There are many schemes launched by the government the fruits of which excluded certain sectors so far. This autonomous financial institution should look into the weak points and the missing links in these schemes and try to find solutions.[13] For example, if the Venture Capital Financing scheme is not taking off because of some problems in the state, this Financial Institution should find ways of getting over these hurdles for the benefit of the region. Again, there are many schemes put up by individual financial institution, which go unheeded because of the lack of information and may be because of lack of concern from the other organizations.[14] For example, various schemes of equity financing may be unknown to the people of some area. The Financial Institution should take upon itself to even spread the schemes and guide the borrowers including organizing relevant educational programmes in obtaining financial and other types of assistance.

Further, regarding the financial schemes that the Financial Institution should take up, the concept of universal banking may be a good base to start with. Term loan, bridge loan, working capital loan, equity support, leasing, and equipment financing—all such activities must be within the purview of this Financial Institution. At present, there is no financial institution that is catering to the needs of all such borrowers in the state. Instead of borrowers changing their project to suit the scheme of the financial institutions as is happening today, the Financial

Institution should be ready to accept any profitable proposition from the borrowers and amend its rules. NEDFi can play a major role in this direction. Just as new processes are being designed based on the new information technology, the Financial Institution should be able to design new products based on the regional characteristics and the changing environment.[15]

Although there are sectoral classification but classification as to business segmentation are not there which is strongly expected at this moment. The government has promoted a number of financial institutions in the formal sector since independence. However, there functioning are not away from debate. One reason is that moneylenders do not distinguish between an agricultural loan and an industrial loan as long as the borrower is good.[16] A good financial institution should come out from the ambiguous terms and conditions and serve the borrowers or potential borrowers on need.

For the educated unemployed having a technological skill suiting at the perception for venture capital financing, the proposed Financial Institution may devise special schemes to enlighten them regarding VCF so that they can be motivated to take up risk to start an enterprise funded through VCF. For all these the proposed Financial Institution should be equipped with technically skilled people to take prudent decision in the direction of VCF. It is observed in the process of interviewing the chiefs of various research laboratories, institutions and universities in this region, that in most of the Financial Institution in Assam do not have officials who are having industry experience. As a result, such officers are neither capable of appraising the technological research and development nor, its future commercial viability.

The Financial institutions operating in the state should think for an ideal model of VCF through which the penetration can be done in the state. In addition, venture capitalists provide a wide range of support for the ventures they finance and sometimes take over day-to-day operations, Sahlman (1990[17]). The issue of control is often difficult since the entrepreneur values the independence of his organization.[18] But according to the present researcher a control by the VCF firm should be taken as a guideline for running the enterprise and should not be taken as a matter of anxiety by the entrepreneurs opting for VCF in Assam. This is because of the fact that the entrepreneurs in this state may possess technical skill to have core-competence but may lack the knowledge of market or other overall aspects of running a business. Most research on the venture capital industry is descriptive in nature, e.g., Tyebjee *et. al.* (1984[19]), Sahlman (1988[20], 1990[21]), and Barry *et. al.* (1990[22]), but some studies attempt to model venture capital contracting. Authors such as Amit, *et. al.* (1990[23]), study a wealthy entrepreneur's decision whether to involve an outside investor or not. But in contrast, a model involving investor from outside of the enterprise is necessary. Hansen (1991[24]), Neher (1992[25]), and Admati *et. al.* (1994[26]), examine the conditions that determine when a project that requires multiple rounds of investment should be continued and when it should be terminated. Trester (1993[27]), Bergl¨of (1994[28]), and Cornelli *et. al.* (1997[29]), compare payoffs and control outcomes under different types of contracts, but do not characterize an efficient contract. As per the findings so far, an efficient contract is also necessary in all the three stages of VCF. However, the proposed VC firm in the state may follow the model of Bergl¨of (1994[30]) shows that debt and equity are complementary in an environment in which control issues are important. Cornelli *et. al.* (1997) show that, in an environment with staged financing, convertible debt is better than a mixture of debt and equity because it reduces the entrepreneur's incentives to focus his/her effort on the short-term success of the project. Although the model, which is, required in the state having only one round of financing, it allows a first-best contract to be characterized rather than just providing comparative results.

The model of Hellmann (1998[31]) shows that an entrepreneur may voluntarily relinquish control rights over his project to the venture capitalist when the venture capitalist must be given incentives to engage in costly search for a new CEO for the project. Other studies that describe how venture capitalists retain control rights over projects include Rosenstein (1988), Sahlman (1990), Gompers (1995), and Lerner (1995).

5.4 CREATION OF ENTREPRENEURS

The movement of entrepreneurship promotion and

development in the past few decades has gone a long way in Assam. Both the State Government and various industrial promotion and support institutions are making considerable efforts to facilitate the process of emergence of new entrepreneurs for setting up enterprises in small-scale sector. These efforts involved making attractive schemes for availability of finance and various other assistances including technical know how, training, sales, purchases, etc. It is believed that these efforts have made a favourable impact on the growth of these enterprises in the State. There are today a large number of organizations like North Eastern Industrial and Technical Consultancy Organization (NEITCO), National Institute of Small Industry Extension Training (NISIET) [until it was merged with the Indian Institute of Entrepreneurship (IIE)] and the North Eastern Industrial Consultants Ltd (NECON) who has been actively involved in entrepreneurship development activities in the state. The North Eastern Council (NEC) has supported their efforts in general and financial institutions like Industrial Development Bank of India (IDBI), Small Industries Development Bank of India (SIDBI), North Eastern Development Finance Corporation Limited (NEDFi) and various commercial banks in particular.

It is observed that India is recognized outside for its high technology and human capital. India has become successful in software and information technology against several odds such as inadequate infrastructure, expensive hardware, restricted access to foreign skills and capital, and limited domestic demand. Some of its management (IIMs) and technology institutes (IITs) are globally known as centers of excellence. Certainly, the younger generation of Assam has the potentiality to grasp the opportunity. Ferris rightly observed that,"(Venture capital) certainly isn't about quick trading profits in the stock market. At its best, it is about helping entrepreneurs grow really great companies."[32] Thus, what member funds are likely to look for when they talk to entrepreneurs with fresh idea are:

- Strong and motivated management teams;
- Clear strategies;

- Large but carefully defined target markets;
- Proven abilities to outperform the competition; and
- Innovation.

The basic things that the entrepreneurs must ensure, to have the VCF support are:

- ❖ Venture capitalists must be confident that the firm has the quality and depth in the management team to achieve its aspirations. Venture capitalists seldom seek managerial control; rather, they want to add value to the investment where they have particular skills including fundraising, mergers and acquisitions, international marketing and networks.
- ❖ In many ways, the introduction of a venture capitalist is preparatory to a public listing. The venture capitalist will want to ensure that the investee company has the willingness to adopt modern corporate governance standards, such as inclusion of representative of the venture capitalist as non-executive directors. Venture capitalists dislike investing in complex corporate structures, changing ownership structure and where personal and business assets are merged in other form of business organizations.
- ❖ Apart from the requirement of an attractive business opportunity, the venture capitalists also seek to structure a satisfactory deal to produce the anticipated financial returns to investors.
- ❖ Lastly, venture capitalists look for clear exit routes for their investment such as public listing or a third-party acquisition of the investee company.

Apart from the above, in order to sustain oneself in the fray one has to look for the application of technology. The entrepreneurs may find it relatively easier to adapt to the innovative situation—the basic requirement for technological evolution, especially when it caters to the need of the largest section of the market. Several aspects where the sector may not; nor had less control like price control, level of government stake and barriers to entry, etc. previously, but with the changes in the global economy, these factors are eased out for them. It seems that Assam has a state-of-the-art or the premium product market. On the other hand, there is a very large base of price sensitive customers who look for quality at an affordable price. Therefore, a firm's strategy towards technology would depend on the influence of these two distinct factors on that industry. Its effects can be analyzed in a matrix as depicted in exhibit 5.1.

EXHIBIT 5.1

The Technology Orientation Matrix

Degree of Control			
	2. Steady State:	3. Modern:	
	Highly regulated production of mass consumption goods; Example: Cement, Sugar etc. Future Trajectory: Upgrading technology to improve production capacity.	Regulated goods, Producers for selected consumer segments; Examples: White goods, cars, branded shoes etc. Future Trajectory: Finding Joint Venture or Strategic Alliance partner to bridge technology gap.	High
	1. Indigenous: Traditional production systems for local markets, often ignored; Examples: Handicrafts, cloth, vegetables etc. Future Trajectory: Finding appropriate technology to enhance quality and output.	4. State-of-the art: Hi-Tech activities often supported by regulations; Examples: Software projects, floriculture, pharmaceuticals (except over-the-counter brands) etc. Future Trajectory: Strengthening R&D to develop world class.	Low

Notes : 1. Indicates low control and mass market,
2. Indicates high control and mass market,
3. Indicates high control and premium market;
4. Indicates low control and premium market.

A firm that seeks to meet the external situation would have to respond by choosing an appropriate technological solution. One way of achieving success seems to be an arrangement of partnership with parties having required expertise. Indian firms in each quadrant in the diagram can find suitable partnership. What most it requires is that of the learning from the experience of other Asian countries like Hong Kong, Malaysia etc. The degree of involvement and scope of collaboration could be attributed in another matrix as depicted in the Exhibit 5.2.

EXHIBIT 5.2

The Strategic Alliance Spectrum Collaboration

INVOLVEMENT	Limited	Wide-Ranging	
	• Consignments • Technical advise	• Advisory Service	Slight
	• Joint Research Development • Long-term Loans • Bye-back arrangements	• Direct Investment • Joint Venture	Moderate
	• Ventrue Capital • Franchising • Turnkey Projects	• Merge • Acquisition	High

Such a type of collaboration will not only enhance the technological sector but also enable to bridge the technology gap. Henceforth, the organization could focus more on cost reduction, expansion etc. This will also encourage the contributors to invest more in these sectors.

Thus given the opportunities available in the state and if those opportunities can be duly utilized, may lead to ample opportunities for growth of Venture Capital here. The information asymmetry problem presently exist in Assam should be reduced and the demonstration effect about VCF should be properly communicated to the entrepreneurs. The security of investment must be protected by way of mutual dependence between the demand and supply side. Role of NGOs cannot be ignored in creation of social capital. At the same time the mutual trust between the entrepreneurs and the financial institutions must be created so that the VCF gets momentum. An intervention from Government of Assam through its various machineries is a must for creation of social capital. It is only when the human, social and financial capital meet together, a conducive atmosphere for VCF in the state shall emerge. Thus from above discussion and findings this can be concluded that: Assam has potential for growth of venture capital financing. It is a fact that environment does change from one place to another. Hence we can not jump to the conclusion that the potentiality available in Assam for VCF would be same to any other unorganized environment. However, it noteworthy to mention that every environment do possess some potentialities, which needs to be explored according to the facilities available.

Notes and References

1. BT Report on "The Hottest States for Business", *"Business Today"*, Vol. 12, No. 19, September 2003.
2. Economic Time Report, "State Consumerism', Brand equity, July 2, 2002
3. Rao, S.; New Industrial Policy for North-East likely, available at www.projectmonitor.com accessed on April 5, 2007.
4. Dossani, R. and Kenney M. (2002); "Creating an Environment for Venture Capital in India"; *World Development*, Vol. 30, No. 2.
5. This also includes Ayurvedic and Homoeopathic medicines.
6. Rao, M.; "Redefining Indian Pharma Industry"; *Business Today*, Vol. 13, No. 2; 2004.
7. Report published in RRL Newsletter, Vol. XXVII No. 6 Nov.-Dec., 2006.
8. RRL Jorhat News, *Regional Research Laboratory*, Jorhat, Vol. XXVII, No. 4, July-August, 2006.
9. Ben Denial, D., Reyes, J. and d'Angelo, M., 2000, "Concentration in the Venture Capital Industry". *Journal of Private Equity*, Summer, 7-13.
10. Sarma, A., "A Financial Institution that may work" available at Assam.org http://assam.org/accessed on April 2006.
11. Sarma, A., "A Financial Institution that may work" available at Assam.org http://assam.org/accessed on April 2006.
12. *Ibid*.
13. Sarma, A., "A Financial Institution that may work" available at Assam.org http://assam.org/accessed on April 2006.
14. Doorlinger, M. (1994), Entrepreneurship: Strategies and Resources, Boston, Mass: Irwin, p. 212.
15. Sarma, A., "A Financial Institution that may work" available at Assam.org http://assam.org/accessed on April 2006.
16. Sarma, A., "A Financial Institution that may work" available at Assam.org http://assam.org/accessed on April 2006.
17. Sahlman, W.A. (1990), The Structure and Governance of Venture-Capital Organizations. *Journal of Financial Economics*, Vol. 27, pp. 473–521, available at www.jse.rochester.edu/jfenh.htm.
18. Refer Perez (1986, pp. 8-9), Gorman and Sahlman (1989, p. 241), and Golder (1991).
19. Tyebjee, T.T., Bruno, A.V. (1984), A Model of Venture Capitalist Investment Activity. *Management Science*, Michigan University, USA, Vol. 30, pp. 1051-66.

20. Sahlman, W.A. (1988) Aspects of Financial Contracting in Venture Capital. *Journal of Applied Corporate Finance*, UK, Vol. 1, pp. 23–36.
21. Sahlman, W.A. (1990) The Structure and Governance of Venture-Capital Organizations. *Journal of Financial Economics*, Vol. 27, pp. 473-521, available at www.jse.rochester.edu/jfenh.htm
22. Barry, C.B., Muscarella, C.J., Peavy, III, J.W., Vetsuypens, M.R. (1990) The Role of Venture Capital in the Creation of Public Companies. *Journal of Financial Economics*, Vol. 27, pp. 447-71, available at www.jse.rochester.edu/jfenh.htm
23. Amit, R., Brander, J., Zott, C. (1997) Why do Venture Capital Firms Exist? Theory and Canadian Evidence. *Journal of Business Venturing*, Elsevier, Netherlands, Vol. 12, pp. 28-42.
24. Hansen, E. (1991) Venture Capital Finance with Temporary Asymmetric Learning, LSE Financial Markets Group Discussion Paper Series #112
25. Neher, D. (1992) Entrepreneurial Human Capital and Financial Contracting. Mimeo, Princeton University, pp. 280-306.
26. Admati, A.R., Pfleiderer, P. (1994) Robust Financial Contracting and the Role of Venture Capitalists. *Journal of Finance*, Blackwell Publishing, American Finance Association, Vol. 49, pp. 371-403.
27. Trester, J.J. (1993) Venture Capital Contracting Under Asymmetric Information. Mimeo, University of Pennsylvania, p. 318.
28. Bergl¨of, E. (1994) A Control Theory of Venture Capital Finance. *Journal of Law Economics and Organization*, Germany, Vol. 10, pp. 247-67.
29. Cornelli, F., Yosha, O. (1997) Stage Financing and the Role of Convertible Debt, CEPR Discussion Paper No. 1735.
30. Bergl¨of, E. (1994) A Control Theory of Venture Capital Finance. *Journal of Law Economics and Organization*, Germany, Vol. 10, pp. 247-67.
31. Hellmann, T. (1998) The Allocation of Control Rights in Venture Capital Contracts. *Rand Journal of Economics*, Santa Monica, CA, Vol. 29, pp. 57-76.
32. Bill Ferris, Executive Chairman, Castle Harlan Australian Mezzanine Partners in a TV Talk in CNN Business hour aired on June 1992 available in archive section at www.cnnnews.com

APPENDIX

INFORMATION TECHNOLOGY POLICY OF ASSAM, 2000 (INDIA)

1. INTRODUCTION

Information Technology (IT) occupies a key position in our modern age and is one of the fastest growing sectors in the world economy. Applications of IT have become pervasive, covering all spheres of life. Government of Assam has recognised this fact and has formulated the policy below keeping in mind all facets of IT.

2. OBJECTIVES OF THE POLICY

The basic objectives of the Information Technology Policy of Assam shall be:

2.1 to accord primacy for the growth of Information Technology industry in the State;

2.2 to accelerate the use of Information Technology at the Government Level with a view to provide better services to the citizens of the state;

2.3 to improve productivity and efficiency of the Government services to the citizens of the state;

2.4 to serve as an important tool to enhance employability as well as to absorb a major portion of the educated unemployed in the state;

2.5 to enable the state reach an eminent position in the Information Technology sector;

2.6 to encourage and accelerate the growth of both the domestic and the export-oriented IT units in the state and make the state an attractive destination for IT investment within India and abroad;

2.7 to encourage and accelerate the use of Information Technology in schools, colleges and educational institutions in the state to enable the youth to acquire necessary skills and knowledge in this sector making them highly employable;

2.8 to set-up specialised training institutes in private sector and the joint sector in order to prepare skilled manpower within the existing system;

2.9 to organise Manpower Development Training Programme (MDTP) in the field of Computer Applications for the successful implementation of the Information Technology Policy of Assam.

2.10 to develop appropriate networks between various departments and different spatially spread out administrative hierarchies through well designed database management system; and

2.11 to encourage the spread of IT in the private sector.

3. SALIENT FEATURES OF THE POLICY

The salient features for the Information Technology Policy of Assam shall be:

3.1 Information Technology Policy for the Government Administration

3.1.1 The Industry & Commerce Department would function as nodal department for implementation of the IT policy, which would co-ordinate with all the other departments of the Government of Assam in order to ensure that the detailed objectives and goals of the IT Policy are achieved.

3.1.2 The Government shall endeavour to have connectivity among all its offices within **2004** so that communication can flow through e-mail/video conferencing etc. to enhance productivity. The Government shall endeavour to provide video conferencing and e-mail facilities in all district head and quarters to enable communication with the State Secretariat.

3.1.3 The Government shall endeavour to improve the process of governance so that citizens could file their documents required by the Government electronically. Web applications would be developed in the local language of the State.

3.1.4 The Government shall endeavour to put in place training programme to enable all government employees to use Information Technology to enhance productivity.

3.1.5 The Government shall make a special budget

allocation of atleast 2-3% of the plan fund allocated to the Government departments every year to complete its computerisation programmes in each Department. An IT sub-plan would be formulated department-wise and closely monitored

3.1.6 The Government shall improve infrastructure such as laying of communication cables for interconnecting the departments, setting up of data transfer exchanges, routers, gateways etc, and ensure reliable power supply, transport system etc to improve the quality of works.

3.1.7 The Government shall encourage the use of Information Technology in all educational institutions by way of giving special grants every year to enable them to put up the necessary infrastructure. Connectivity between the various educational institutions would also be established by **2004.**

3.1.8 The Government shall with the help of the industry start training programmes for teachers to help them use information technology in the teaching process.

3.1.9 The Government shall endeavour to teach the school level children the use of computers and to impart training through computers. All college students in the state of Assam would be encouraged to undertake three months course in the use of information technology and in working on computer by **2004**.

3.2.0 The Government shall endeavour to increase the number of college students specialising in Information Technology to meet the needs of the Information Technology industry to cater to both the export and domestic market. The syllabi for specialisation in computer education would be standardised and recognised to make in more relevant. The education department would monitor the placements on offer and make suitable changes in the design of courses according to the needs of the jobs.

3.2.1 The Government shall strengthen the Assam Electronic Development Corporation Ltd. (AEDC Ltd). AEDC will play the role of facilitator and assist various Government departments in selection of appropriate Hardware, Software and training programmes in accordance with their needs.

3.2.2 For specialised training in emerging areas of Computer and Communication Technology the Government shall consider sponsoring employees of various Government departments, undertakings, autonomous organisations and other non-governmental organisations to institutions situated within or outside the State. All efforts would be made to set-up an autonomous IIIT at Guwahati with assistance from Private sector and Union Government.

3.3 Information Technology Policy for the Industry

3.3.1 Government shall set-up a Software Technology Park (STP) at Guwahati in the first phase with comprehensive infrastructural facilities inclusive of adequate power, water and telecommunication facilities. Adequate residential areas shall also be developed in and around the STP to enable easy accessibility to the professionals working in the STP units.

3.3.2 Government shall encourage the private sector for establishment of STPs in the State of Assam.

3.3.3 Government shall permit establishment of the IT industries in residential areas.

3.3.4 The Government shall endeavour to set up an electronic sub-urban town in an appropriate location having fully developed integrated infrastructural facilities. This Electronic City shall be solely for the use of the Information Technology Industry and allied services. The State Government will encourage private sector participation in development of such infrastructure.

3.3.5 The Government shall co-ordinate and liaison with the Software Technology Park of India (STPI), the nodal agency for development for the software industry and organisations such as Videsh Sanchar Nigam (VSNL), Department of Electronics, Department of Telecommunication, National Informatic Centre, and other such organisations of Government of India to expand communication links in the state of Assam. These agencies shall be encouraged to set-up gateways and earth stations and Government shall try to provide land/ building/spaces and other facilities whenever needed on priority basis.

3.3.6 In order to ensure that the Information Technology industries in the state are in a position to meet international quality certification like ISO 9000 etc. and Software Engineering

Institute (SEI) certification insisted by International companies, efforts would be made to establish such an organisation or its branch at Guwahati which shall be authorised to issue such certification as may be necessary.

3.3.7 For development of 100% Export Oriented Unit (EOU) in Assam, Government of India would be requested to designate an Officer at Guwahati to grant necessary clearances/ and approvals under 100% Export Oriented Scheme.

3.3.8 Information Technology industries in the State would be assisted with the development of telecommunication network in the state for which Government and its agencies would constantly liase and co-ordinate with Department of Telecommunication and draw up time bound action plans for up-gradation and strengthening of telecommunication net works. As a short term measure, development agencies of the Government of Assam viz. Assam Industrial Development Corporation Ltd, Assam Small Industries Development Corporation Ltd, Assam Electronic Development Corporation Ltd and Assam Industrial Infrastructure Development Corporation Ltd shall make block bookings for telecommunication connections in potential areas and locations so that entrepreneurs who come forward to set-up Information Technology Industry can be sanctioned telecommunication facilities immediately on application.

3.3.9 Government shall endeavour to arrange financial assistance to the Information Technology industries to be established and set-up in the state. Government will initiate dialogue with the Banks and Financial Institutions to evolve a suitable procedure for obtaining finance for the units on a priority basis. The State Government would create a corpus of funds as venture capital fund with AIDC to provide assistance to the IT sector.

4. DEFINITIONS AND ELIGIBILITY

Information Technology includes Information Technology and Telecommunications.

Information Technology industry includes hardware and software industries, IT software industry includes IT software,

IT service and IT enable services but excluding training institutions in this field.

New unit means an IT unit which has commenced commercial production on or after the date on which the policy has been notified.

Existing unit means an IT unit, which is or was in commercial operation at any time prior to the date on which the policy has been notified.

100% Export Oriented Unit means an IT unit, which undertakes to export its entire value, added goods subject to relaxation as permitted by the Government of India from time to time.

Fixed Capital means and include cost of land and its development, building including

operational space, godown, laboratory, plant and machinery and its installation cost, pre-operative expanses capitalised, Electrical and such other equipment which are directly related to operational activity.

Expansion on an IT unit means additional fixed capital investment exceeding at least 25% of the capital investment of the existing unit. For the purpose of calculation, gross value of all capital investment made on land, building and plant and machinery of the existing unit will be taken into consideration. Expansion shall also imply an increase of 25% in the existing installed capacity as well as increase an in additional employment by at least 10%.

Modernisation means separately identifiable investment made by an industrial unit involving new/improved technology having definite advantages in reduction of cost of production provided the additional investment in fixed assets should not be less than 25% of the gross fixed capital.

4.1 Eligibility

All industries defined as IT industries shall be eligible for the incentives enumerated.

The units undergoing expansion/modernisation shall be eligible for incentives for the increased capacity created after expansion/modernisation of the existing unit

4.2 Incentives for Promotion of Investment in it Sector

Incentives shall be available to the new units as well as existing units undergoing expansion/modernisation. The package of incentives shall be as follows:

4.2.1 Sales Tax Exemption

All new units and existing units undergoing expansion/ upgradation/diversification shall be granted sales tax exemption on sale of finished products, value added products and purchase of capital goods and raw materials for the following period. However, sales tax exemption for purchase of capital goods will be given only if such goods are purchased locally:

1. New units 10 years
2. Existing units 10 years

(A separate notification will be issued by the Finance (Taxation) Department in this regard.)

However, the sales tax exemption will reviewed by the Industries and Commerce Department after 5 years to decide their continuation or otherwise.

4.2.2 Power Subsidy

Power subsidy shall be available for a period of 5 years from the date of going into commercial production. The amount of subsidy shall be 50% subject to a ceiling of INR 5.00 lakhs per year.

4.2.3 Subsidy on Generating Set

The subsidy on captive generating set including non-conventional energy generation set shall be 50% of the cost of the generating set subject to a ceiling of INR 10.00 lakhs per industrial unit.

4.2.4 State Capital Investment Subsidy

State Capital Investment subsidy of 30% on the capital investment on land, building, plant and machinery, etc. subject to a ceiling of INR 10.00 lakhs shall be provided to an IT unit under the policy. For 100% EOU and for units run by women,

SC and ST entrepreneurs the amount of subsidy shall be INR 15.00 lakhs.

4.2.5 Subsidy Infrastructure

50% subsidy on shed rent payable to STPI shall be available for a period of three years from the date of going into commercial operation subject to a ceiling of INR 2 lakhs per annum.

4.2.6 Subsidy on Hot line/Lease line connectivity

30% subsidy on Hot line/Lease line connectivity paid to STPI shall be available for a period of three years from the date of going into commercial operation subject to a ceiling of INR 2.00 lakhs per annum.

4.2.7 Manpower Development Subsidy

Subsidy on Manpower development shall be provided in respect of training/technical upgradation/Skill upgradation of local persons in a recognised training organisation/institution or in house training subject to following ceiling :

Investment in fixed capital Total ceiling
Up to INR 20.00 lakhs Rs. 1.50 lakhs
INR 20.00 lakhs to INR 25.00 lakhs INR 2.00 lakhs
INR 25.00 lakhs to INR 50.00 lakhs INR 3.00 lakhs
INR 50.00 lakhs to INR 100.00 lakhs INR 5.00 lakhs
*Above INR 100.00 lakhs Rs. 10.00 lakhs

The above amount shall be available for a period of five years from the date of commercial operation of the unit only.

4.2.8 Subsidy on Quality Certification

50% of the cost for getting ISO: 9000, Software Engineering Institute (SEI) certification and Quality Assurance Institute (QAI) certification shall be subsidised subject to a ceiling of INR2.00 lakhs.

4.3 For *mega projects* the Government would consider special incentives on a case by case basis in addition to the benefits already provided. A Mega project may be define as one having investment of 100 crores and more.

5. SPECIAL INCENTIVES FOR IT ENABLED INDUSTRIES

In addition to the benefits provided to IT Industries the following benefits shall be provided for IT enable services.

5.1 Power subsidy shall be available for a period of 5 years from the date of going into commercial production. The amount of subsidy shall be 60% subject to a ceiling of INR 10.00 lakhs per year.

5.2 The subsidy on captive generating set including non-conventional energy generation set shall be 60% of the cost of the generating set subject to a ceiling of INR 15.00 lakhs per industrial unit.

5.3 State Capital Investment subsidy of 40% on the capital investment on land, building, plant and machinery etc., subject to a ceiling of INR 15 lakhs shall be provided to an IT unit under the policy.

5.4 60% subsidy on shed rent payable to STPI shall be available for a period of three years from the date of going into commercial operation subject to a ceiling of INR 5.00 lakhs per annum.

5.5 40% subsidy on Hot Line/Leased line connectivity piad to STPI or VSNL, subject to a ceiling of INR 10.00 lakhs per annum shall be vailable to the unit for a period of three years from the date of commercial production.

The eligibility criteria specifically for the *IT enabled sector* are as follows:

(a) The unit should provide employment for minimum 100 local person.
(b) Employment should be provided for a minimum period of three years.
(c) A minimum wage of at least INR4500 per month per employee shall be provided by the unit.

6. The Government would take all necessary steps to exempt the IT Industry from the relevant provisions of the following regulations:

(a) Factories Act, 1948.

(b) Employment Exchange (Compulsory notification of vacancies) Act, 1959
(c) Payment Wages Act, 1936
(d) Minimum Wages Act, 1948
(e) Contract Labour (Regulation and Abolition) Act, 1970
(f) Workmen Compensation Act, 1923
(g) Shops and Establishment Act, 1971
(h) Employees State Insurance Act, 1948
(i) Zonal Regulation under the Gauhati Metropolitan Authority Act, 1985 (Notification for zoning vide TCP.79/83/56 dtd 25.9.1986 publish in Gazette on 24.12.1986)

7. IMPLEMENTING AGENCY

The Industries & Commerce Department would be the nodal agency for implementation of Information Technology Policy of Assam on behalf of the Government. The Policy shall come into effect from the date of notification of this policy till such time, the Government may consider fit and proper. The Government also reserves the right to make any amendments in the policy.

8. ELIGIBILITY CERTIFICATE

4.1 Eligibility Certificate is a certificate which shall be issued by the *Udyog Sahayak Cell* to be constituted at the Assam Electronic Development Corporation Ltd for the purpose of implementation of this policy.

4.2 No right or claim for any incentives under the scheme shall be deemed to have been conferred by the scheme mearly by virtue of the fact that the unit has fulfilled on its part the conditions of the scheme.

4.3 The incentives under the scheme cannot be claimed unless the Eligibility Certificate has been issued under the scheme by the implementing agency and the unit has complied with stipulations/conditions of the Eligibility Certificate.

4.4 The decision of the implementing agency, subject to such direction as Government may issue from time to time in this regard shall be final and binding.

9. PROCEDURES FOR APPLICATION

Separate guidelines for issuance of Eligibility Certificate & submission of claims for incentives would be issued.

10. PRIORITY FOR DISBURSEMENT

The disbursement of the incentives by the implementing agency shall be in accordance with the chronological order of approved claims. Priority shall however be given to 100% Export Oriented Units.

11. INTERPRETATION

The decision of the Industries & Commerce Department, Government of Assam, as regards interpretation in this policy resolution/incentive scheme shall be final. The state Government reserves the right to increase or decrease incentives or frame new guidelines, amend and provision(s) including withdrawal of any of the incentives/subsidies provided in this policy.

12. IMPLEMENTATION AND MONITORING OF THE POLICY

12.1 Information Technology Cell (ITC)

In order to provide various information and facilities to the IT industry and to ensure proper delivery of all services a separate Cell known as *Information Technology Cell (ITC)* shall be created at the Assam Electronics Development Corporation Ltd (a Government of Assam undertaking). The primary objective of the *ITC* shall be to provide adequate information to the entrepreneurs, identification of projects and its implementation and also to keep in touch with similar organisation/institution on the line of IT within and outside the state.

12.2 Function of ITC

All administrative Departments shall refer all issues related to implementation of the Information Technology Policy to the *ITC* and keep the *ITC* apprised of all actions taken in this regard. *ITC* will perform the following functions:

(i) Ensure adequate publicity of the Information Technology Policy of Assam, 1999 as well as render all assistance to the entrepreneurs to avail the benefit of the incentives.

(ii) Identification of prospective entrepreneurs, building up a data bank to guide and motivate the entrepreneurs and also to prepare viable project profiles in different categories of investment.

(iii) Enlistment of applications and issuance of eligibility certificate under the policy.

(iv) Co-ordinating with the connected agencies/ administrative departments for implementation of the IT Policy.

(v) Proper and effective implementation of all incentives and issuance of sanctions thereof.

(vi) To refer all relevant issues to the Government or to the Committees framed there under for any matter connected with implementation of the policy.

(vii) To take up any other matter entrusted by the Government from time to time.

12.3 Procedures for Issuing Eligibility Certificate

The application for issuance of eligibility certificate shall be submitted to the Assam Electronic Development Corporation Ltd directly for issuance of Eligibility Certificate. The Government shall issue a separate notification on constitution of a committee entrusted with the powers of approval on the proposals.

---

* Amended vide notification No: MI.102/99/142 dtd 25th July, 2000.

CHAPTER 6

The Synthesis

In the foregone chapters, an attempt has been made to understand the problems and prospects of growth of VCF in Unorganized environment by considering Assam as a representative state. While analyzing the same, a brief study about the concept, origin of VCF along with its practices, growth, and development in some part of the world has been elaborated. The experiences of VCF in Karnataka have been utilized in the study to have a proper understanding of the growth, development, and problems associated with VCF in Assam. Some of the potentialities of growth of VCF in Assam have also been identified. The objective of the present chapter is to present a synthesis of the details enumerated in the forgone chapters. Therefore, in the ensuing paragraphs summarized observations have been furnished.

6.1 VENTURE CAPITAL IN A NUTSHELL

- Venture capitalists are higher risk investors and, in accepting these higher risks, they desire a higher return on their investments. The venture capitalist manages the risk/return ratio by only investing in businesses that fit their investment criteria and after having completed extensive due diligence.

- Venture capitalists have different operating approaches. These differences may relate to the location of the business, the size of the investment, the stage of the company, industry specialization, structure of the investment and involvement of the venture capitalists in the company's activities. The entrepreneur should not be discouraged if one venture capitalist does not wish to proceed with an investment in the company. The rejection may not be a reflection of the quality of the business, but rather a matter of the business not fitting with the venture capitalist's particular investment criteria.
- However, it has been observed that the concept of Venture Capital Financing varies from place to place due to its practice process as well as the socio-economic consideration of the practiced environment. The Venture Capital Financing concept in US is quite different from that of European practice and at the same time the Asian concepts of Venture Capital Financing is also quite different. As the development process of Venture Capital Financing is in different stages throughout the world, the very concept of the same also keep on changing from one place to another so as to suit the local requirements and needs.

6.2 FINDINGS ON EUROPE

- European venture capitalists consider themselves as intermediaries who often refer to venture capital as a prerequisite for productivity and employment growth to young enterprises in combination with management support for these enterprises. The role of venture capital in facilitating employment and productivity growth has made venture capital a major target of financial market policies by European Governments.
- Unlike other continents, the European venture capitalist seems to be not focusing exclusively on high technology. The coverage of industries is broad-based

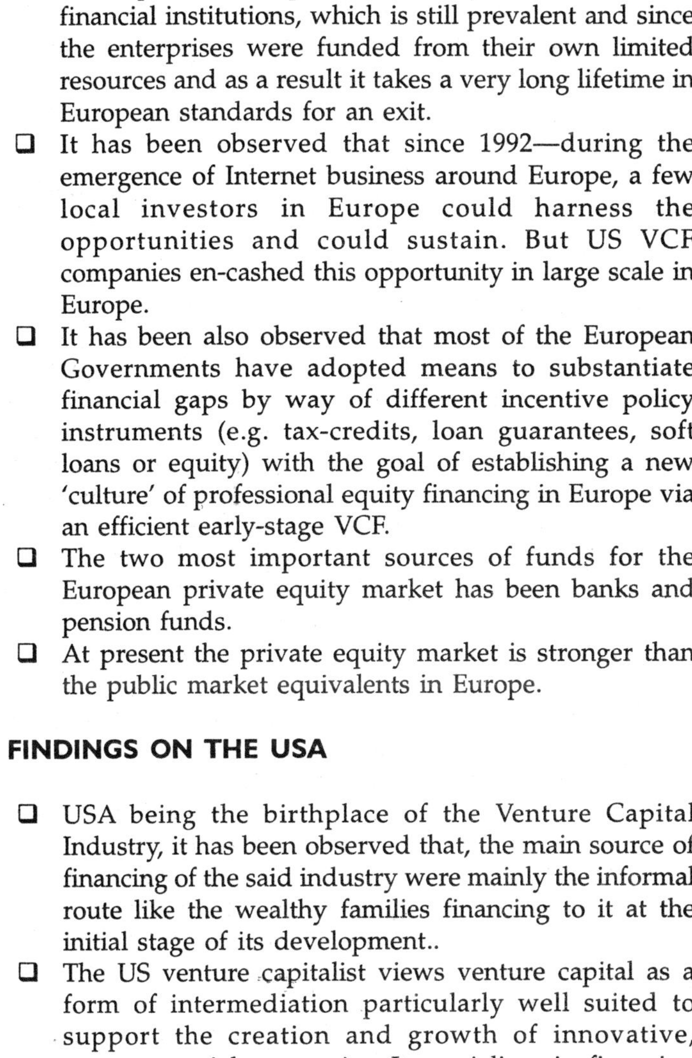

and in some countries of Europe, the prime focus is on growth of economy rather then micro level gain.

- During 1970s till late 1980s the Venture capital funds developed in Europe were mainly from banks and financial institutions, which is still prevalent and since the enterprises were funded from their own limited resources and as a result it takes a very long lifetime in European standards for an exit.
- It has been observed that since 1992—during the emergence of Internet business around Europe, a few local investors in Europe could harness the opportunities and could sustain. But US VCF companies en-cashed this opportunity in large scale in Europe.
- It has been also observed that most of the European Governments have adopted means to substantiate financial gaps by way of different incentive policy instruments (e.g. tax-credits, loan guarantees, soft loans or equity) with the goal of establishing a new 'culture' of professional equity financing in Europe via an efficient early-stage VCF.
- The two most important sources of funds for the European private equity market has been banks and pension funds.
- At present the private equity market is stronger than the public market equivalents in Europe.

6.3 FINDINGS ON THE USA

- USA being the birthplace of the Venture Capital Industry, it has been observed that, the main source of financing of the said industry were mainly the informal route like the wealthy families financing to it at the initial stage of its development..
- The US venture capitalist views venture capital as a form of intermediation particularly well suited to support the creation and growth of innovative, entrepreneurial companies. It specializes in financing and nurturing companies at an early stage of development ('start-ups') that operate in high-tech

industries and later on the growth financing once the enterprise is established.

- It was observed that the US environment for VCF is more specific to high technology driven projects as they envisaging fast growth. It is observed that from 1992 to 1998, venture-backed companies saw their turn over growth, on an average, by 66.5 per cent per annum as against five per cent for Fortune 500 companies.
- It seems that the US venture capitalist often go for long-term horizons classified into specific defined phases.
- Venture capital funds brought their passive investors high returns, resulting in a considerable re-investment of money; especially institutional investors reinvested large amounts of their funds. Secondly, the development of stock markets resulted in a restructuring of institutional investors' portfolios so as to invest more money in venture capital funds. As a result, the US government also has supported the creation of venture capital companies.
- The US venture capitalist primarily focusing on start up stage investment. They normally go for equity financing and risk sharing.
- Pension fund is one of the major sources of VCF. Pension funds contributed between 35 and 60 per cent of the new funds raised between 1990 and 1998. In 1999, however, only 23 per cent of the capital was contributed by pension funds.
- The US venture capitalists syndicate their investments, i.e., several venture capitalists finance a single enterprise and only one of them takes on the monitoring of the enterprise. This venture capitalist is called the lead venture capitalist. Both, specialization as well as syndication reacts rather sensitively to cyclical changes.
- Of late, the focus of venture capitalist in US has been changing from IT sector to Life Sciences sector, which include biotechnology and medical devices.

6.4 FINDINGS ON ASIA

- Most of the venture capitalist of Asia describes VCF, as a means of financing fast-growing private companies.
- The VCF environment in Asia is relatively newer than that of US and Europe.
- Asian countries like Japan, South Korea, Singapore, Hong Kong, Thailand and Malaysia fosters the venture capital environment due to its technological advancement.
- Some of the Asian countries like Taiwan, Israel etc are primarily got influenced by the US environment of VCF and some other countries like Hong Kong, Malaysia, etc. got influenced by the European environment of VCF.
- It has been observed that the stress of VCF institutions in Asia was put on expansion or later stage financing.
- Unlike the VCF firms in UK and the USA, Asian VCF firms prefer for lower risk taking (with sustainable profit) than high risk taking (higher profit).
- It has been observed that the VCF firms in the continent depend more on macro level observation (in lieu of minutest micro-analysis), hard work and limited participation in management.

6.5 FINDINGS ON INDIA

- The earliest discussion of venture capital in India came in 1973, when the government appointed a commission to examine strategies for fostering small and medium-sized enterprises.
- In 1988, the Indian government issued its first guidelines to legalize venture capital operations (Ministry of Finance, 1988). These regulations were aimed at allowing state-controlled banks to establish venture capital subsidiaries, though it was also possible for other investors to create a venture capital firm. But the responses were minimal including the private sector.

- The Government of India issued guidelines in September 1995 for overseas investment in Venture Capital in India. For tax-exemption purposes, guidelines were also issued by the Central Board of Direct Taxes (CBDT) and the investments and flow of foreign currency into and out of India have been governed by the Reserve Bank of India's (RBI) requirements. Further, as a part of its mandate to regulate and to develop the Indian capital markets, the Securities and Exchange Board of India (SEBI) framed the SEBI (Venture Capital Funds) Regulations, 1996. These guidelines were further amended in Apr. 2000 with the objective of fuelling the growth of Venture Capital activities in India.
- The venture capital industry, which is understood globally as "independently managed, dedicated pools of capital that focus on equity or equity-linked investments in privately held, high-growth companies", is relatively in a nascent stage in India.
- From 2000 onwards however, it has been observed that there is an emergence of successful India-centric VCF firms. It is also seen that there is an increasing US VCFs' appetite to invest in India.
- The major portion of the VCF investment in India is in the field of IT more specifically in the field of software development. The Indian software sector had crossed the Rs. 100 billion-mark turnover during 1998. The sector grew 58% on a year-to-year basis and exports accounted for Rs. 65.3 billion while the domestic market accounted for Rs. 35.1 billion. Exports grew by 67% in rupee terms and 55% in US dollar terms. The strength of software professionals grew by 14% in 1997 and has crossed 1,60,000 by 2005. The global software sector is expected to grow at 12% to 15% per annum for the next few years.
- Socio-economic environment in India is not compatible to American methodology of VCF.
- Control and ownership of enterprise is the inherent management practice with investors' limited access

(with few exceptions) to it in the corporate sector in India.

- For high technology products in India there are absence of local/regional market, however, the potential of export market cannot be denied. But the simplification of export procedures can have the VCF to access to export market.
- It has been observed that in case of the VCF with government stake emphasize more on the overall development (macro-level) of the economy of the country/region than emphasizing on ROI of the projects (micro-level)—seems to be not pragmatic in approach.

6.6 THE FIs VIEW ON VENTURE CAPITAL FINANCING IN KARNATAKA

- Although the entrepreneurial qualification is not considered as the major criterion for judging the entrepreneurial skills as expressed by the financial institutions; but the presence of such attribute was not totally ignored by them.
- Mental attributes and the behavioral attributes, which can be generated from the social capital, receive less importance from the financial institutions operating in Karnataka.
- Since the social atmosphere of Karnataka is very conducive, less importance has been given on those attributes; which can easily be acquired from the social environment for judging the entrepreneurial skills.
- So far entrepreneurial ability and family background is concerned, the financial institutions have put least weigtage.

6.7 VIEWS OF THE FIs (OPERATING IN ASSAM) ON VENTURE CAPITAL FINANCING IN ASSAM

- 83.33 percent of the Financial Institutions operating in Assam have a clear view that they do not have any plan to introduce VCF in the state at present. Only

16.67 percent reveals that they are planning to introduce venture capital financing in Assam but when is quite uncertain.

- To the reason for not introducing venture capital financing in the state, 50 percent of them were of the opinion that they have not yet opened up their subsidiaries or any SPV in the state for such financing. 33.33 percent maid their respective head offices responsible for this decision. 16.67 percent of the COOs have stated that they have not yet created a separate fund exclusively for venture capital financing due to absence of proposals from the demand side.
- 33.33 percent Financial Institutions were in the opinion that Assam is quite premature (lack of concept) for VCF and another 33.33 percent of them believe that Assam is quite under-prepared (absence of conducive environment) for VCF. On the other hand 16.67 percent of them were of the opinion that entrepreneurial skill is missing in Assam and another 16.67 percent says that the youth are not properly motivated due to absence of social linkages.
- 83.33 percent of the Financial Institutions believe that lack of financial sustainability of the entrepreneurs in Assam has been one of the pervasive reasons for discernible VCF formation in the state. Almost all the financial institutions were of the opinion that there is a lack of ventured entrepreneurs in the state. It is mainly because that there is substantial brain drainage occurred in the state since 1990. Such brain drainage leads to dearth of skilled entrepreneurs (supported by new technology and innovative skill), which is an essential for VCF.
- All the financial institutions are of the opinion that the present social system of Assam is also not conducive. 50 percent of them are of the opinion that poor repayment of conventional loans has become a part of the culture leading to financial discord in Assam. On the other hand rest 50 percent believes that since the entrepreneurial activities are receiving second status (an off-shoot of the prevalent social texture) than that

of a job in the state. Consequencing to preference for jobs by the major portion of the youths in Assam.

- Regarding the business risk, almost all the financial institutions were of the opinion that they are ready to fund the projects even though the business risk is high. However, on the matter of the present social texture they were found to be quite defensive.

6.8 VIEWS EXPRESSED BY VENTURE CAPITAL FIRMS (OPERATING IN KARNATAKA) ON ASSAM

- Almost all the Venture Capital Firms were of the opinion that the socio- economic environment of Assam is not conducive enough for starting VCF. 66.67 percent of them also believe that there is a lack of entrepreneurial prospects in Assam. 50 percent of them were in the opinion that there are often some social risk factors associated with any investment in Assam and 33.33 percent believes that there is a poor support from the government side to develop an atmosphere for VCF. As per the present researcher the above comments seems to be superficial in nature because the VCFs operating in Karnataka have made these comments without any practical experience as their exist no similar counterparts in Assam.
- 75 percent Venture Capital Firms believe that geographical remoteness in the region is not a major problem now a days. 8.33 percent believes that it is one of the vital problems and rest 8.34 percent believes that it may be a problem but could not be treated as a serious problem.
- Referring to the financial sustainability for VCF growth, 66.67 percent respondents were of the view that it is somewhat missing in Assam. Another 16.67 percent believes that the Government role in creating an environment of financial sustainability is much to be desired in Assam and the rest Venture Capital Firms were of the view that exposer to industries and technologies has been discernible in Assam.

- 58.33 percent of them hold the opinion that there is a lack of entrepreneurs seeking VCF (without having any VCF counterparts) in Assam and almost 75 percent of them believed that honesty is measured in terms of financial discipline and it is missing among a portion of the entrepreneurs in Assam.
- Regarding the overall view on VCF in Assam, the Venture Capital Firms have been almost unanimous in stating that the social atmosphere in the state is not conducive enough to have VCF in the state. They believe that a portion of the youths of this region is not financially disciplined enough to create the environment required for VCF. They believe that for a VCF, at first it should be a win-win situation for both the parties and to have such a situation the entrepreneurs should come up with good proposals, create an environment of trust and profitability and at the same time the intervention of the state machineries should also be there to ensure social harmony.
- It can be inferred that in comparison to Karnataka or any other leading states of India in terms of VCF growth, Assam is suffering from poor diffusion of venture capital, which is at present mainly due to discernible Human and Social Capital formation in the state. As a result, it has also reflected in terms of releasing the venture capital by the FIs operating in the state. However, the state enjoys certain potentialities, which if well utilized than the growth of venture capital in the state is possible in the near future.

6.9 MAPPING THE KEY FACTORS FOR GROWTH OF VCF IN ASSAM

- It has been observed from the study that the formation of financial capital in the state of Assam suffers due to some poor track record of repayments in conventional type of loans. This creates a sense of lack of confidence among the Financial Institutions in the state towards the budding entrepreneurs. At the same time in order to protect their risk involvement in financing a project so as to get the repayment on time, the Financial Institutions prefer to finance only those projects, which are backed by some existing successful enterprises. This could be of any form like experienced entrepreneurs, entrepreneurial Klan, conventional type of businesses where a steady earning can be obtained or stake of successful business houses in the proposed enterprise. Such an attitude though provides a good support for the Financial Institutions to safeguard their business risk but it also subjected to some negative impacts. One of them is relating to formation of VCF. Because VCF is generally provided to a sunrise industry having no experience of any actual performance unless it is started and/or to those entrepreneurs who have for the first time ventured into the project. Such prejudice view has some negative impact on the budding entrepreneurs as they were deprived of getting their venture financed.

- It was observed from the study that the formation of Human Capital in Assam in comparison to Karnataka is somewhat unorganized. Though Assam has enough potentiality to form such Human Capital but due to the information asymmetry, social attitudes, educational programmes, etc. the proper development of such capital is not there in the state at present. At the same time the brain drainage (exodus of brilliant and bright students to outside the state) could be another problem patronizing the low formation of Human Capital in the state. However, a detail analysis reveals that such problem exist because of low formation of Social Capital here. Interestingly, in case of Karnataka it was found that the Financial Institutions are least bothered to analyze the human capital while receiving a proposal because the Social Capital in that state is encouraging as perceived by them.
- It was also observed that, as a compensating strategy that entrepreneurs can adopt, is to have a wide range of contacts in their social networks. It can be felt that when networks contain people from a verity of work backgrounds, especially those beyond the immediate

work group, they tended to be more powerful. In Karnataka, it has been observed that most of the IT based VC receivers are previously having working experience mostly in the Silicon Valley as highly paid executives. There is a positive relationship between prior work experience and venture survival and success and this view was supportive in the state specially IT and IT enabled VCF. Thus, network diversity enhances the chances of accessing a wide array of resources. However, the socio-economic environment of Assam is reacting slowly to these developments.

- In case of Karnataka, it has been found that the financial institutions were keen in financing VC due to the presence of human and social capital. Apart from education and training, human capital is derived from work environment. In Karnataka such environment is created not only from the efforts of people of the state but also by the government. However, in Assam the governmental effort receives lesser success due to the existing negative atmosphere in developing entrepreneurial skills. This apart the matter of financial discipline has to be insisted upon.
- An interesting finding of this study emerges that bootstrapping and loan financing provide a foundation for gaining experience and legitimacy that position ventures to secure equity financing. In Karnataka, almost all the Financial institutions were pursuing equity financing and for that they consider only the presence of Human and Social capital. However, in Assam, the loan financing itself gives such a gloomy picture to the financial institutions. Under the circumstances to pursue equity financing tends to be illusory.
- In Assam, the concept of supporting entrepreneurs and innovators with Venture Capital funds has not yet developed. Even though development funds have been available from various Financial Institutions and Development Banks, they are largely to support proven technologies whether indigenously developed

or imported. Support by funding "Home grown technologies" are though available, Government and other sources still follow the pre-condition of validating the technology but at least at the laboratory stage. Even today, most of the Venture Capital firms whether attached to large financial institutions such as IDBI or ICICI or to State and Central Governments are varying in supporting very early stage projects, primarily due to the fear of failure.

6.10 VCF GROWTH POTENTIAL IN ASSAM

- Assam has a Strategic location - access to the vast domestic and South Asian market.
- Assam has every potentiality to become an investor's destination provided the diffusion of human and social capital is in the proper direction.
- Assam has potentiality to explore VCF in some of the areas like Pharmaceuticals including Ayurvedic and Homeopathic medicines, IT and IT-enabled services including software Products (Mainly Enterprise-focused), Agro-based industries including Horticulture, Sericulture, Media/Entertainment, Bio Technology/Bio Informatics, carbon, SME exclusive and Retails.
- In Assam, there is an urgent need to develop a Financial Institution, which will work exclusively to promote Venture Capital Financing in the state. The AIDC in collaboration with other Financial Institutions can create such fund to facilitate the venture capital growth in the state. A combination of Equity and Debt financing support could be the ideal form of Venture Capital Financing. The VCF prospects in the state include equity support to Pharmaceutical industry, IT enabled industry, indigenous engineering process in Oil, Tea, Natural Gas production, Carbon-based industries, exclusive SME financing, etc.
- Role of NGOs cannot be ignored in creation of social capital. Assam has enough potentiality to utilize the services of NGOs to create a conducive social

environment. At the same time the mutual trust between the entrepreneurs and the financial institutions must be created so that the Venture Capital Financing get momentum.

- An intervention from state government machineries is necessary for creation of social capital. The convergence of human and social capital with the financial capital only will have an environment favourable to Venture Capital Financing.

The Final Word

From the forgone chapter, it can be inferred that the growth of venture capital in Assam in comparison to other states is poor in the present day context. However, by looking at the potentialities of the state, the diffusion of Venture Capital Financing can at any time change its' trajectory. Until now, Assam has not witnessed any Venture Capital firm coming up to promote such finance in the state. It is true that the demand and supply should match for the growth of VCF, yet, the role of Venture Capital suppliers are found more important for the growth of VCF in the state.

The information asymmetry, brain drainage, as well as absence of social network are some of the hindrances preventing the entrepreneurial development in an unorganised environment especially for VCF like Assam. The governmental effort receives lesser success due to mismatch of planning and implementations. The institutional complementarities in creating proper human and social capital suffer due to poor diffusion of knowledge particularly entrepreneurial knowledge, experiences and social linkages. It is no doubt that a disciplined approach is necessary for venture capital financing, which is possible only when the social and human capital work together.

It was observed that in Karnataka, almost all the financial institutions were pursuing equity financing and for that, they apart from the venture plan put more thrust on the presence of human and social capital. It is interesting to note here that some of the attributes of human capital has been less emphasized by the FIs operating in Karnataka while analyzing the entrepreneurial quality; because they feel that these can be acquired from the social capital, the status of the same is satisfactory to their perception. At the same time some of the attributes of social capital has been ignored due to their deemed presence in the human capital. However, in Assam, the experience of loan financing gives a very gloomy picture to the financial institutions, leading to a gap of reliability which in turn leading to the gap between the supply and demand of lendable funds. As a consequence, going for an equity financing in the state at this moment, seems to be illusory. So it can also be inferred that since the human as well as social capital formation in the state is very low (as highlighted in Chapter-4 in detail), the financial institutions are not interested to go for venture capital financing at present.

It has been observed that the opportunities available in Assam if can be duly utilized, may lead to creation of ample scope for VCF. The demonstration effect* about VCF should be properly communicated to the potential entrepreneurs by various institutional complementarities* in the state. Such effect not only calls for drawing experiences from other successful VCF promoting states but also creating an environment of diffusion of social and human capital. Assam has enough

---

* Demonstration effect: For example, the Entrepreneurial Development Foundation in Lebanon offers training modules in basic business and accounting skills to adults with a high school education, but not necessarily a university degree, and encourages them to submit business plans by the end of their training workshop. Some of these plans receive loans, with a ceiling of US $ 10,000. The businesses proposed range from Internet cafes; babysitting services and wedding dress rental shops, to proposals to expand existing farms with additional cattle or set-up jam production facilities or apiaries in rural areas.
* Includes governmental and non-governmental institutions, financial institutions, educational and training centers, and all other institutions working for upliftment of the society, e.g. Clubs, entertainment organizations, etc.

potential for creation of human capital. The role of institutional complementarities is to organize and implement the various factors influencing the development of human capital *per se*. However, in Assam, it is basically the creation of social capital, which requires prudent consideration. The security of investment must be protected by way of mutual dependence between the demand and supply side. Role of NGOs cannot be ignored in creation of social capital. An intervention from Government of Assam through its various machineries is a must for creation of social capital. It is only when the human, social and financial capital meet together, a conducive atmosphere for VCF in the state shall emerge.

7.1 CONCLUSION

Finally it has been made clear by the study that the market does not function at the lower end every time and that FIs are increasingly becoming the first investor for starting companies in some states of India. The venture capitalists are moving towards the later stage financing, with a noticeable preference for Bridge Financing and towards bigger deals. On the other hand, some of the states are still at the verge of introducing this financing concept. Therefore, renewed public attention has been for the VCF as an alternative to conventional financing. This has also being revealed that so long sanction of public initiatives to rescue the non-performing PSUs in the country by launching expensive subsidy schemes. Such subsidy amounts spent could have been diverted for initiation of Government sponsored VCF. The non-performing PSUs according to the present researcher could have been perhaps be revamped by following well-planned disinvestments path. But till the date of the present study the Government of Assam has not looked into harnessing these alternatives. It has also been revealed by the study that coping with the information asymmetry problem is a crucial one. Initiatives aiming at stimulating the syndication process, the investors' readiness, the location (and revelation) of the potential VCF, the involvement of sound FIs, the setting up of efficient network for VCF and the integration of financial resources are totally absent in the state. In this context to overcome the above, efforts from various segments of the society at large and also the State Government have been discernible.

7.2 SUGGESTIONS

Considering the elaborate findings in Chapter-2 through Chapter-5 and pointed findings highlighted in Chapter-6, the following suggestions has been put forward. It is worth stating here that the global experiences including India in general and the experience of Karnataka has been extensively used for suggesting the initiation, growth and sustainability of VCF in Assam as a representative of unorganised environment.

1. For the State Government

The Government of Assam can play an important role in floating a Venture Capital firm in the state to promote the Venture Capital Financing in the state and in case for any unorganised environment for VCF. The Proposed Venture Capital Firm may come up under the aegis of Assam Industrial and Development Corporation (AIDC), and could turn out to be a venture capital company focused on funding small and medium, technology-based enterprises. The proposed firm may raise at least five Venture Capital Funds to start with considering the present potentiality available in the state with a cumulative corpus fund and may mainly focus on raising SME Funds.

The First of the proposed Five Venture Capital Funds may be meant for the formation of Capital like equity support in the form of convertible preferred securities. By creating a corpus fund primarily being sponsored by some financial institutions like SIDBI, NEDFi, etc. working together with AIDC as the settler and by creating a Trustee company taking the fund duration comparatively a longer one may be around 10 to 15 years. The proposed Venture Capital firm may go on exploring the research findings of various bodies in the state to convert the same for the commercial purpose. Like this way, the other types of Venture Capital Funds could be focusing on specific areas like Pharmaceutical & Health Care Venture Fund, Horticulture Venture Fund, IT Venture Fund and Biotechnology Venture

Fund. In addition, the firm may think for exclusive launching of a SME Fund with a target corpus.

As highlighted in the conclusion part regarding the diversion of funds out of subsidy allocated for survival of the state level PSUs, the Government of Assam for creating funds for VCF can utilize such diverted amount. PSUs may be revamped by following the alternative path of right disinvestments path. However, to comment on PSUs has been kept outside the purview of the present study.

To justify the suggestion to establish a separate VCF firm, it is worthy to reiterate that effectiveness of commercial banks in this context is limited because of the fact that they cannot come out of the system of traditional loan financing based on collateral. An entrepreneur having a technology back up, willing to start up own enterprise usually does not have collateral to get financial support from commercial banks. Under the situation for various positive reasons as referred to in above, the VCF is the right option for such budding entrepreneurs. At the same time the commercial banks are not empowered through various statutes affecting them to hold controllable volume of equities in the enterprises financed by them to have surveillance and control on them. This is one of the reasons to comment that the scope of the commercial banks in the state to invest in enterprises is limited. Banks are allowed to extend loans to industrial firms, but they cannot hold controlling amounts of equity in investee enterprises. This view has been upheld in a study on banking and venture capital in USA, (Pozdena, 1990[1]). Thus, equity financing is not presently an option for commercial banks in India.

The present researcher proposes the framework developed by Marco Da Rin, Giovanna Nicodano and Alessandro Sembenelli (2005), to use the notion of 'innovation ratios,' which is defined as the ratio of early stage (or high-tech) investments to total venture investments. A higher magnitude of innovation ratio is the indicative of the extent to which the VCF is active. This is useful for studying how strategy can make venture capital not only larger but also focused on those firms, which can most benefit from the support of a venture capitalist. As a result the rationality of the ratio in the state of Assam is evident. Apart from being simple, this framework is effective enough to point to several potential drivers of active venture capital environments, which are under the influence of policy-makers.

Further, the present researcher utilized a simple extension of the seminal double moral hazard model of financial intermediation by Holmstrom *et. al.* (1997) to study the structure of venture capital investment.* By summarizing the key ingredients of the model, which formalizes the idea that the ability to pledge collateral (the technology/innovation/invention) determines both the amount and the type of financing that a firm can obtain, it can be used to determine the innovation ratio, and extend the model to stimulate further supply of venture capital by other venture capital firms. This model lasts two periods. In the first period financial contracts are signed and investments are implemented (Seed Stage). In the second period uncertainty about project returns is resolved and payments are made to VC firm (Start up Stage).

In addition, venture capitalists are largely unrestricted in the financial relationship between them and the entrepreneurs, Pozdena (1990[2]). Because venture capitalists can have rights of control over their investments and can utilize financial arrangements that involve both debt and equity, they have a comparative advantage in venture capital investing.[3]

The equity component of the financing arrangement between a venture capitalist and an entrepreneur generally takes the form of equity support. However, for the case of Assam, it is suggested to use preference shares convertible to equity shares in course of time. Preference shares gives the venture capitalist some debt-like priority over equity share-holders, while the requirement that the preference share be convertible to equity provides some of the upside potential of equity share. Testa (1988[4]), Silver (1987[5]), and Sahlman (1990[6]) argue that the possibility of the venture capitalist receiving both fixed payments and a share of the project's remaining return is a key characteristic of convertible preference shares. Preference shares offer a fixed dividend like debt, but typically the decision

* The double moral hazard model, where both the entrepreneur and the venture capitalist exert non-contractible effort, has become the workhorse of the theoretical venture capital literature (see Casamatta (2003), Inderst and Müller (2004), Repullo and Suarez (2004), Schindele (2004), and Schmidt (2003) among others).

whether to pay dividends or allow them to accrue is at the discretion of the directors. This will definitely enable to bridge the gap between the receivers (Venture Capital Receivers here) and providers (VC firms here) of financial products leading to a faithful situation. In Assam, the creation of such faithful situation is the need of the hour. Conversion typically occurs when the firm holds an initial public offering or when the firm consistently generates more than a target level of earnings.[7] In addition to receiving equity, venture capitalists usually obtain inside management rights, for example, the right to appoint one or more directors or to serve as an officer of the company.[8] Gompers (1997)[9] shows that, in a sample of fifty convertible preferred equity venture investments, contracts usually explicitly allocate control rights to the venture capitalist, which includes providing them with enough board seats to control the board of directors.

In the line of Marx (2002) model, the researcher proposes a model, which is an extension of the original model that seeks the optimal contract between a wealth-constrained entrepreneur and a risk neutral venture capitalist; the project is financed through a mixed debt-equity sharing rule. Since intervention by the venture capitalist is sometimes efficient and contracts can provide proper incentives for it, so it is justifiable to give the venture capitalist the same right.

However, in order to fit the model in the environment of Assam, the venture capitalist should allow separating the debt and equity components of the project's financing. Then one would need to consider the incentives for the venture capitalist to see either the debt or the equity component and how that affects their incentives to intervene in the project. Another extension includes relaxing the all-or-nothing nature of intervention by the VC firm to allow their own degrees of intervention with varying investment to the entrepreneurs. On the other hand, the VC firm may go for more than one alternative for infusing funds to enterprises they finance. So, the proposed model allows staged financing, or if the project has returns in more than one period, one must consider when payments to the venture capitalist should be made and how the venture capitalist's incentive to intervene changes over time. If projected data of the project's performance are available in multiple periods, then, as in Cornelli *et. al.* (1997[10]), the sharing rule may need to provide incentives that prevent the entrepreneur from being overly focused on short-term results (for the models refer appendix 1 and 2). Thus in a nutshell the specific suggestions based on above are:

(i) The State Government should take initiative to create a separate venture capital firm.
(ii) Mobilize financial resources to create such fund out of subsidies creating budgetary provisions.
(iii) Follow innovation ratio as a parameter for extended VCF.
(iv) Pursue both debt and equity financing or initial financing in convertible debt instruments or investment in convertible preference shares for VCF.
(v) While financing the enterprises through the VCFs in equity or convertible debt or preference shares, the State Government should have adequate surveillance and control by inducting its representative in the Board of Directors of the said enterprises.

2. For the Entrepreneurs in Assam

This study has been conducted focusing only the supply side. Yet the presence of the demand side cannot be ignored. The entrepreneur needs to be somewhat competent in all aspects of the business to get the VCF support. Investors are likely to be impressed by entrepreneurs who are particularly knowledgeable about their technology/innovation and about the business environment too.

For an entrepreneur of a sunrise industry it is always better to seek investors for the long-term. Especially the entrepreneurs of Assam have to seek investors who bring more than money. They have to seek investors who will be able to bring in other investors at a later date if that will be necessary. Therefore, the entrepreneurs have to be specific about their talents and qualities before entering the deal.

They have to be very careful about the valuation of the firm. A valuation that is too high may make raising money difficult. A valuation that is too low effectively reduces the amount that can be raised. The investors will perform due diligence prior to an investment in the enterprise. The entrepreneurs must perform due diligence on the investors. It is advisable to talk with their current portfolio companies. Capital raising which is an ongoing process, where prudent financial planning by the entrepreneurs is a pre-requisite. Wherever possible, the entrepreneurs have been suggested to start-up and generate satisfactory IRR before seeking VCF for further growth. This will make the negotiation process with the VC firm easier.

The entrepreneurs should assemble a competent management team. Management is the single attribute of the company that is most important for VCF. If such assembling of management teams the entrepreneurs should identify their weaknesses and advise to develop an alternative plan to the satisfaction of VC firms.

Many successful entrepreneurial firms develop strategic alliances with major players in the industry for the purpose of marketing its products. The name recognition and experience of the larger partner will help in getting the product to market. The VC firms are often impressed by strategic alliances.

The entrepreneurs should try to avoid a concentration of sales with a single customer, if possible. They should be prepared for contingencies, which may occur due to various reasons beyond their control. They should also develop a sustainable business plan. It should not be prepared solely to satisfy investors.

The entrepreneurs are suggested to maintain adequate business and financial records. The VC firms may avoid considering enterprises, which cannot demonstrate clear and reasonable record-keeping as well as legal compliances.

3. For Financial Institutes Operating in Assam

A venture capital investment is a partnership between the investors and the management. It is therefore important that management wants the involvement of the investors, not simply their capital. From the study, it was observed that in Assam the Financial Institutions are putting less emphasis to a management team when they would go for Venture Capital Financing. Hence, it is advisable that they should consider this attribute seriously for assessing the Venture Capital proposals by exposing themselves to the realities.

From the study, it was also observed that the exit route receives less importance among the attribute that the Financial Institutions consider. The goals of the investor and the entrepreneur need to be aligned—although not necessarily the same. They should finalize the matter at the time of negotiation to determine if their interests are compatible. Since the timing of an exit is a key factor so, the FIs are also suggested to pursue this critically.

It has been observed from the study that the officials working in the Financial Institutions of the state have less exposure to the business activities. It is therefore suggested that the FIs in the state should expose themselves to VCF by perceiving rightly the quality deal flow and due diligence.

The FIs should emphasize with minority stake in a firm, which will enable to give two-dimensional effect. One is safeguarding the social risk and in the other case, it gives the entrepreneur the incentive to work hard.

The FIs should emphasize on strategic sale as a viable exit opportunity. The FIs needs to be prepared to "open doors" to make this happen. FIs with minority investment should be cautious about sale of assets, excessive compensation of executives, payment of dividends, etc. by the investee enterprises. The valuation should be discounted if the investment is perceived to be not liquid enough.

The Financial Institutions should make sure that the entrepreneur is deeply involved in the plan. Problems with valuation may be remedied with earn-out* provisions. They should also agree to liquidate shares (i.e., accept a higher valuation in case of a company) if the entrepreneur is successful.

The IRR of some invested enterprises may erode over time. Thus, the Financial Institutions should seek portfolio of enterprises that can provide higher IRR in order to achieve satisfactory margin against the fund they have invested. The Financial Institutions should seek maximum gross margins wherever possible.

---

* The contract between the entrepreneur and the buying corporation that provides for the entrepreneur to earn additional money on the sale of his/her company, if operating earnings are in excess of a specified amount during the future years.

4. For the NGOs

The role of NGOs cannot be ignored in creation of social capital in the state. As it was stated by most of the financial institutes, operating in Assam that the social risk is high in the state and they are not ready to take such risk in the context of venture capital financing. Hence, the NGOs should empower themselves to create a strong social capital in the state by reducing the social risk.

The social risk starts with poverty, leading to poor economic condition that ultimately has an impact on the human capital. The NGOs operating the state has been suggested to elevate the poverty by promoting the micro- finance, which is a classic example of poverty elevation theorem proved in many third world countries like Bangladesh. Such effort in the long-run can able to minimize the social risk associated in the state. At the same time the NGOs are suggested to accelerate spread of entrepreneurial education and training to usher in the information symmetry, which will enable to strengthen the linkages between Human and Social Capital with Financial Capital in the state.

5. Education System

The education system has a long lasting relationship in formation of Human Capital, Becker (1964[11]). Introduction of entrepreneurship development and conceptual learning should be made in the curriculum of at least VIIIth Standards so that the students can develop some interest into the subject.

At the same time knowledge related to the human rights, right to information etc. should be incorporated in the Xth Standard curriculum. This will enable the budding entrepreneurs to reduce the problem of information asymmetry as well as generation of interest in the field of entrepreneurial activities to stimulate interest for VCF.

6. Indian Venture Capital Association

Mason *et. al.*. (2002[12]) have reported investment outcomes for business angel investors in the UK, one of the very few investigations of performance data for these informal venture capitalists. Regarding the worth of the study, they raised several concerns about the risk profile of angel investors, where investment failures are the rule rather than the exception. However, their results relative to formal venture capital outcomes Murray (1999[13]) showed significantly lower proportions of investment failure and comparable 'homerun' outcomes. It may be worthy, but significantly more information is still needed. India is also not an exception in this direction. So far no such records on Informal Inventors in VC are available to facilitate comparison between formal and informal VCF performances. Hence, it is suggested that the Indian Venture Capital Association should incorporate data of Informal Investors (popularly known as Private Angels in the Country) to monitor their performances in India like that of National Venture Capital Association, USA.

7.3 SCOPE OF FUTURE STUDY

This is a research-based book and I wish, the budding researchers must carry on the research with new vistas. In future research, it would be useful to more tightly specify the definition of financial capital as well as equity funding while analyzing the growth prospects of Venture Capital Financing in India. Such differentiation will provide wider scope for interpreting the problems associated with the Venture Capital Financing in India. The understanding of the subject will be more fruitful if the study is extended to look from the demand side by way of considering the concepts of Behavioural Finance. The Entrepreneurs' expectations, needs and actual performance should be taken into cognizance in order to give a comprehensive view. The so-called 'regional location quotient' presented by Martin *et. al.* (2003[14])—incorporating the size of regional economies in the comparison of the distribution of venture capital investments across regions—is a helpful preparatory indicator. Although the present study has not examined the implicitly smoothing out the quotients between regions. This measure should best be seen as a precursor for further and more sophisticated econometric analyses. Such quantitative models can be applied to ascertain correlations of region-specific factors and VC activities/outcomes in future studies. This will enable them to assess impacts of region-specific factors on the regional VCF including its impact on entrepreneurship, economic growth or regional employment growth.

According to Engel (2003[15]), a count data model* is suitable to assess the influencing factors on the number of VC-backed firms in a county. Another means to examine regional differences is the control group approach where the assessment of regions can be done by comparing employment growth; Wallsten (2004[16]), economic growth or firm growth; Almus *et. al.* (1999[17]). The underlying assumption would be that VC-backing is favourable to all of these factors. The data may also contain failure rates. With these rates, a duration analysis can be done to reveal the probability of survival for VC backed SMEs. It can be convincing that such analyses will improve the current findings and would give further insights in the mechanisms of venture capital in India in future studies.

A future study may also be conducted on the companies, which are included in the portfolios of the VC firms. To maintain the portfolio of companies has been a usual practice in developed countries. This apart there is a practice of building up syndicates of VC firms where decisions of intra and inter project financing is taken on agreed upon basis. A similar practice has been absent in India. A future study may also be undertaken to reveal the potential of syndication of VC firms in India.

Notes and References

1. Pozdena, R.J. (1990) Banking and Venture Capital. *Federal Reserve Bank of San Francisco Weekly Letter*, June 1.
2. Pozdena, R.J. (1990) Banking and Venture Capital. Federal Reserve Bank of San Francisco Weekly Letter, June 1.
3. Amit *et. al.* (1997) Argue that venture capitalists' advantage lies in their ability to reduce information-based asymmetries, particularly through their selection and monitoring of entrepreneurial projects.
4. Testa, R.J., Esq. (1988) The Legal Process of Venture Capital Investment. In: Morris, J.K. (ed.) Pratt's Guide to Venture Capital Sources, 12th edn. Venture Economics, Wellesley Hills, Mass., pp. 67-78.
5. Silver, A.D. (1987) Who's Who in Venture Capital, 3rd edn., John Wiley & Sons, New York.

* Engel (2003), Assesses for Germany the relevance of factors determining the regional distribution of VC backed firms, Haus Des Osten, Bremen, Germany, pp. 170-91.

6. Sahlman, W.A. (1990) The Structure and Governance of Venture-Capital Organizations. *Journal of Financial Economics*, 27: 473–521.
7. See Testa (1988), Sahlman (1990), Brealey and Myers (1991), and Golder (1991).
8. See Perez (1986), Pozdena (1990), and Brealey and Myers (1991).
9. Gompers, P. (1997) Ownership and Control in Entrepreneurial Firms: An Examination of Convertible Securities in Venture Capital Investments. Mimeo, Harvard University.
10. Cornelli, F., Yosha, O. (1997) Stage Financing and the Role of Convertible Debt, CEPR Discussion Paper No. 1735.
11. Becker, G.S. (1964), "Human Capital", Columbia University Press, New York.
12. Mason, C.M. and Harrison, R.T. (2002) Is it worth it? The rates of return from informal venture capital investments, *Journal of Business Venturing*, 17, pp. 211-36.
13. Murray, G. (1999) Seed capital funds and the e.ect of scale economies, Venture Capital, 1, pp. 351-84.
14. Martin, R., Berndt, C., Klagge, B., Sunley, P. and Herten, S. (2003) Regional Venture Capital Policy: UK and Germany Compared, Report for the Anglo-German Foundation for the Study of Industrial Society (http://www.agf.org.uk/pubs/publications.shtml).
15. Engel, D. (2003), Determinanten der regionalen Verteilung Venture Capital-.nanzierter Unternehmen, Jahrbuch fu¨r Regionalwissenschaft, Vol. 23, pp. 155-81.
16. Wallsten, S. (2004), Do Science Parks Generate Regional Economic Growth? An Empirical Analysis of their E.ects on Job Growth and Venture Capital, Brookings Working Papers 04-04.
17. Almus, M., Enge, D. and Nerlinger, E.A. (1999), Wachstums determinanten junger Unternehmen in den alten und neuen Bundesla¨ ndern: Ein Vergleich zwischen innovativen und nicht-innovativen Unternehmen, ZEW Discussion Paper No. 99-109.

APPENDIX I

MARCO DA RIN, GIOVANNA NICODANO AND ALESSANDRO SEMBENELLI'S MODEL

This model lasts two periods. In the first period financial contracts are signed and investments are implemented. In the second period uncertainty about project returns is resolved and payments are made. There is a continuum of firms—or, equivalently, entrepreneurs—which have access to a project that delivers a payoff equal to $R > 0$ with probability pH and to 0 otherwise. The cost of the investment is I. Firms need to borrow the amount I—A > 0, where A denotes a firm's own equity capital which is pledged as collateral. G(A) denotes the cumulative uniform density of collateral for all firms, which is assumed to be continuous. Entrepreneurs are able to divert resources from the project and extract private benefits equal to $B > 0$, which reduces the probability of success to pL < pH.

Firms can borrow from arms' length ('uninformed') investors or from ('informed') financial intermediaries. Uninformed investors simply provide funds and require a return ã, which reflects their opportunity cost of funds. In addition to providing funds, financial intermediaries can also monitor, which reduces private benefits to $0 < b < B$ and mitigates the entrepreneur's moral hazard problem.

The present researcher identifies two linking variables i.e. financial intermediaries with venture capital firms. Finally, it is assumed that only the good project is economically viable, which can be written as: $pH\ R - \gamma I > 0 > pLR - \gamma I + B$.

Direct finance: It is easy to show that some firms with low equity capital will not be financed by uninformed investors, because their capital is not enough to generate the correct incentives for entrepreneurs to behave diligently. Let Rf be the share of the payoff retained by the firm, and Ru=R–Rf the share paid out to uninformed investors. A necessary condition to obtain finance is that the entrepreneur prefers not to shirk, i.e.

$pH\ Rf = pLRf + B.$

A necessary and sufficient condition to obtain finance from uninformed investors is then:

γ(I – A) = pH Ru = pH ·R – (B/pH – pL), which says that the market value of the loan (the left hand side) cannot exceed the firm's expected income (the right-hand side). Firms are then able to raise finance from uninformed investors if:

$$A \geq \bar{A}(\gamma) = 1 - \left(\frac{pH}{\gamma}\right)\left[R - \frac{B}{pH - pL}\right]$$

where A is increasing in γ.

Venture capital finance

Credit rationing of firms with A<A creates a role for monitoring by venture capital firms.

In this case, a monitored entrepreneur chooses not to shirk only if pH Rf =pLRf+b. Let Rvc be the share of the payoff paid out to the venture capital firm. It is assumed that monitoring has a private cost c >0, so that the venture capitalist will monitor only if their expected payoff compensates for the private cost of monitoring: pHRvc-c =pLRvc.

The rate of return to venture capital, denoted by β, is given by β = pH Rvc/Ivc, where Ivc is the amount of funds borrowed by monitored firms. We then see that the value of Ivc adjusts to satisfy the incentive compatibility constraint of the venture capitalist, so that:

$$I_{vc}(\beta) \geq \frac{cpH}{\beta(pH - pL)}$$

Venture finance costs more than uniformed capital, since it must compensate for monitoring effort. It follows that in equilibrium Ivc takes the lowest possible value, which allows venture capitalists to recover the monitoring costs, the residual financing needs of a firm being served by cheaper uninformed capital. The above equation thus holds as equality.

A necessary and sufficient condition for a firm to be financed by both uninformed investors and venture capitalists is then:

$$A \geq \underline{A}(\gamma, \beta) = I - I_{vc}(\beta) - \left(\frac{pH}{\gamma}\right)\left[R - \frac{b + c}{pH - pL}\right]$$

where it can be shown that A increases in both its arguments, so that more credit constrains become tighter as the rate of return required by either type of investor increases. Panel (a) of Figure 1 represents the firms 'financing choices, depending on their own equity capital.

Figure 1 shows the equilibrium in financial markets when the supply of funds to venture capital is fully invested in montored finance. A represents firm equity capital, γ is the rate of return to uninformed financing, β is the rateof return to venture capital, R is the return on investments, D_w and K_w are the demand and supply of venture capital, S is the supply of uninformed capital.

FIG. I

Panel (a), Firms' Financing Choice as a Function of their Equity Capital, A

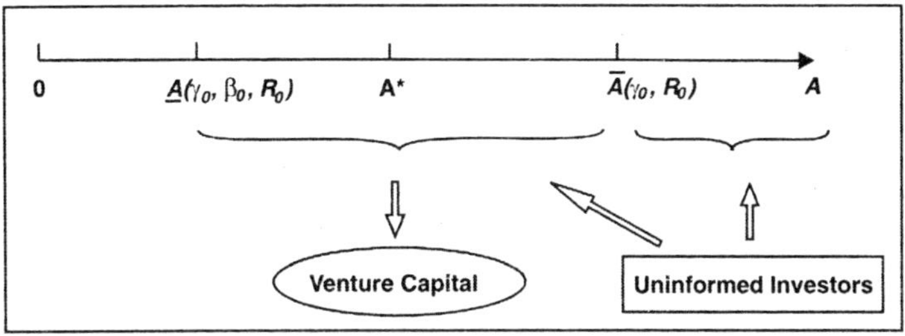

Panel (b), Equilibrium in the Venture Capital Market when K_w is fully Invested in Monitored Finance

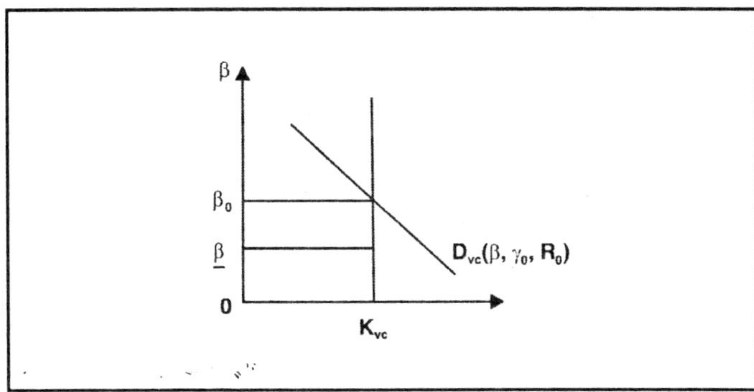

Panel (c), Financial Market Equilibrium when S(γ) is Infinitely Elastic at γ_0

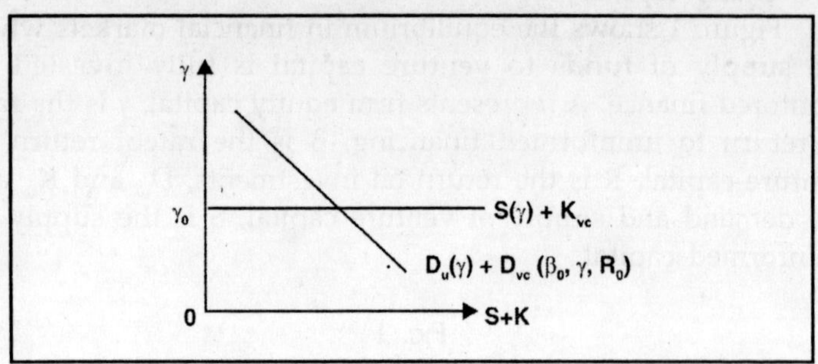

APPENDIX 2

THE PROPOSED VENTURE CAPITAL FINANCING MODEL (DESIGNED IN THE LINE OF LESLIE M. MARX MODEL)

The model has three periods, $t = 0; 1; 2$. There is a venture capitalist and an entrepreneur. The entrepreneur "owns" the rights to the return of a project. The entrepreneur can trade rights to the return to the venture capitalist in exchange for investment capital. In order for the project to be executed, at $t = 0$ the entrepreneur and venture capitalist must sign a contract, and the venture capitalist must provide investment I 0. The entrepreneur proposes a contract and the venture capitalist accepts if they has nonnegative expected payoff. The venture capitalist can, at a cost, affect the distribution of the project's return by intervening in the project, but then the entrepreneur loses his non-pecuniary benefits of control.

The need to balance intervention by the venture capitalist with control for the entrepreneur forms the primary contracting problem in this model. The venture capitalist does not internalize the full cost of intervention because they do not take into account the entrepreneur's loss of benefits of control. It is assumed that intervention by the venture capitalist is a sufficiently complex action that contracts cannot be contingent on intervention. Thus, it is not possible to enforce contracts that make the venture capitalist internalize the full cost of intervention by requiring that they pay an amount equal to the entrepreneur's benefits of control when they intervenes. In the model, there is no effort choice by the entrepreneur. Although providing incentives for the entrepreneur to work hard may be important, it is desired to focus on other issues. If the entrepreneur is sufficiently motivated by the private benefits of control or other self-motivation, then the venture capitalist need not offer additional incentives for high effort.

Figure 1 shows the timeline for the model. At $t = 1$, the state *!* is revealed. The state *!* is observable to both the venture capitalist and the entrepreneur, but it is not verifiable, so contracts cannot be contingent on the observed value of *!*: The state *!* is an element of the set, which is a compact interval of the

FIG. 1

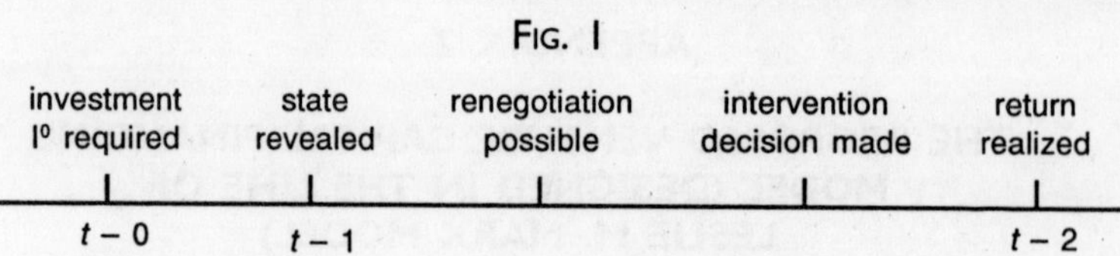

real line, [!, ¯!]. Let ! > !0 indicate that ! is a "better" state than !0 in the sense that returns in state ! first-order stochastically dominate returns in state !0 (see Assumption 3): Ex ante, the distribution of ! is given by the differentiable function *h*, which is common knowledge. After the state is revealed, the contract can be renegotiated, with the entrepreneur making offers that the venture capitalist must accept or reject, and then the venture capitalist chooses whether or not to intervene. Intervention reduces the venture capitalist's payoff by $c > 0$, the cost of intervening, and deprives the entrepreneur of his benefits of control, $b > 0$:

The variable _ 2 *f*0; 1*g* represents the intervention decision, with _ = 1 if the venture capitalist intervenes and _ = 0 if they does not. For monetary return *r* and intervention decision _; the entrepreneur's utility is *r* + (1 - _)*b*. For monetary return *R* and intervention decision _; the venture capitalist's payoff is *R* - _*c*.

At $t = 2$, the project's payoff *y* 2 [0;1) is realized. The distribution of the project's payoff depends on the state and the intervention decision _. Given the state and the intervention decision, the cumulative distribution function for the project's return is denoted by *F*(_ *j* !; _). The following assumptions are made regarding the distribution of the project's return and the distribution of the state.

Assumption 1. For all ! 2 ; F(_ j !; 0) *is absolutely continuous and has continuous density function f* (_ *j* !; 0).

Assumption 2. For all ! 2 ; the support of f (_ *j* !; 0) *is an interval of the form* [0; *x*!], *where x*! > *I* 0.

Assumption 3. For all !; !0 2 , if! > !0 then the distribution F(_ *j* !; 0) *firstorder stochastically dominates F*(_ *j* !0; 0). *Furthermore, given ! and y* 2 (0; *x*!),

F(*y j* !; 0) *is differentiable with respect to* !.

Assumption 4. R!2 R1

0 *yf* (*y j* !; 0)*h*(!)*dyd*! > *I* 0.

Assumption 1 is a technical assumption. Assumption 2 has the important implication that there is always positive probability of low returns if the venture capitalist does not intervene. In the absence of intervention, failure is always possible. Further, the assumption implies that, regardless of the state, recovery of the initial investment is also possible. Assumption 3 says that the distributions *F*(_ *j* !; 0) are ordered according to first-order stochastic dominance, with distributions for larger, "better" states first-order stochastically dominating distributions for smaller, "worse" states. The assumption of differentiability is for convenience. Assumption 4 is a feasibility assumption and ensures that the project has positive expected return when the venture capitalist does not intervene.

INTERVENTION

Intervention by the venture capitalist improves the project's prospects for success, but it can be assumed that only the entrepreneur has the creative or project-specific abilities necessary to achieve high returns, so intervention by the venture capitalist can prevent some bad returns but cannot affect the probabilities of high returns. The venture capitalist brings managerial and organizational skills to the project, not new creative ideas or initiatives. The venture capitalist may be able to salvage a struggling venture with good administration and marketing or by using her contacts with suppliers and other businesses; however, she cannot affect the probability of high returns because these depend on the quality of the entrepreneur's idea and other factors beyond her control.

Specifically, assume intervention does not affect the probabilities of returns above some amount *L*; where *L* _ *I* 0. Although the basic results of this paper hold as long as intervention results in a first-order stochastic dominance improvement for returns below *L*,[8] for simplicity I assume that whenever the project would have produced a return less than *L* without intervention, the project returns exactly *L* with intervention. So for all ! 2 ; *F*(*y j* !; 1) = 0 for *y* < *L* and *F*(*y j* !; 1) = *F*(*y j* !; 0) for *y* _ *L*: Under these assumptions, one can take two possible views of intervention. First, one can view intervention as bringing additional skills to the project so that, the project will return at least *L*. Second, one can view intervention as putting the venture capitalist in a position to assess whether the project's return will be less than *L;* in which case the venture capitalist liquidates the project's assets at liquidation value *L* rather than allowing the project proceed.

CONTRACTS

A contract requires payment of *I* 0 by the venture capitalist, and it specifies a sharing rule for the final return. Sharing rules are written as functions *s*(_), where if the project's return is *y*, the venture capitalist receives *s*(*y*) and the entrepreneur receives *y* – *s*(*y*). In order to incorporate wealth constraints on the entrepreneur, sharing rules are restricted to satisfy *s*(*y*) _ *y* for all *y*.

Three types of sharing rules can be defined: debt, equity, and mixed debt-equity. A *debt* sharing rule with debt level ˆ *d* _ 0 is defined by *sd* (*y j* ˆ *d*) _ min*fy;* ˆ *dg:* An *equity* sharing rule with share _ 2 [0; 1] is defined by *se* (*y j* _) _ _*y:* A *mixed debt-equity* sharing rule with dividend *v* _ 0 and share 2 [0; 1] is defined by *sm*(*y j v;*) _ min*fy; v* + (*y* - *v*)*g*. Note that the mixed debt-equity sharing rule can be written as *sm*(*y j v;*) = _ *y; y* < *v v* + (*y* – *v*)*; y* _ *v;* so it can be viewed as a fixed dividend payment *v* in conjunction with a proportional sharing rule for returns in excess of the dividend. If = 0, then the mixed debt-equity sharing rule is actually a debt sharing rule, and if *v* = 0, then it is an equity sharing rule.

The mixed debt-equity sharing rule can be interpreted, as convertible preferred equity or participating preferred equity, whose holders receive a preferred dividend and then share equally with the common shareholders in the remaining dividends. To see this, note that, in a model in which returns are available in only one period, a mixed debt-equity sharing rule captures the basic characteristics of convertible preferred equity financing. With returns possible only at *t* = 2, the decision to allow dividends to accrue and decisions on the timing of conversion can be ignored. One can view *v* as the level of accrued dividends at *t* = 2. When the project's return at *t* = 2 is less than the level of accrued dividends, the preferred shareholder has priority and receives all of the project's returns.

When the project's return is greater than the accrued dividends, the investor receives the accrued dividends and converts her preferred stock into the fraction *of* the common stock in the venture, which has value (y - v).

Note that the sharing rule of Proposition 1 is optimal for the entrepreneur in the class of mixed-debt equity contracts, and since the sharing rule achieves the first best, there is no sharing rule that makes both the entrepreneur and the venture capitalist better off, and thus there is no scope for renegotiation. While the results of this section show that the contract with sharing rule *sm*(_ *j v_; _*(*v_*)) is optimal, it has not been shown that equity and debt contracts are not also optimal. Debt and equity are also optimal if, after the state is revealed and before the intervention, decision is made, they are renegotiated to new contracts that give the venture capitalist proper incentives for intervention.

If the initial sharing rule is debt, the venture capitalist has the incentive to intervene in states in which intervention is inefficient, and if the initial sharing rule is equity, the venture capitalist has the incentive not to intervene in states in which intervention is efficient. If, in these situations, the entrepreneur can propose a new contract under which intervention occurs if and only if it is efficient, then debt and equity can be optimal initial contracts. However, transfers are a necessary part of the renegotiation—from the entrepreneur to the venture capitalist when renegotiating debt and from the venture capitalist to the entrepreneur when renegotiating equity. Wealth constraints may prevent the first type of transfer.[1]

Thus, even considering renegotiation, a debt-sharing rule may not be efficient. Furthermore, if renegotiation is costly, both parties prefer that the initial sharing rule be mixed debt-equity. The result on the optimality of mixed debt-equity requires that the same investor hold the debt and equity and that the debt have priority. The inseparability of the fixed component and the proportional component of mixed debt equity is crucial for the optimality result. Once the two features are separated, the holders of the separate instruments have different incentives for intervention than a single investor holding mixed debt-equity.[2] Even if debt and equity are issued to the same investor, if the two securities are separable, they might have the incentive to sell one or the other. In addition, the implications of defaulting on debt may be quite different from those of deferring or cancelling dividend payments.

An important additional point is that the venture capital project of this model is distinct from the investment project of a pre-existing firm, and thus it should not be interpreted as suggesting that all firms should finance their projects with mixed debt-equity. First, if a firm already has outstanding debt or equity, mixed debt-equity may not be optimal. Second, if the value of a pre-existing firm is in its continuing existence and profitability, then reinvesting it in the company might best use any income from a new project. In the case of a venture capital project, the $t = 2$ return is typically the result of an initial public offering, and thus the venture capitalist can cash out their investment without adversely affecting the future of the firm.

Notes and References

1. If the venture capitalist made additional payments to the entrepreneur at $t = 0$, then renegotiation to an optimal contract might be possible since the entrepreneur could compensate the venture capitalist for accepting the new sharing rule.
2. Incentives for intervention will also be different if there are multiple investors. However, Barry *et. al.* (1990, p. 462) finds that when more than one venture capitalist invests in a venture-backed firm, one venture-capital investor typically takes the lead role in coordinating the investors and working with the firm. Brander *et. al.* (1997) view having multiple venture capitalists as potentially valuable since then the entrepreneur benefits from the expertise of more people.

Glossary

Some common terms used by venture capitalists.

Acquisition: Purchasing a business or acquiring interest in business.

Bollerplate: Standard paragraphs containing safety provisions in venture capital and investment documents.

Bootstrap Financing: Financing from internal sources like accounts receivables or advanced payment for future sales.

Bricks and Mortar: Creation of assets of the company. The term is derived from a building that is built of bricks and mortar.

Bridge Financing: Finance for temporary period provided to a company until it can go public and raise equity capital.

Break-even: Volume of sales needed to cover fixed and variable expenses.

Burn Rate: The monthly rate at which a company is spending cash.

Buy-out: Buying controlling interest in a business; when the buyer of a business buys it, he 'buy out' the seller.

Buy-back Agreement: Entrepreneurs agree to buy the shares or properties of the venture capitalist.

Buy-sell Agreement: Buy-sell agreements are two-pronged arrangements negotiated between the entrepreneur and venture capitalist wherein the former agrees to buy out the latter's stake or *vice-versa.*

British Venture Capital Association (BVCA): BVCA was established in 1983 as a self-regulatory body to represent the views and interests of the UK-based venture capitalists.

Business Expansion Scheme (BES): This scheme was introduced in the UK in 1983 to encourage private investors to invest in unquoted companies by offering tax relief at a marginal rate for up to 40,000 investment a year.

Business Plan: Information about future business of the firm.

Capital Gains: Profits derived from sales of capital assets.

Capital Appreciation: The difference between selling price and acquisition price of an asset, where selling price is greater than the other.

Capital Assets: Fixed assets of long-term standing, viz. land, buildings, equipments, furniture and fixtures.

Capital Depreceiation: Depreciation in value of capital assets.

Capital Formation: Collection of monies, both equity and loan for startup of a business.

Cash Flow: Actual movement of cash within a business. The money coming in and the money going out constitute the flow of cash that determines the future of a business.

Cash-out: Quick sale for money.

Closing: The signing of legal documents by a company in favour of venture capitalists and getting funds transferred from the venture capitalists to the company.

Collateral: Assets pledged as a secondary security for a loan made to the company.

Compounding: The addition of interest on an investment to the principal each month or year so that interest is earned on interest during the succeeding period.

Contract: Agreement for exchange services, acts deeds and rights for payment.

Control: Position to exercise authority over financial matters resulting from owning 51 per cent of the stock of a company or owning enough stock in the company so as to carry on the management thereof.

Convertible Security: Debt or preferred stock, each of which is convertible into common stock of the company.

Covenant: Legal statements detailing the things, which have been agreed, will be done or will not be done.

Current Ratio: The ratio obtained by dividing current assets by current liabilities to measures ability of the firm to pay short-term debt from readily available funds.

Current Return: Income that is received monthly, quarterly, or annually as interest, or dividends as opposed to the capital gain portion received on an investment at the end of the investment period.

Current Yield: Rate of return investment at the present time expressed as an annual percentage.

Captive Organisations: Venture capital organizations which from part of larger financial services groups and draw on the resources of their parents for all or most of their funds for investment.

Corporate Venturing: The practice of a large company taking an equity stake in, or establishing a joint venture with, a smaller business with the objective of developing the letter's specialist skills.

Deal: Agreement to perform a business transaction, for example, an agreement between a venture capitalist and an entrepreneur where the former agrees to provide financial facility and the latter agrees to accept the same.

Debenture: Document or written note as evidence of a debt or loan.

Debt Service: The amount of money due in the form of interest of instalment of repayment one has to pay on a debt in order to keep it from being in default.

Default: Default occurs on non-performance of obligations for example, non-payment of monies on due dates which are part of investment agreement. It is also called breach of contract.

Discount Rate: The interest rate used in calculations of present value of convert future cash flows into present value.

Downside Risk: The worst case of risk where the investor is sure to lose.

Due Diligence: The process of investigating a business venture to determine its feasibility.

EBIT (Earnings before Interest and Tax): The bottom line before interest and Tax payments.

Earn-out: The contract between entrepreneur and the buying corporation that provides for the entrepreneur to earn additional money on the sale of his company, if operating earnings are in excess of a specified amount during the future years.

Equity: Normally described as owner's capital invested in business. Also, it is frequently used to described the amount of ownership of one person or a venture capitalist in a business.

Evaluation: Assessment of performance or projection.

Exit: The sale of equity or ownership in the enterprise for cash.

Exit Route: The means by which a venture capitalist realizes his investment, usually by way of initial public offering or trade sale or buy-back.

Face Value: Amount printed on the security showing nominal value of the instrument.

Fully Diluted Ownership: Ownership assuming the exercise of all common stock options, warrants, and the conversion of any convertible securities.

Future Value: Present value plus amount of accumulated interest that would be earned at a specified rate in future period.

Going Public: Raising funds through initial public offerings of the equity shares.

Good People: Term used by venture capitalist for honest and loyal entrepreneur.

Grace Period: The period of time given to correct a default.

Hurdle Rate: The return on investment (ROI) necessary to compensate the investor for the risks involved in investment.

Incubation Investment: Investment made in new business struggling for survival.

Internal Rate of Return (IRR): The discount rate that equates the present value of cash outflows with the present value of cash inflows.

Infant Industry: New business or industry which is of recent origin.

Instrument: Document with legal bindings and contractual relationship.

IPO (Initial Public Offering): The initial offer made to sell a company's stock to the public.

Junior Securities: Securities with claims subordinated to the senior creditors in liquidation.

LBO (Leverage Buy-out): A buy-out or acquisition of a business using mostly debt and a small amount of equity. The debt is secured by the assets of the business.

Lead Investor: The investor who leads a group of investors into a syndicated investment. In venture investment one venture capitalist will be the lead investor while a group of venture capitalists invest in a single business.

Leverage: Synonymous with debt. Borrowings are referred to as leverage when used with equity. With a small amount of equity and a large amount of debt, one can leverage a business on the basis of its assets.

Management Buy-out: The buy-out where buyer is the incumbent management.

Mezzanine Financing: It is later stage venture capital financing envisaging low risk. The level of financing is chosen between debt and equity to lower the risk of investment.

Net Present Value: The discounted present value of an investment minus the required initial investment.

NOL (Net Operating Loss): The balance remaining after deduction of cost of goods sold and overhead expenses from gross income.

NOI (Net Operating Income): Cumulative operating losses that may be carried back and/or forward to othe. tax years to offset taxable income for those years.

Note: A business loan for a term, written as promissory note to evidence a debt.

Options: The right given to the venture capitalist to buy stock in assisted company.

Outstanding: Unpaid obligation which has fallen due for payment.

Paper: Form of money, other than cash, like notes, bills, stock, bonds, mortgage, etc.

Payback Period: The number of years required to recover the initial cash investment.

Present Value: The value today of future payments reduced by the interest at an appropriate compound rate known as discounted value of a series of future cash flows so as to account for the time value of money.

Price-Earnings Ratio: The market price of a share divided by the earnings per share.

Pricing: Determining the price that an investor will pay to purchase shares of stock in an enterprise. Price is determined on the basis of the full value of the company.

Proposal: The document prepared by an entrepreneur to propose an investment to a venture capitalist or other investors.

Public Offering: The selling of shares to the general public as a means of raising equity funds.

Quote: To specify a price at which a company will perform a given amount of work.

Return on Investment (ROI): The internal rate of return on an investment.

Second and Third-round Financing: The later rounds of expansion financing that follow the start-up round of financings.

Secondary Market: Market for sale of corporate securities.

Sensitivity Analysis: Analysis to determine the sensitivity of return on investments to the changes which expectedly or unexpectedly occur in key variables like sales growth, margins, interest rates, etc.

Syndication: The process of contributing financial assistance by a group of venture capitalists in portions of the amount of money required by an enterprise to finance its project cost.

Seed-corn Capital: Often referred to as pre-start-up capital, seed capital usually involves quite small amounts to turn a good idea into a prototype, business plan or marketable product or service.

Start-up: The stage at which a business is being formed or the earliest stage at which venture capitalist provides funds to an enterprise.

Threshold Company: Company striving to achieve long-term growth and prosperity.

Trade Sale: The purchase of a venture-capital-backed company by another business, often in the same, or related, industrial sector.

Turnaround: Term used to described business in the process of getting out of trouble.

Unlocking: A legal provision in venture capital investment agreement stipulating that one party may require the other to buy it out under certain circumstances.

Up-front Cost: Start-up cost in the beginning of a new project.

Upside: The amount of money that one makes by investing in a certain deal is the upside potential.

Value-Added: The increase in worth of a product due to change in its form or function by manufacturing, packaging or other method, the difference between the amount a company sells a product for what was paid for materials and labour used to manufacture the product.

Warrant: A stock option given by a company to an outsider that entitles him or her to purchase stock in that company.

Warranty: A promise that certain facts are true. A promise by a seller covering title, performance and physical condition of a product or service.

Yield: In the business of investing, the amount of return (profit) expressed as an annual percentage rate of the amount of capital invested.

Yield to Maturity: The return on an interest bearing investment, usually applied to a bond. Yield to maturity measures the rate of return of the bond if held to maturity, considering purchase price, redemption value, time to maturity, coupon yield and the time between interest payments.

Zoning: The regulation of structures and uses of property within designated boundaries, usually within local governmental jurisdictions. Generally the classifications of zones are: heavy industry, light industry, commercial, residential and farm.

Bibliography

Books

Aldrich, H., (1989), "Networking among Women Entrepreneurs"; Women-Owned Business eds.: O. Rivchun and D. Sexton , NY: Praeger, New York.

Armour, John, and Douglas Cumming (2003), "The Legal Road to Replicating Silicon Valley," Mimeo, USA.

Avnimemelech, Gil, and Morris Teubal, (2002), "Israel's Venture Capital Industry: Emergence, Operation and Impact, "The Growth of Venture Capital: A Cross Cultural Analysis", ed.: David Citendamar, Westport, Praeger.

Becker, G.S., (1964), "Human Capital", Columbia University Press, New York.

Bygrave, W.D., (1992), "Venture capital returns in the 1980's", The State of the Art of Entrepreneurship, eds.: D.L. Sexton and J. Kasarda, PWS Kent, Boston.

Bygrave, W.D. and J.A. Timmons (1992), Venture Capital at the Crossroads. Harvard Business School Press, Boston, MA.

Bottazzi, Laura, and Marco Da Rin (2004), 'Financing European Entrepreneurial Firms: Facts, Issues and Research Agenda' Venture Capital, Entrepreneurship and Public Policy, eds.: Christian Keuschnigg and Vesa Kanniainen, MA, MIT Press, Cambridge.

Bottazzi, Laura, Marco Da Rin, and Francesco Giavazzi (2003), 'Research, Patents, and the Financing of Ideas: Why is the EU Growth Potential so Low?' Economic Policy-Making in the European Union, eds.: André Sapir and Mario Nava, Brussels, European Commission.

Coopers and Lybrand (1998), Venture Capital: Der Einfluß von Beteiligungskapital auf die Beteiligungsunternehmen und die deutsche Wirtschaft. Frankfurt/a.M.: Fachverlag Moderne Wirtschaft.

Chowdhuri, S.N. (1996), "India's North-East Industrial Resources and Opportunities", Devi Prasad Bagrodia, Laser King, Tinsukia.

Chitale, V.P. (1983), Risk capital for industry. New Delhi: Allied Publishers.

Carter, Lawrence, Teresa Barger, and Irving Kuczynski (1996), 'Investment Funds in Emerging Markets,' Washington, D.C., International Finance Corporation.

Doorlinger, M. (1994), Entrepreneurship: Strategies and Resources, Boston, Mass: Irwin.

Engel, D. and Heger, D. (2005), Return-Orientation of Venture Capital Companies and Its Importance for Venture-backed Firm Performance in the Early Stage: Empirical Evidence for Germany, mimeo, Hamburg.

Frrear, J. Sohl, J. and Wetzel, W.E. Jr, (1997), The informal venture capital market: milestones passed and the road ahead. Entrepreneurship 2000, Eds: D.L.Sexton and R.W.Smilor , Chicago: Upstart Publishing.

Feldman, M.P. (2001), The Entrepreneurial Event Revisited: Firm Formation in a Regional Context, Industrial and Corporate Change, Upstart Publishing, Chicago.

Gromb, Denis, and David Scharfstein (2002), 'Entrepreneurship in Equilibrium', CEPR DP 3652, UK.

Gill, D. (2003), 'Venture Capital in Selected Countries'. Washington D.C., IFC.

Hisrich, R.G. and Brush, C.G. (1983), The women entrepreneur: implications of family, educational and occupational experience, Frontiers of Entrepreneurship Research, eds.: N.C. Churchill, S. Birley, W.D. Bygrave, D.F. Muzyka, C. Wahlbin and W.E. Wetzel, Jr., Wellesley, MA: Babson College.

Hugot, J.B. (2000), *Le Guide des Sociétés de Capital-Investissement.* 3rd edition, Paris.

HM Treausury (2003), 'Bridging the Finance Gap: A Consultation on Improving Access to Growth Capital for Small Businesses,' Oxford Press, London.

Hirukawa, Masayuki, and Masako Ueda (2003), 'Venture Capital and Productivity', Mimeo, University of Wisconsin-Madison.

Henderson, J.W. (1998), 'Obtaining Venture Financing : Principles and Practices' , Massachusetts, Lexington Books.

Kulicke, M. (1997), Beratung junger Technologieunternehmen, *Technologieunternehmen im Innovationsprozess: Management, Finanzierung und regionale Netzwerke.* Ed.: K. Koschatzky, Fraunhofer-Institut für Systemtechnik und Innovationsforschung (ISI). Heidelberg.

Laan, van der, S. and B. Cornelius (2000), The Role of Government Policy in Economic Growth Through Venture Capital: Lessons From The German Experience., *SMEs in East Asia in the Aftermath of the Asian Financial Crisis,* Ed.: C. Harvie and B. Lee, Von Publication; Hamburg.

Leopold, G. and H. Frommann (1998), *Eigenkapital für den Mittelstand-Venture Capital im In-und Ausland.* Verlag C.H. Beck, Munich.

Lessat, V., J. Hemer, T. Eckerle, M. Kulicke, G. Licht, E. Nerlinger, F. Steil and M. Steiger (1999), *Beteiligungskapital und technologieorientierte Unternehmensgründungen: Markt—Finanzierung—Rahmenbedingungen.* Wiesbaden: Gabler.

Lumme, A., C.M. Mason, and M. Suomi (1998), Informal Venture Capital: Investors, Investments and Policy Issues in Finland, Boston.

Lindsey, Laura (2003), 'The Venture Capital Keiretsu Effect: An Empirical Analysis of Strategic Alliances among Portfolio Firms', mimeo, Stanford University.

Mishra, Asim Kumar (2003), 'Venture Capital Financing'. New Delhi, Shipra Publications.

Maula, M. and Murray, G.C. (2001), Corporate Venture Capital and the Creation of US Public Companies: The Impact of Sources of Venture Capital on the Performance of Portfolio Companies. In: Creating Value: Winners in the New Business Environment. Eds: Hitt, M.A., Amit, R., Lucier, C., Nixon, R.D., Blackwell Publishers: Oxford, UK.

Narasimham, M. (1995), 'The Financial System'. New Delhi, Nabhi Publications.

Nelson, Richard, and Paul Romer (1996), 'Science, Economic Growth, and Public Policy,' Technology, R and D, and the Economy, eds.: Bruce Smith and Claude Barfield; Washington, DC, Brookings Institution.

Olm, K., Carsurd, A. and Alvey, L., (1988), 'The Role of Networks in New Venture Founding for the Female Entrepreneur : A Continuing Analysis', 'Frontiers of Entrepreneurship Research', (eds).: W.A. Long, E. McMullan, K.H. Vesper and W.E., Wetzel Jr, Wellesy, M.A.: Babson College.

Pfirrmann, O., U. Wupperfeld and J. Lerner (1997), *Venture Capital and New Technology Based Firms: An US-German Comparison*. Heidelberg: Physica-Verlag.

Poterba, James (1989), 'Venture Capital and Capital Gains Taxation' Tax Policy and the Economy, ed. Larry Summers, Cambridge, MIT Press.

Prantl, S., Engel, D. Almus, M. and Egeln, J. (2005), Intermediation von Kreditinstituten und die Rolle ö .entlicher Fö rderkredite bei der Finanzierung junger Unternehmen: Eine Empirische Untersuchung, mimeo.

Quindlen, R., "Confession of a Venture Capitalist", Warner Books, NY.

Rao, P.M. and Jain, T.K. (2002), "Venture Capital Financing: Profile and Strategic Issues", Ed. Vol. Strategic Management: Current Trends and Issues; Deep and Deep Publications Pvt. Ltd., New Delhi.

Ramesh, S. and Gupta, A. (1995), Venture Capital and the Indian Financial Sector. Delhi: Oxford University Press.

Schindele, Ibolya (2003), 'Advice and Monitoring: Venture Financing with Multiple Tasks', mimeo, Amsterdam University.

Saxenian, A.L. (1998), Regional Advantage. Cambridge: Harvard University Press.

Van Osnabrugge, M. and Robinson, R.J., (2000), Angel Investing: Matching Start-up Funds with Start Up Companies [San Francisco: Jossey-Bass].

Verma, J.C. (2000), "Venture Capital Financing in India", Sage Publication.

Weimerskirch, P. (1998), *Finanzierungsdesign bei Venture-Capital-Verträgen.* Deutscher Universitäts Verlag. Wiesbaden.

Wupperfeld, U. (1994), Die Betreuung junger Technologieunternehmen durch ihre Beteiligungskapitalgeber. Empirische Untersuchung. Arbeitspapier. Institut für Systemtechnik und Innovationsforschung (ISI). Karlsruhe.

———, (1997), Der Beteiligungskapitalmarkt in Deutschland. In K. Koschatzky (ed.), *Technologieunternehmen im Innovationsprozeß: Management, Finanzierung und regionale Netzwerke*. Heidelberg: Physica-Verlag.

Zemke, I. (1995), Die Unternehmensverfassung von Beteiligungskapital-Gesellschaften. Analyse des institutionellen Designs deutscher Venture Capital-Gesellschaften. Wiesbaden: Gabler.

Journals

Aldrich, H., Reese, P.R. and Dubini, P., (1989), "Women on the verge of a break throught: networking among entrepreneurs in the United States and Italy", 'Entrepreneurship and Regional Development', Routeledge Publication, UK, Vol. 1. pp. 339-356.

Altimansky, B., (2000), "Eight ways to ruin your chances of raising equity capital", 'Journal of Private Equity', USA, Summer, Vol. 3, No. 3, pp. 78-83.

Almus, M., Enge, D. and Nerlinger, E.A. (1999), "Wachstumsdeterminanten junger Unternehmen in den alten und neuen Bundesla¨ ndern: Ein Vergleich zwischen innovativen und nicht-innovativen Unternehmen", ZEW Discussion Paper No. 99-109.

Audretsch, D.B. and Fritsch, M. (2002), "Growth Regimes over Time and Space", 'Regional Studies', U.K., Vol. 36, pp. 110-32.

Alesina, Alberto, Silvia Ardagna, Giuseppe Nicoletti, and Fabio Schiantarelli (2003), 'Regulation and Investment,' NBER WP, No. 9560, pp. 208-24.

Buttner, E.H. and Rosen, B.H. (1988), "Bank Loan Officer's Perceptions of Characteristics of Men, Women and successful entrepreneurs", *Journal of Business Venturing,* Elsevier, Netherland, Vol. 3, No. 3, pp. 233-59.

Brush, C.G., (1992), "Research on Women Business Owners: Past Trends, a New Perspective and Future Directions"; Entrepreneurship Theory and Practice, Baylor University, Waco, Vol. 16, pp. 5-30.

Bruderl, J. Preisendorfer, P. and Zeigler, R., (1992), "Survival Chances of Newly Founded Business Organizations"; *American Sociological Review,* USA, Vol. 57, pp. 227-42.

Ben Denial, D.; Reyes, J. and d'Angelo, M, (2000), "Concentration in the Venture Capital Industry"; *Journal of Private Equity,* USA, Summer, pp. 7-13.

Brass, D.J., (1985), "Men's Women's Networks: A Study of Interaction Patterns and Influence in an Organization"; *Academy of Management Journal,* Academy of Management, NY, Vol. 28, pp. 344-74.

Baker, M., and P.A. Gompers (1999), "An Analysis of Executive Compensation, Ownership, and Control in Closely Held Firms"; Working Paper. Harvard Business School, Boston, MA., pp. 187-205.

Baker, M., and P.A. Gompers (1999), "The Determinants of Board Structure and Function in Entrepreneurial Firms". Working Paper. Harvard Business School, Boston, MA. pp. 232-50.

Barry, C. (1994), "New Directions in Research on Venture Capital Finance". *Journal of the Financial Management Association,* Vol. 23, No. 3, pp. 447-71, available at www.jse.rochester.edu/jfenh.htm

Baygan, G. and M. Freudenberg (2000), The Internalisation of Venture Capital Activity in OECD Countries: Implications for Measurement and Policy. DSTI/DOC (200), Vol. 7, Paris, OECD Publication, pp. 21-52 available at www.oecd.org.

Brav, A., and P. Gompers (1997), Myth or Reality? The Long-Run Underperformance of Initial Public Offerings: Evidence from Venture and Non-venture Capital-Backed Companies. *The Journal of Finance,* Blackwell Publishing, *American Finance Association,* Vol. 52, No. 5, pp. 114-35

Black, B. and R. Gilson (1998), Venture Capital and the Structure of Capital Markets: Banks versus Stock markets. *Journal of Financial Economics*, Vol. 47, No. 3, pp. 180-207, Available at www.jfe.rochester.edu/jfenh.htm

Brouwer, M., and B. Hendrix (1998), Two Worlds of Venture Capital: What Happened to US and Dutch Early Stage Investment? *Small Business Economics*, UK, Vol. 10, No. 4., pp. 156-79.

Bygrave, W.D. (1987), Syndicated Investments by Venture Capital Firms: A Networking Perspective. *Journal of Business Venturing*, Elsevier, Netherlands No. 2, pp. 132-38.

BVK (Bundesverband Deutscher Kapitalbeteiligungsgesellschaften) (various issues). *BVK-Statistik*. Berlin.

———, (2001). *Mitgliederverzeichnis in alphabetischer Reihenfolge*. Access on March 6th 2001 via http://www.bvk-ev.de/suchen/mitglieder.cfm.

Blau, J.R. and Alba, R.D.; (1982), "Empowering nets of Participation". *Administrative Science Quarterly*, USA, Vol. 27, pp. 363-79.

Baskaran, A. (2000), "Duality in national innovation systems: the case of India", *Science and Public Policy*, UK, Vol. 27, No. 5, pp. 367-74.

Barry, C. (1994), "New Directions in Research on Venture Capital Finance", *Journal of the Financial Management Association*, USA, Vol. 23, No. 3, pp. 447-74.

Brouwer, M., and B. Hendrix (1998), 'Two Worlds of Venture Capital: What Happened to US and Dutch Early Stage Investment?' *Small Business Economics*, UK, Vol. 10, No. 4, pp. 198-224.

Bade, F.-J. and Nerlinger, E.A. (2000), 'The spatial distribution of new technology-based firms: Empirical results for West-Germany', Papers in Regional Science, Germany, Vol. 79, pp. 87-103.

Bottazzi, L. and Da Rin, M. (2002), 'Venture Capital in Europe and the Financing of Innovative Companies', *Economic Policy*, UK, Vol. 17, pp. 123-45.

Bottazzi, L. and Da Rin, M. (2002a), 'Venture Capital in Europe: Europiun firm and the Financing of European Innovative Firms,' Economic Policy, UK, Vol. 17, No. 1, pp. 134-50.

Bottazzi, L., Da Rin M. and Hellmann, T. (2004), 'Active Financial Intermediation: Evidence on the Role of Organizational Specialization and Human Capital,' RICAFE WP, No. 12, pp. 87-106.

Brau, James, Bill Francis and Ninon Kohers (2003) 'The Choice of IPO versus Takeover: Empirical Evidence,' *Journal of Business*, Vol. 76, No. 4, pp. 82-102.

Barry, C. (1994). New Directions in Research on Venture Capital Finance. *Journal of the Financial Management Association*, USA, Vol. 23, No. 3, pp. 202-36.

Carter, N.M. and Allen, K.R., (1997), 'Size Determinants of Women-owned Business: Choice or Barriers to Resources?' Entrepreneurship and Regional Development, Vol. 9. pp. 211-20, Available at www.erd.com./journal

Coleman, S., (2000), Access to Capital and Terms of Credit: a Comparison of Men and Women-owned Small Business. *Journal of Small Business Management*, UK, Vol. 38, pp. 48-52.

Coleman, J., (1988), Social Capital in the Creation of Human Capital. *American Journal of Sociology*, NY, Vol. 94, pp. S95-S120.

Carter, N.M., Williams, M. and Reynolds, P.D. (1997), Discontinuance among new firms in retail: the Influence of Initial Resources, Strategy and Gender. *Journal of Business Venturing*, Elsevier, Netherland, Vol. 12, pp. 125-46

Carter, N.M. and Allen, K.R., (1997), Size Ddeterminants of Women-owned Business : Choice or Barriers to Resources? Entrepreneurship and Regional Development, Vol. 9, pp. 211-20, Available at www.erd.com./journal.

Coleman, S., (2000), 'Access to Capital and Terms of Credit: a Comparison of Men and Women-owned Small Business.' *Journal of Small Business Management*, Vol. 38, pp. 48-52.

Cooper, A.C., Gimeno-Gascon, F.J. and Woo, C.Y., (1988), 'Survival Failure: A Longitudinal Study', Frontiers of Entrepreneurship Research, Babson College, Wellesley, M.A., Vol. 1, pp. 225-37.

Carter, N.M., Williams, M. and Reynolds, P.D. (2003), Discontinuance among New Firms in Retail: The Influence of Initial Resources, Strategy and Gender. *Journal of Business Venturing*, Elsevier, Netherland, Vol. 18, pp. 235-59.

Casamatta, Catherine, (2003), 'Financing and Advising: Optimal Financial Contracts with Venture Capitalists', *Journal of Finance*, Blackwell Publishing, American Finance Association, Vol. 58, No. 5, pp. 213-34.

Dossani, R. and Kenney, M. (2002); "Creating an Environment for Venture Capital in India"; *World Development*, USA, Vol. 30, No. 2, pp. 227-53.

Doran, A. and Bannock, G. (2000), Publicly Sponsored Regional Venture Capital: What can the UK Learn from the US Experience?, *Venture Capital*, Routledge Publication, UK, Vol. 2, pp. 213-54.

EVCA (European Venture Capital Association) (various issues). *Yearbook*. Zaventem, Belgium.

———, (2001), Pan-European Survey of Performance. ENN Supplement, October 2001. Access on March 6th 2001 via: http://www. evca.com/publications.html.

Engel, D. (2003), Determinanten der regionalen Verteilung Venture Capital-.nanzierter Unternehmen, Jahrbuch fu¨r Regionalwissenschaft, Vol. 23, pp. 155-81.

Fried, V.Hisrich, R.D. (1988), Venture Capital Research: Past Present and Future. Entrepreneurship—Theory and Practice, Baylor University, Waco, Vol. 13, pp. 15-29.

Gilson, Ronald (2003), 'Engineering an Venture Capital Market: Lessons from the American Experience', *Stanford Law Review*, USA, Vol. 55, No. 4, pp. 287-312.

Gompers, Paul (1994), 'The Rise and Fall of Venture Capital', *Business and Economic History*, Vol. 23, No. 2, pp. 143-67.

Gompers, Paul (1995), 'Optimal Investment, Monitoring, and the Staging of Venture Capital,' *Journal of Finance*, Blackwell Publishing, *American Finance Association*, Vol. 50, No.4, pp. 1461-90.

Gompers, Paul, and Josh Lerner (1997), 'Risk and Reward in Private Equity Investments: The Challenge of Performance Assessment', *Journal of Private Equity*, USA, Vol. 1, No. 2, pp. 235-64.

Gompers, Paul, and Josh Lerner (2000), 'Money Chasing Deals? The Impact of Fund Inflows on Private Equity Valuations', *Journal of Financial Economics*, Vol. 55, No. 1, pp. 178-92, Available at www.jfe.rochester.edu/jfenh.l.tm.

Gompers, P.A., and J. Lerner (1996), 'The Use of Covenants: An Empirical : Analysis of Venture Partnership Agreements', *The Journal of Law and Economics,* Vol. 39, No. 2, pp. 245-56.

———, (1998a). What Drives Venture Capital Fundraising? Working Paper. Harvard University, Cambridge, MA.

———, (1998b), The Determinants of Corporate Venture Capital Success: Organizational Structure, Incentives, and Complementarities. In: R.K.

Gompers, P. (1995), Optimal Investment, Monitoring, and the Staging of Venture Capital, *Journal of Finance,* Vol. 50, No. 5, pp. 123-43.

Gompers, P. (1995), Optimal Investment, Monitoring, and the Staging of Venture Capital, *Journal of Finance,* Blackwell Publishing, *American Finance Association,* Vol. 50, No. 5, pp. 67-120.

Gifford, S. (1997), Limited Attention and the Role of the Venture Capitalist. *Journal of Business Venturing,* Elsevier, Netherlands, Vol. 12, pp. 167-93.

Gompers, P.A. (1995), Optimal Investment, Monitoring, and the Staging of Venture Capital. *The Journal of Finance,* Blackwell Publishing, *American Finance Association,* Vol. 50, No. 5, pp. 1461-89.

———, (1997), Ownership and Control in Entrepreneurial Firms: An Examination of Convertible Securities in Venture Capital Investments. Working Paper. Harvard University, Cambridge, MA.

———, (1998), Venture Capital Growing Pains: Should the Market Diet? *Journal of Banking and Finance,* Vol. 22, pp. 1089-1104.

Gompers, P.A., and J. Lerner (1996), The Use of Covenants: An Empirical Analysis of Venture Partnership Agreements. *The Journal of Law and Economics,* Vol. 39, No. 2, pp. 142-50.

———, (1998a), What Drives Venture Capital Fundraising? Working Paper, Harvard University, Cambridge, MA.

———, (1998b), The Determinants of Corporate Venture Capital Success: Organizational Structure, Incentives, and Complementarities. In: R.K. Morck (ed.), Concentrated Corporate Ownership, Chicago Press, Chicago.

Gorman, M., and W. Sahlman (1989), What Do Venture Capitalists Do? *Journal of Business Venturing*, Elsevier, Netherlands, Vol. 4, No. 4, pp. 34-38.

Gupta, A.K., and H.J. Sapienza (1992), Determinants of Venture Capital Firms' Preferences Regarding the Industry Diversity and Geographic Scope of their Investments. *Journal of Business Venturing*, Elsevier, *Netherlands*, Vol. 7, pp. 347-62.

Honig-Haftel, S. and Martin, L., (1986), is the Female Entrepreneur at a Disadvantage? Thrust: *The Journal for Employment and Training Professionals*, Vol. 7, pp. 49-67.

Heitzer, B., and C. Sohn (1999), Zur Bedeutung des Neuen Marktes für die Venture Capital-Finanzierung in Deutschland. Finanz Betrieb, Vol. 1, No. 11, pp. 76-90.

Herring, R (1977), 'Venture Capital Finance: A Security Design Approach,' *The Review of Finance*, Vol. 8, No. 1, pp. 75-108.

Harding, R. (2000), Venture Capital and Regional Development: Towards a Venture Capital 'System', *Venture Capital*, Routledge Publication, UK, Vol. 2, pp. 287-311.

Hellmann, Thomas, and Manju Puri (2000), 'The Interaction between Product Market and Financing Strategy: The Role of Venture Capital,' *Review of Financial Studies*, Vol. 13, No. 4, pp. 959-84.

Hellmann, Thomas, and Manju Puri (2002), 'Venture Capital and the Professionalization of Start-up Firms: Empirical Evidence', *Journal of Finance, Blackwell Publishing*, American Finance Association, Vol. 57, No. 1, pp. 169-97.

Holmstrom, Bengt, and Jean Tirole (1997), 'Financial Intermediation, Loanable Funds, and the Real Sector,' *Quarterly Journal of Economics*, Vol. 112, No. 3, pp. 87-101.

Inderst, Roman, and Holger Müller (2004), 'The Effects of Capital Market Characteristics on the Value of Start-up Firms', *Journal of Financial Economics*, Vol. 72, No. 2. pp. 293-316, Available at www.jfe.rochester.edu/jfenh/htm.

Jeng, L.A., and P.C. Wells (2000), The Determinants of Venture Capital Funding: Evidence Across Countries. *Journal of Corporate Finance*, UK, Vol. 6, No. 3, pp. 45-78.

Just, C. (2000), *Business Angels und technologieorientierte Unternehmensgründungen-Lösungsansätze zur Behebung von Informationsdefiziten am informellen Beteiligungskapitalmarkt aus Sicht der Kapitalgeber.* Fraunhofer IRB Verlag, Stuttgart, Vol. 5, pp. 345-89.

Kortum, S. and J. Lerner (2000), Assessing the Contribution of Venture Capital to Innovation. *The Rand Journal of Economics,* Santa Monica, CA, Vol. 31, No. 4, pp. 674-92.

Kelly, M. (1993), Towanda's triumph: social and culture capital in the transition to adulthood in the urban ghetto. International Journal of Urban and Regional Research, Vol. 18, march, pp. 88-111. Available at www.blackwell-publishing.com/journal.asp?ref=0309-1317.

Lerner, J. (1994), The Syndication of Venture Capital Investments. *Journal of the Financial Management Association,* USA, Vol. 23, No. 3, pp. 293-316.

———, (1995), Venture Capitalists and Oversight of Privately-Held Firms. The Journal of Finance, Blackwell Publishing, *American Finance Association,* Vol. 50, No. 1, pp. 124-45.

Lerner, J. (1994), 'Venture Capitalists and the Decision to go Public', *Journal of Financial Economics,* Vol. 35, No. 1, pp. 293-316.

Lerner, J. (1995), 'Venture Capitalists and the Oversight of Private Firms,' *Journal of Finance,* Blackwell Publishing, American Finance Association, Vol. 50, No. 1, pp. 132-42.

Lerner, J. (1999), 'The Government as a Venture Capitalist: The Long-run Impact of the SBIR Program,' *Journal of Business,* Vol. 72, No. 3.

Lerner, Josh and Antoinette Schoar (2004), 'Does Legal Enforcement Affect Financial Transactions? The Contractual Channel in Private Equity,' *Journal of Economics,* Vol. 67, No. 4, pp. 212-32.

Megginson, William (2004) 'Towards a Global Model of Venture Capital?', *Journal of Applied Corporate Finance,* Vol. 17, No. 1, pp. 56-78.

Mahanta, V. (1996); "Shifting Paradigm of Venture Capital"; *Business Today,* Vol. 5, No. 19, pp. 17-62.

Mittal, R. (2005); "Karnata Boom", *Business World,* Vol. 25, Issue 3, pp. 23-45.

Mason, C. and Harrison, R., (2002), Venture Capital: Rationale, Aims and Scope. *Venture Capital*, Routledge Publication, UK, Vol. 1, pp. 211-36.

Mason, C.M. and Harrison, R.T. (1995) Closing the Regional Equity Capital Gap: The Role of Informal Venture Capital, *Small Business Economics*, Vol. 7, pp. 153-72.

Mason, C.M. and Harrison, R.T. (2003) 'Closing the Regional Equity Gap? A Critique of the Department of Trade and Industry's Regional Venture Capital Funds Initiative', Regional Studies, Vol. 37, pp. 855-68.

Murray, G.C. (1998) A Policy Response to Regional Disparities in the Supply of Risk Capital to New Technology-based Firms in the European Union: The European Seed Capital Fund Scheme, *Regional Studies*, Vol. 32, No. 5, pp. 56-84.

Murray, G.C. and Lott, J. (1995) Have UK Venture Capitalists a Bias against Investment in New Technology-based Firms?, *Research Policy*, Vol. 24, pp. 213-53.

Megginson, William (2004) 'Towards a Global Model of Venture Capital?', *Journal of Applied Corporate Finance*, Vol. 17, No. 1, pp. 143-76.

Mayer, Colin, Koen Schoors, and Yishay Yafeh (2002) 'Sources of Funds and Investment Activities of Venture Capital Funds: Evidence from Germany, Israel, Japan, and the UK', *Journal of Corporate Finance*, Vol. 71, pp. 63-89.

Michelacci, Claudio, and Javier Suarez (2004) 'Business Creation and the Stock Market,' *Review of Economic Studies*, Vol. 71, No. 2, pp. 459-81.

Nicoletti, Giuseppe, and Stefano Scarpetta (2003) 'Regulation, Productivity, and Growth: OECD Evidence,' *OECD Economics WP*, No. 347, pp. 345-67 Available at www.oecd.org

Neher, D. (1999), Staged Financing: An Agency Perspective. *Review of Economic Studies*, Vol. 66, pp. 67-83.

Norton, E. (1994), Venture Capitalist Attributes and Investment Vehicles: An Exploratory Analysis. *The Journal of Small Business Finance*, UK, Vol. 3, No. 3, pp. 124-44.

Norton, E., and B.H. Tenenbaum (1993), Specialization versus Diversification as a Venture Capital Investment Strategy. *Journal of Business Venturing*, Elsevier, Netherlands, Vol. 8, No. 5, pp. 234-54.

Poterba, James (1989b), 'Capital Gains Tax Policy Toward Entrepreneurship', *National Tax Journal*, USA, Vol. 42, No. 3, pp. 121-34.

Powell, W.W., Koput, K.W., Bowie, J.I. and Smith-Doerr, L. (2002), The Spatial Clustering of Science and Capital: Accounting for Biotech Firm-Venture Capital Relationships, *Regional Studies*, Vol. 36, pp. 113-42.

Pramanik, A.K.; (1998), "Venture Capital Financing: An Emerging Issue in Financial Service", *Indian Journal of Public Enterprise*, UP, Vol. 13, No. 24, June, pp. 102-20.

Riding, A. and Swift, C., (1990), Women Business Owners and Terms of Credit : Some Empirical Findings of the Canadian Experiences. *Journal of Business Venturing*, Elsevier, Netherlands, Vol. 5, pp. 327-440.

Schmidt, Klaus (2003), 'Convertible Securities and Venture Capital Finance,' *Journal of Finance*, Blackwell Publishing, American Finance Association Vol. 58, No. 3, pp. 124-46.

Sahlman, W.A. (1990), The Structure and Governance of Venture Capital Organizations. *Journal of Financial Economics*, Vol. 28, No. 2, pp. 102-24, Available at www.jfe.rochester.edu/jfenh.htm.

Singh, J.K. (2002), "Regulatory framework of venture capital financing in India", *The Journal of Accounting and Finance*, RDA, Rajasthan, Vol. 16, No. 2 Apr.-Sept., p. 53.

Tyebjee, T.T. and Bruno, A.V., (1984), A Model of Venture Capitalist Investment Activity. *Management Science*, Vol. 30, pp. 1051-66.

Watson, W., Ponthieu and Critelli, J., (1995), Team Interpersonal Effectiveness in Venture Partnerships and its Connection to Perceived Success. *Journal of Business Venturing*, Elsevier, Netherlands, Vol. 10, pp. 393-411.

Westhead, P. and Wright, M., (1998), 'Novice Portfolio, and Serial Founders in Rural and Urban Areas', *Entrepreneurship Theory and Practice*, Baylor University, Waco, Vol. 22, pp. 132-56.

Wright, M. and Robbie, K., (1998), 'Venture Capital and Private Equity: A Review and Synthesis', *Journal of Business Finance and Accounting*, Vol. 25, pp. 521-70, Available at www.blackwellpublishing.com/journal.asp?ref=0306-686X

Wright M., Rooobbie, K and Ennew, C. (1997), 'Venture Capital and its Serial Entrepreneurs', *Journal of Business Venturing*, Elsevier, Netherlands, Vol. 16, pp. 311-32.

Zacharakis and Shepherd (2001), 'The Nature of Information and Overconfidence on Venture Capitalist's Decision-making, *Journal of Business Venturing*, Elsevier, Netherlands, Vol. 16, pp. 311-32.

Reports

Association Francaise des Investisseurs en Capital (2000), Annuaire des Membres, Paris.

Arora, A., and Arunachalam, V.S. (2000), The Globalization of Software: The Case of the Indian Software Industry. Report Submitted to the Sloan Foundation. Available: http://www.heinz.cmu.edu/project/india/.

CDC (2001), *Profile.* Access on November 15th 2004 via http://www.cdcpart.com. cdcenglish/pres.htm.

Danish Growth Fund (2003), 'Vaekstfonden: Background and Overview,' mimeo, Copenhagen.

EASDAQ (European Association of Securities Dealers Automated Quotation System) (2001), *Primary Market Statistics.* Access on October 12th 2004 via: http://www.easdaq.com.

Euronext (2001), *IPOs.* Access on October 14th 2004 via: http://www.euronext. com.

EBAN (European Business Angels Network) (1998), Dissemination Report on the Potential for Business Angels Investments and Networks in Europe. 6

European Commission (2004), EC Report of the CREST Expert Group on SME and Research: Open Method of Coordination (OMC) 3% Action Plan. (Brussels: European Commission).

European Commission (1994), European Report on Science and Technology Indicators, EUR 15897, Brussels.

European Commission (1998), Risk Capital: A Key to Job Creation in the European Union, COMM (1998) 522, Brussels.

European Commission (2002), More Research for Europe: Towards 3% of GDP, COMM (2002) 499, Brussel.

European Commission (2003), Communication on the Implemenation of the Risk Capital Action Plan, COMM (2003) 654, Brussels.

European Investment Fund (2002), 'Annual Report 2001,' Luxembourg.

French Ministry of Industry (2003), 'Plan Innovation,' Paris.

IVCA Report, various volumes.

IDBI: Report on Development Banking, 1998-99.

"Karnataka Boom", BW-Report, *Business World*, 2004.

London stock exchange (2001), List of Companies on AIM. Access on October 12th 2003 via: http:// www.london stockexchange.com.

MacMillan, H. (1931), Report of the Committee on Finance and Industry. Cmnd 3897, (London: HMSO).

Martin, R., Berndt, C. Klagge, B. Sunley, P.J. Herten S. and Sternberg, R. (2003), Regional Venture Capital Policy: UK and Germany Compared, Report for the Anglo-German Foundation for the Study of Industrial Society.

NEIBM Report: *An Enquiry into the Institutional Credit Flow in Assam,* (1998).

Nasscom, (1998), Enabling a Quantum Leap in Successful Indian Venture Creation. New Delhi: Nasscom.

Neuer Markt (2001), *IPO Archiv*. Access on October 10th 2003 via: http://www. neuermarkt. com.

Nouveau Marché (2001), *Introductions*. Access on October 12th 2001 via: http://www. bourse-de-paris. fr.

OECD (Organisation for Economic Co-Operation and Development) (1997), Government Venture Capital for Technology-Based Firms, OECD/GD 201, Paris.

OECD (2000), A New Economy? The Changing Role of Innovation and Information Technology in Growth. Paris: OECD

SBA (Small Business Administration) (2001), *SBIC Venture Capital,* Access on November 14th 2001 via: http://www. sba. gov/inv.

Monographs

Assam 2000—A Hand Book : Directorate of Information and Public Relations, Govt. of Assam.

German Federal Ministry of Economy and Techonology (1999), 'Innovation and Jobs', Bonn.

India (2000), Observer Statistical Handbook, Observer Research Foundation, 2000.

K+V organisatie adviesbureau, Entrepreneurial Holding (1996), The role of informal investors in the Dutch Venture Capital Market: Unknown but much in Demand, Study Commissioned by the Ministry of Economic Affairs, Arnhem, The Hague.

National Venture Capital Association (2003), The 2003 Yearbook, Arlington.

North Eastern Industrial Policy 2003, DIandCC Publication, Dibrugarh; Published under the Ministry of Industry, Government of Assam.

State Finances—The Factual Position : Finance (Economic Affairs) Department, Govt. of Assam, 1999.

Seminar and Working Papers

Bascha, A., and U. Walz (2001), Financing Practices in the German Venture Capital Industry: An Empirical Assessment. Paper presented at the Weekly Seminar in honour of Erich Schneider, Kiel.

Berwin and Co (1997), Venture Capital Incentives in Europe: Outlines Fiscal and Legal Incentives Specifically Relating to Venture Investing in 10 European Countries. Access on September 18th 2001 via: http://www.evca. com/publications.html.

Bürgel, O., A. Fier, G. Licht and G. Murray (2000), Internationalisation of High-Tech Start-ups and Fast Growth-Evidence for UK and Germany, ZEW-Discussion Paper, No. 00-35, Mannheim.

Baker, M. and P.A. Gompers (1999a), An Analysis of Executive Compensation, Ownership, and Control in Closely Held Firms. Working Paper. *Harvard Business School*, Boston, MA.

———, (1999b), The Determinants of Board Structure and Function in Entrepreneurial Firms. Working Paper. *Harvard Business School*, Boston, MA.

Bascha, A., and U. Walz (2001), Financing Practices in the German Venture Capital Industry: An Empirical Assessment. Paper presented at the Weekly Seminar in honour of Erich Schneider, Kiel.

Baygan, Gunseli and Michael Freudenberg (2000), 'The Internationalisation of Venture Capital Activity in OECD Countries: Implications for Measurement and Policy,' OECD-STI Working Paper n.7.

Bottazzi, Laura, and Marco Da Rin (2002b), 'Europe's 'New' Stock Markets', CEPR Discussion Paper n. 3521.

Cochrane, J. (2001), The Risk and Return of Venture Capital. NBER Working Paper W8066, Bosten.

Cornelli, F., and O. Yosha (1997), Stage Financing and the Role of Convertible Debt. CEPR Discussion Paper 1735. *Centre for Economic Policy Research*, London.

Champenois, C., Engel, D. and Heneric, O. (2004), The Importance of Venture Capital Companies and Corporate Investors as Equity Partners of German Biotechnology Start-Ups: An Econometric Investigation, RWI Discussion Paper No. 16, Essen and ZEW-Discussion Paper No. 04-09, Mannheim, revised version from March 2005.

Cochrane, J. (2001), The Risk and Return of Venture Capital, NBER Working Paper W8066, Bosten.

Cornelli, F., and O. Yosha (1997), Stage Financing and the Role of Convertible Debt. CEPR Discussion Paper 1735. *Centre for Economic Policy Research*, London.

Dalal, Y. (2000), Email communication to Martin Kenney, August 14. available in note on paper of Dossani R. and Kenney M.(2002), "Creating an Environment for Venture Capital in India"; *World Development*, Vol. 30, No. 2.

Engel, D. (2001a). The Impact of Venture Capitalist's Role on Firm Performance. Paper presented in E.A.R.I.E. Zentrum für Europäische Wirtschaftsforschung (ZEW), Mannheim.

———, (2001b), Höheres Beschäftigungswachstum durch Venture Capital? Discussion Paper 01–34. Zentrum für Europäische Wirtschaftsforschung (ZEW), Mannheim.

Engel, D. and Keilbach, M. (2002), Firm Level Implications of Early Stage Venture Capital Investments—An Empirical Investigation, ZEW Discussion Paper, No. 02-82, Mannheim.

EVCA—European Venture Capital Association (2003), 'Benchmarking European Tax and Legal Environments,' Benchmarking Paper, Zaventem.

Gompers, Paul, and Josh Lerner (1998), 'What Drives Venture Capital Foundraising?,' Brookings Papers on Economic Activity—Micro-economics.

Hart, M. (1995), Founding Resource Choices: Influences and Effects. Doctoral Dissertation. *Harvard Graduate School of Business.*

Hellman, Thomas (1998), 'Comment on 'What Drives Venture Capital Fundraising?', Brookings Papers on Economic Activity—Microeconomics.

Kaplan, S.N., and P. Strömberg (2000), Financial Contracting Theory Meets the Real World: An Empirical Analysis of Venture Capital Contracts. NBER Working Paper 7660. *National Bureau of Economic Research*, Cambridge, MA.

Mitta, S. (1999), India's Technological Potential. Paper presented at Asia/Pacific Research Center Conference, January 11.

Mayer, C., K. Schoors and Y. Yafeh (2001), Sources of Funds and Investment Strategies of Venture Capital Funds: Evidence from Germany, Israel, Japan and the UK (preliminary draft).

Naqvi, R. (1999), Business Support Center of STPI: Proposal for an India InfoTech center in Silicon Valley, US, Unpublished manuscript. Available at www.elsevier.com/locate/worlddev.

Posner, E. (2000), Is there a revolution in European venture capital? Berkeley Roundtable on the International Economy Conference Paper Number 4, University of California, Berkeley, CA.

Schertler, A. (2001), Venture-Capital-Investitionen in Deutschland: Welche Rolle spielen staatliche Fördermaßnahmen? Die Weltwirtschaft 2001(1).

Schmidt, K.M. (1999), Convertible Securities and Venture Capital Finance. CESifo Working Paper 217, Munich.

Verma J.C., 'A study on Venture Capital in the Promotion of Industrial Growth in India', *Senior Fellowship of Indian Council of Social Sciences Research*, New Delhi, 1995.

Websites

Online official site www.sebi.net.in originated from SEBI, Mumbai

Online official site www.ivca.com originated from Indian Venture Capital Association, New Delhi.

Online official site www.avca.com originated from Asian Venture Capital Association, Hongkong.

Index